A Soldier's Song

The World War II Diary of
Sergeant Jack Anderson

John "Jack" Charles Anderson
September 16, 1921 – December 6, 2009

A Soldier's Song

The World War II Diary of Sergeant Jack Anderson

Jason Grom

LEARN IN THE
FLOW OF LIFE

Published by Learn In the Flow of Life

ISBN 979-8-9903710-0-2

Library of Congress Control Number: 2024906648

Editing, design, and illustration by Kim Rodgers

First Edition

For my gramma, Annette Anderson.

May this book honoring Grampa bring you many
moments of happiness.

Contents

"I'm OK now!"

— *Jack Anderson*

Preface

It was December 2009, and the day had come to lay to rest my grandfather John "Jack" Charles Anderson. I was wondering if I could muster the strength to get up in front of our family church to say the words I had prepared to honor a man I looked up to my entire life.

He had passed away the prior Sunday, shortly after my niece Miah's birthday party where he collapsed. My brother-in-law, Matt Buenning, and my sister's mother-in-law, Donna Andrist, tried to revive him via CPR. He was then rushed to the hospital where a doctor asked my mom, Barb Grom, and grandma, Annette Anderson, questions about his care and why he hadn't been given a pacemaker when according to the doctor it was obvious he had needed it for quite awhile after being diagnosed with congestive heart failure. Of course, this line of questioning didn't provide comfort, but instead questions about "what if" and "if only" he might have lived.

At 88 years old, he had lived a full life. He was born in 1921, grew up during the Great Depression, graduated from high school as Adolf Hitler was rising in power, served our country during WWII and the Korean War, built a house with his own two hands, raised a family in his hometown of Marinette, Wisconsin, worked his entire career at Scott Paper Company, hosted thousands of people at our beloved family cottage, spent almost 30 years as a snow bird in Arizona, and so much more.

The one constant with my grandpa Jack Anderson was music. He took piano lessons briefly, but because of his musical talent he learned to play by ear. He added the tuba in high school including performing in the annual smelt festival where someone threw a smelt into his tuba one year and, after weeks of noticing a terrible smell, he had to have a janitor use a compressor to blow out the decaying fish. Later he was gifted an organ from his friend Linky and learned the autoharp to accompany sing-a-longs and various performances.

Although he played many instruments, his voice was his favorite — singing in barbershop choruses and quartets, church choir, weddings, funerals, and at almost every family gathering. "Let Me Call You Sweetheart," "Down By the Riverside," "The Green, Green Grass of Home," "Swing Low, Sweet Chariot" and "Silver Bells" were just a few that many of us know by heart because of him. Based on his talent and love of music, it's fitting that my mom picked out the poem "Each Life Is a Song" by Charles Little Jr. to hand out at his funeral.

I planned on including a song in his eulogy "Megan Megan I've been thinking...," a little ditty he would sing to my sister Megan Buenning. I still wasn't sure if I would be able to speak.

I cried every day since he passed away. The last time I spoke with him, I was driving home from work that Friday before he died. I remember stopping at a Red Box to pick up a DVD to watch with my fiancée Heather. He seemed reflective in the conversation, making comments about all the fun times he had and indicating it was time to pass on the torch to the next generation. Of course I didn't know at the time it was the last time I would talk to him, nor that the last time I would see him was a few weeks earlier when he gave me a big hug in his and my grandma's kitchen as Heather and I headed back to Minnesota after Thanksgiving and deer hunting season.

I didn't have regrets about our last connections nor about my time with him. It was a blessing to live only two houses from my grandparents. We spent a lot of time together at our house and their house as well as The Cottage. The Cottage is where he taught me to golf, and I helped him with handiwork or cutting the grass. One time he commented that he could hear me singing Willie Nelson's "On the Road Again" hundreds of yards away as I cut the grass on a riding lawnmower.

I followed in his musical footsteps with the tuba starting in sixth grade. In high school, faced with the question of whether or not it was "cool" to be in the band, he offered his support regardless of my decision even though he was so proud of seeing me play.

I remained in the band which turned into a successful four-year tenure in the University of Wisconsin Marching Band with countless moments of happiness including two Rose Bowls, A Final Four, lifetime friends, and a mentor in Mike Leckrone.

I had so many things to thank him for that I wanted the world to know about, and his eulogy was a step toward sharing that, although I didn't know if I was going to be able to get the words out.

My cousin Chris Anderson was first to speak, and he called grandpa his "hero" which reminded me that he wasn't important to only me. He was married to my grandma for over 60 years. They started dating after standing up in my grandma's brother's wedding three days before he was discharged from the Army after three years of active duty, including two of those years overseas. They were engaged six weeks later, married the next year, and raised two kids (my mom and uncle Steve Anderson) in the house they built where my grandma still lives today.

My mom and grandpa sang together hundreds of times in choir, church, and weddings. Later when my mom married my dad, Gary Grom, my grandpa became a second father to my dad. My dad's mother passed away at 39 and his father at 48, so he didn't really know an adult life with parents other than my grandparents. My dad looked up to his patience, handiness, and how he focused on everyone having a good time.

I could go on forever talking about his impact on others from swimming with my sister, Kirsten Tuyls, to the joy he brought to so many when he would greet you in response to "How Are You?" with joy and enthusiasm: "I'm OK now!!!!" My eulogy needed to be relatively short, and I needed to be able to say the words and not break down to a puddle overwhelmed with emotion.

After my cousin finished, I gave the OK to the pastor that I was good to go. I walked up to the front and spoke from the heart with enthusiasm, confidence, and not one single breakdown. I felt a responsibility to tell everyone about the special man he was, what he meant to me, and help family and friends heal from his loss.

While it's almost 15 years later, I still feel compelled to tell his story, inspiring me to complete the project that began with journaling during his service in World War II. He started with his training in Illinois, Georgia, and Florida, and then continued throughout his travels through North Africa, Italy (Battle of Anzio), France, and Belgium (the Battle of the Bulge), and finally Germany as the United States and the Allies claimed victory over the Axis powers led by Adolf Hitler.

My mom, uncle, and I transposed his diary while he was still alive. He reviewed the details and guided my mom where to add pictures he took while there. As you read his entries, you may notice terms you haven't seen before that were more common during this time, as well as misspellings on occasion. We tried to keep the diary as true to his written word as possible in keeping with the original pocket-sized diary booklets.

Since then, his diary has been read by dozens of family members, loaned to friends and colleagues, included in the curriculum of Mark Scott in the high school World War II history class he taught for eight years in West Lafayette, Indiana, and recently was the basis for a talk I gave at my son Jack's school during Veterans Day week. And yes, my son is named after my grandpa, another demonstration of his impact.

As you read his diary, I encourage you to view it from the perspective of my great-grandma, Esther, and great-grandpa, John, who were his primary audience when he wrote it. Their eldest son was in the thick of battle, right behind the front lines in his 40 mm gun pit, leading his crew to shoot down enemy planes and jump into countless foxholes to stay out of danger as the enemy dropped buzz bombs and other weapons to try to take out their anti-aircraft guns.

Their only way to communicate was through letters that arrived on a significant delay traveling across the Atlantic Ocean and through military security. I imagine there were lots of prayers and instead of waiting for a text or a call, they were likely waiting for the mail each day with bated breath.

In closing, you will notice the cover of the book has a picture of my grandpa playing a piano in a blown-out building. I mentioned that music was a constant in his life. That was true even in World War II. He would play this piano and sing to entertain his fellow troops during downtimes, and they even moved this piano around on the back of their truck. It seemed fitting that the title of the book capture his connection to music and the spirit of Charles Little, Jr.'s poem "Each Life Is a Song." I hope you enjoy *A Soldier's Song: The World War II Diary of Sergeant Jack Anderson.*

— *Jason Grom (Jack Anderson's grandson)*

Introduction

September 22, 1942 to February 15, 1943

The diary of my life in the service

By the fall of 1942, the United States was almost a year into its declaration of war which the attack on Pearl Harbor the prior December made unavoidable. As the war effort continued, in 1942 over three million men were inducted into military service through the Selective Service System including Jack Anderson.

The Introduction section of Jack's diary contains what he sent home to his parents with an intent to finish some day, but not a clear plan of how. Once on his way overseas, he began using small pocket notepads to document his experience throughout the rest of his service.

I was inducted into the Army on September 22, 1942, had a two-week furlough, and then went to Fort Sheridan, Illinois. Two days later I was shipped to Camp Stewart, Georgia. I have finished my five weeks of basic training and my training on the range. On the range with the 40 mm gun which is our main weapon, in our record fire we made the best record ever made at this camp.

New inductees at Fort Sheridan, Illinois (I am on the right)

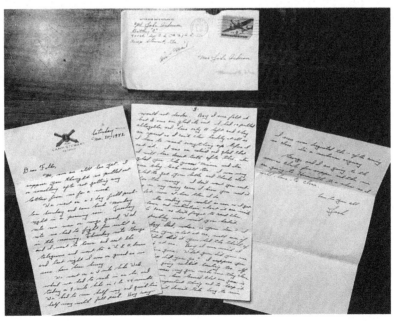

Letter to me from my parents dated September 9, 1942

Upon hearing about my draft status, my mom wrote me a letter. This started regular correspondence between my parents and me including my diary journaling my daily experiences.

Letter from me to my parents dated November 28, 1942

Dec. 14, Mon. – The day before yesterday we just came back from a three-day field problem, and yesterday which was Sunday, I was on range guard. I was to the dentist today so I had a pleasant day. OUCH! (My past again.) We went on a 28-mile hike with full pack and also a nine-mile hike in 1 hour 38 minutes with full pack and blankets. More blisters.

Dec. 15, Tue. – Went out to the range today and fired the 50 caliber machine gun and rifle. I managed to get about 80 rounds of tracers, so I had lots of fun. We were issued our own guard rifle tonite. We also were restricted to leave our area tonite 'cause someone hadn't made their bed this morning.

Dec. 16, Wed. – Out to the range again. We're range guard tonite, and is it going to be cold.

Dec. 17, Thu. – Out at the range shooting 50 caliber and rifles. Security guard tonite.

Dec. 18, Fri. – Sixteen-mile hike in four hours with a five-minute break. Full pack and blankets.

Dec. 19, Sat. – Dentist, had a parade, inspection of hutments, and mass games. Oh yes, we had a big party in the day room last nite. Most fun I had in a long time. Lots of singing!

Dec. 20, Sun. – Went to Savannah Saturday afternoon until Sunday nite. Spent most of our time with Bill Kulick, my pal from home. Boy, George and I were sure glad to see him, and we had a perfect time.

I'm with Bill Kulick at Camp Stewart, Georgia

Dec. 21, Mon. – Went on a 25-mile hike, stayed overnite. The whole battalion went.

Dec. 22, Tue. – Came back from our hike. My feet were OK, but I was plenty tired. Went to Hinesville to mail my Xmas packages.

Dec. 23, Wed. – Rained again this morning, but cleared up and got nice and warm. Went out to the range, didn't do much except clean the 40 mm and 50 caliber machine gun. Then went with George P. and our officers to see how we are supposed to load our trucks on freight cars when we leave.

Dec. 24, Thu. – Hiked out to the range again but didn't do much except drill the men and lay around. Then went in to camp about 3:30. Went to the Xmas dance at the U.S.O. and had lots of fun. We were last to leave the range as usual too.

Dec. 25, Fri. – Had Christmas off and got out of range guard too tonite. Had turkey and punkin pie and a lot of other stuff. Had a good supper, too. Going to see *Hellzapoppin'* tonite on the stage at No.1 theater. Stage show was very good. George, Danny, George P. and I went to a U.S.O. dance after at Hinesville. Wrote a letter to Carol.

Dec. 26, Sat. – Inspection this morning. Played football in the afternoon and went on security guard at 5:00.

Dec. 27, Sun. – Security guard yet until 5:00 tonite then to the show.

Dec. 28, Mon. – Seven-mile hike this morning and stayed at the range all day and CQ tonite. Wrote a letter to Carol.

Dec. 29, Tue. – Nine-mile hike this morning, then went home for dinner for once from the range. Went to the theater to a special show this afternoon. It was beautiful out this morning but then it started to rain, and it lasted all day.

Dec. 30, Wed. – Went on a hike then to the range and went on security guard at 5:00 for 24 hours.

Dec. 31, Thu. – Came off of security guard at 5:00 tonite. New Years Eve, didn't leave camp, but did we have fun in camp!

Jan. 1, 1943, Fri. – New Years, went out to the range all day. Came back and scrubbed the hutment for inspection tomorrow.

Jan. 2, Sat. – Personal inspection at the parade grounds and hutment inspection. Played football this afternoon and going on range guard at 5:00. The 378th pulled out for parts unknown with some of our men. Sure seems dead over there with them gone.

Jan. 3, Sun. – Range guard until 5:00 tonite. Played football in camp until dark, took a shower, wrote a letter to Carol and home.

Jan. 4, Mon. – Went to the range. Fired at sleeve with 50 caliber, also fired at rocket with 50 caliber and 40 mm. Had march order at 4:00 took guns and everything in the truck and went about 10 miles and came back right away and unloaded everything again. It sure seemed dumb to me.

Jan. 5, Tue. – Went on a 16-mile hike in four hours this morning. We sure are getting tougher each hike 'cause only one dropped out. Goldbricked at the range all afternoon and spent the evening playing the piano and singing in the day room with George P.

Jan. 6, Wed. – Went to the range and then all of the section chiefs went on a reconnaissance tour to find our gun positions for our field problem. Packed all of our equipment and guns. Leaving 5:00 a.m. tomorrow.

Jan. 7, Thu. – I was section chief with a crew of my own. Rained all nite.

Jan. 8, Fri. – The colonel inspected our gun emplacement and said, "Very good corporal." Ahem—! It rained nearly all day, and we were wet all through. Had march order about 3:00 p.m., so we came back today. Boy it never fails to rain every time we go on a field problem, but we just grin and bear it!

Our gun and crew on a field problem at Camp Stewart

Jan. 9, Sat. – Went to the range this morning and unloaded our trucks and cleaned our guns from the field problem. This afternoon our battalion went to the theater where the colonel talked to us on how good we were and how bad we were on the field problem. Our battery "C" he said was the best in the outfit. Boy, are we proud! Tonite we had a farewell on Lt. Carey as he is leaving us. He sure was a good Soldier. I'm on battalion guard tonite. Wrote a letter to Carol and home.

Introduction

Jan. 10, Sun. – Came off of guard at six, so I slept all morning. Played football in the afternoon. Went to the show in the evening.

Jan. 11, Mon. – Went out to the range all day and shot the 40 mm at a rocket. Hit it? Heck no, it travels around 450 miles per hour. We had another party tonite in the day room and had lots of fun.

Jan. 12, Tue. – Went to the dentist to see if I could get my teeth (partial) but not much luck yet. We drew for furloughs yesterday too so I hope I have my teeth (partials) before then. I goldbricked all day today.

Jan. 13, Wed. – Didn't feel so good so stayed in my hutment all day and went on security guard at 5:00. I was promoted to sergeant today. Oh boy!

Jan. 14, Thu. – Still on security guard until 5:00 tonite. Played football again until dark.

Jan. 15, Fri. – Went out to the range, but first we had a 10-mile hike. Fired the 40 mm and 50 caliber at the sleeve and rockets. Cleaned equipment and hutments for inspection tomorrow.

Jan. 16, Sat. – Went to the small arms range and fired Garands all day. Sure was a lot of fun. It's raining like mad out now, and I'm on CQ.

Jan. 17, Sun. – Played football all afternoon, went to church in the morning, and went to the show tonite.

Jan. 18, Mon. – Went to the range and shot at rockets then came in early in the afternoon, and we had a dress parade at the parade grounds. Going to Hinesville tonite.

Jan. 19, Tue. – Went on a 10-mile hike today and about half way it started raining in sheets. Boy did it rain. It was warm though, and we sure had a lot of fun singing and splashing water all over everybody. Our officers started the splashing, so we finished it. We were soaked all over but Oh— what fun!

Jan. 20, Wed. – Took all of our guns and equipment back to camp and cleaned them all and are checking up on everything to see what is missing or we need. Cleaned guns until 11:00 tonite.

Jan. 21, Thu. – Reveille was early this morning as we are having a showdown on all equipment issued us. We went to the theater this morning where the colonel announced we are ready to leave. All furloughs canceled, so I won't be getting one. Gee, I sure wish I could get one!

Jan. 22, Fri. – Went out to the range then came in early, and we all went to the theater to see a movie on camouflage.

Jan. 23, Sat. – Went out to the range, and I helped fire rockets. Boy they sure do throw up the dirt when they take off. We loaded up our trucks and guns and took everything off of the range for our trip to Florida on Monday.

Jan. 24, Sun. – Went to church this morning, and this afternoon our quartet practiced a number for the program they are going to have on the field problem. This one is for a morale builder, so we should have a lot of fun. I tried to call home today, but I couldn't get through.

Jan. 25, Mon. – We left this morning for Fernandina, Florida at 6:30 and got there around 4:00 this afternoon. Our camp is outside of town around 200 yards from the ocean. I went to town with Danny and George and had some fun. The town is lit up with dim red lights and people walk out nites with big dogs. It is very dark, and they are scared of being robbed or something. Danny and I had to stop quite a few fights. Too much celebrating for those guys.

Jan. 26, Tue. – Drilled a squad of men in how to crawl without exposing too much of the body. Practiced crawling under barbed wire this afternoon then played football against the officers — 6 to 6 score. After, we went for a swim in the ocean. It was cold at first, but it sure was swell after we got ducked. Boy and does that water ever taste salty. I was sergeant of the guard so I had to stay in camp tonite.

Jan. 27, Wed. – Set the "40's" on the beach and fired at a target out on the water. Our gun was the only one to hit it first and blew it all apart so all that was left was part of the frame. We fixed that too. In the afternoon we fired the 50's on the trucks moving along the beach at the target on the water. Had a party at the state park in Fernandina and went through Fort Clinch, which was built in 1850 under the supervision of General Lee. Very interesting place. Rained tonite.

Jan. 28, Thu. – Left our camp at 9:30 this morning and got back to Camp Stewart at 6:00 tonite. Boy, were we hungry as we had a sandwich on the fly for dinner. I had a swell time, and am now drying out my clothes as the tent leaked last nite. I got a letter from Carol today, and I sure am relieved and happy again. Gee, it sure is funny what a letter means from one you love, and when you don't get one, —oh gee!?

Jan. 29, Fri. – Went out to the range and dug an emplacement for the 40 mm and camouflaged it for tomorrow. This afternoon we went through the obstacle course we helped make. We crawled about a hundred yards through barbed wire and over ditches with machine guns blazing away 30 inches above the ground and dynamite charged mines that were set off at different places. It was a lot of fun, but we sure kept our noses to the ground.

Jan. 30, Sat. – We fired the 40 mm for service record again and an inspection on our camouflage to see how fast we could get into action. We knocked our camouflage off and got the gun on the target by the director in a bit over 20 seconds, so it was very good. We are supposed to be through with the range now, and we have no more security guard to pull. Sgt. Moor, Danny, Todd, and I went to a U.S.O. dance at Hinesville, and after we got a crazy idea and took a bus to Savannah. We met some of the other fellows there, and we had a swell time. We finally got a bus which took us back to camp at 7:00 a.m. Sunday morning.

Jan. 31, Sun. – All section chiefs had to go on a reconnaissance tour at 8:00 a.m., and we didn't get back until 2:00 this afternoon so we sure are sleepy, and there is a non-com meeting to get last instructions on our field problem for tomorrow.

Feb. 1, Mon. – Left on our field problem. After we arrived at our position, we dug our emplacement and camouflaged our guns. We sure did a swell job, and our gun position was the best camouflaged one. We sure worked hard on it.

Our 40 mm and part of a slit trench

Feb. 2, Tue. – Our gun and two other guns fired today at a plane towing a target.

Feb. 3, Wed. – Moved last nite after dark and drove in blackout and put our guns down in the dark ready to fire at daylight.

Feb. 4, Thu. – Came back to camp and took a long way home about 65 miles. Gee it was swell riding in new country.

Feb. 5, Fri. – Went on an endurance test, the whole 45th Brigade. We were supposed to run 300 yards in 45 seconds, carry someone on your back 75 yards and change off on the way back. We had to run all the way. We did a lot of other tiresome running events and then went over the obstacle course and after that a four-mile hike which we did in 38 minutes with full pack. Went to the show with George tonite, going to write some letters now.

Feb. 6, Sat. – Went through the gas chamber this morning, yak and cried some more — tear gas. Four deadly gases which we got a sniff of, and it was plenty! Went and got my impressions at the dentist this afternoon.

Feb. 7, Sun. – Went to the dentist early this morning then went to church. Going to the show tonite.

Feb. 8, Mon. – Packed machine guns with cosmoline and crated them. Bill Kulich came to camp yesterday morning and looked around a bit and then had chow with us. He left early in the afternoon. Sure was good to see him again. Danny, Todd, and I went to see George P. at the hospital. He was looking good.

Feb. 9, Tue. – Packed some more things today.

Feb. 10, Wed. – Went to town with the boys tonite, took in a show.

Feb. 11, Thu. – Fired grenades from the rifle today.

Feb. 12, Fri. – Fired the 37 mm and 50's today at "E" range. Left on a two-day pass after retreat.

Feb. 13, Sat. – Savannah.

Feb. 14, Sun. – At Savannah yet and church.

Feb. 15, Mon. – Showdown inspection today. Issued our guns and the rest of our equipment. Have to send everything home with any address or anything important written on it. When the time gets this short, you get a rather hollow feeling inside of you, but we still are anxious to go.

Have to send you home diary, so — so long for the time being 'cause I'll be back and finish someday.

Here I am at Camp Stewart, Georgia before heading overseas

The diary continues on six small booklets covering the next two and a half years overseas and then back home.

Jack Anderson's diaries (all six editions)

1st Edition

February 20 to October 29, 1943

Our important events during our campaign in North Africa and Italy

In January 1943, Allied leaders Winston Churchill and Franklin D. Roosevelt met in Casablanca where they issued an "unconditional surrender" demand to the Axis powers, demonstrating their commitment to fight to the finish. Jack was only four days away from getting a furlough from the military when his battalion was put on alert and started their journey to North Africa where the United States would join the British battling against the Axis powers. During this time, Jack and his fellow Soldiers trained and prepared for battle while experiencing their first live action as the fighting in North Africa wound down. From here, they boarded the *Empire Perdita* ship and headed east along the shoreline of North Africa toward Italy where they would spend the next year.

Feb. 20, Sat. – Left Camp Stewart, Georgia for embarkation point at Camp Kilmer, New Jersey.

Mar. 4, Thu. – Left Camp Kilmer for overseas.

Mar. 5, Fri. – Name of our boat was the SS *Mexico*. Came in contact with subs twice. Good food on board. Participated in a military funeral at which a captain was buried at sea.

Mar. 18, Thu. – Arrived at Casablanca, North Africa. Bivouacked at k-port, a place outside of town.

Mar. 21, Sun. to Apr. 11, Sun. – Pulled port guard.

Apr. 12, Mon. to Apr. 23, Fri. – Stationed at the docks in gun positions in Casablanca.

Apr. 24, Sat. to Apr. 26, Mon. – Took over prison guard and a large group of German prisoners around 20 miles from Casablanca.

Apr. 26, Mon. – Left the prison camp and went back to Casablanca where we were issued new guns and equipment again and then left for Oran. Went thru Rabat, Fes, Taza, and Guercif. Went thru beautiful country and the Atlas Mountains. Camped on the steeple chase track one nite.

May 1, Sat. – Arrived in Oran after four days travel.

May 2, Sun. to May 18, Tue. – Learning invasion tactics from barges (landing ship tanks "LSTs") at Arzew. Note: African campaign was officially over May 13, 1943, although mopping up still continues.

North Africa 1943

May 19, Wed. – Our first air raid which occurred at 9:45 p.m., and the all clear sounded at 10:05 p.m. A number of Army and Navy fellows killed at Arzew. Direct hit on tent, men and everything blown to bits.

May 20, Thu. – Left our area at Arzew and bivouacked outside of Mostaganem overnite. The Germans came over again that nite, but we didn't see them.

May 21, Fri. – Left our bivouac area to take gun positions around city of Mostaganem. The Germans came over again, and this time we were right in the thick of it. We couldn't see them 'cause of low clouds, so we had to send up a barrage, and there really was a lot of lead and steel in the air. One man from "B" Battery was killed and a few wounded. They came over at 11:35 p.m., and the all clear sounded at 12:10 a.m. We saw one plane go down in flames. Lenard Neville injured.

May 24, Mon. – Red alert but they weren't near us — darn it!

May 28, Fri. to May 29, Sat. – Equipment inspected by General Rutledge.

Jun. 6, Sun. – Inspected by General Star. We've had an inspection every week now since May 29. If they think we can win a war by inspections, well, I guess we'll have to then.

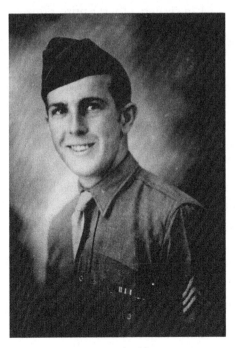

Me in North Africa, 1943

Jun. 13, Sun. – The island of Pantelleria was taken the other day and heard that Sicily was taken yesterday. I sure hope so. (It was just another latrine rumor.) Going to church with George now. Red alert early this morning.

Jun. 14, Mon. – All the section chiefs went to Antemouchant to school on identification of aircraft for a week. Passed the examination OK at a 100th of a second.

Jun. 17, Thu. – Our battalion left Mostaganam and bivouacked about 10 miles from there between mountains which are on all sides of us. We call it death valley or "dust bowl."

Jun. 21, Mon. – We left Antemouchant and returned to the bivouac area. On the way home we sideswiped into a General Grant tank. No one was hurt, but it sure was a close call. We are getting set to move up but not sure where.

Jun. 23, Wed. – Every afternoon since we've been here the wind starts down the mountain on one side of us and blows the sand and dust everywhere, gets half way up the other one and back she comes. Every supper we eat half a mess kit of sand, but it goes down OK if it is mixed up. We had a contest today to see whose gun crew could raise and lower the gun in the least time. My crew won and holds the record with the time of 43 seconds to lower and level and 31 seconds to raise the gun. Each man on my crew got a pack of cigarettes for the prize, donated by the officers.

Jun. 27, Sun. – Our captain (Losson was his name and one peach of a fellow), left our battery to be the battalion adjutant. We had a parade review in his honor conducted by Sgt. Todd, myself, and Corp. Chapeman. After it was over he wanted to say something to us, but he couldn't as he started to cry. That meant more to us than anything he could have put in words. We all are mighty proud of him, and we sure hated to see him go. Our battery commander now is Lt. Carey.

Jul. 2, Fri. – Went swimming again today in the Mediterranean, and the waves were about 10 feet high! What fun!

Jul. 3, Sat. – Artillery and inspection in ranks today. This afternoon our battery left the bivouac area in "dust bowl" and took a bivouac area just outside Mostaganam.

Jul. 4, Sun. – This used to be a day we always looked forward to back home but as all the other important dates go while in the Army, it's just another day. We are pulling aircraft guard on the divisional headquarters (General Patton's headquarters) while here.

Jul. 5, Mon. – Cleaning our guns and all equipment to be ready to move out at a moment's notice. A lot of troops are on boats or ready to hit Europe. The invasion is pulling off very soon.

Jul. 6, Tue. – We got another shot in the arm today and one that really is a lou-lou. It must have been a double dose, 'cause none ached so before (tetanus).

Jul. 7, Wed. – I feel pretty sick today, and my arm is like a toothache. Went into town for a shower. Bought muskmelons, watermelons, and grapes and took back to camp to eat. Boy and are they good.

Jul. 8, Thu. – George, Nachtwey, and I went out to the old bivouac area in "dust bowl" and practiced for a show that's being put on for the battalion.

Jul. 9, Fri. – Practiced again this afternoon and gave the show tonite. We had a stage made from one latrine and cans of gasoline for footlights and mountains on all sides for a background. It went over good.

Jul. 10, Sat. – Practiced in an old French opera house in Mostaganem and put the show on for a bunch of Army and Navy officers. Our Lt. Hedricks from our battery sang also in the show, and has he a wonderful voice. After the show he brought his girl (a lieutenant nurse) backstage and introduced us to her. She sure was a doll! Invasion of Italy was started at 4:00 a.m. this morning, and Holland and France were invaded. Sicily was supposed to be taken by 1:45 p.m. (it wasn't though).

Jul. 11, Sun. – Sunday, went to church this morning, sergeant of the guard tonite. Boy, the mail sure must be screwed up as I haven't had any from Carol for almost a month. The letters from home are also late.

Jul. 12, Mon. – Getting our guns and equipment set to move at a moment's notice.

Jul. 13, Tue. – Put our show on this afternoon again at the Collisea Show House. Expect to leave for Bizerte tomorrow by boat. I sure hope we leave.

Jul. 14, Wed. – Packed up and left, are bivouacking at Port aux Poule.

Jul. 15, Thu. to Jul. 20, Tue. – Been working on our guns and devising new ideas in order to fire the gun while moving in convoy. We are waiting for boats to take us to Bizerte and from there to Sicily.

Jul. 21, Wed. – Figuring out a new camouflage for our gun.

Jul. 22, Thu. – Got it finished today, and it really would give Hitler a nitemare if he saw it. The name we put on it is "paper hangers nitemare." My first truck or the one I ride in is named "Carol." She better appreciate it.

Jul. 23, Fri. – Had an inspection this morning.

Jul. 24, Sat. to Jul. 27, Tue. – Drill, maintenance of material. On the 23rd we fired all of our guns in a barrage fire.

Jul. 28, Wed. – Took a hike and fired our guns.

Jul. 29, Thu. – Went to a dance and had a swell time in Oran.

Jul. 30, Fri. – Had a swimming contest between our battalion and the 92nd Field Artillery in which six fellows and myself represented our battery. It was an endurance test, and most of us swam 8 to 8 ¹/₂ laps with a lap being around 500 yards. We won the contest, 93 ¹/₂ laps to 66 laps for the field artillery. I came in second for the dash in our battery (quit the bragging).

Jul. 31, Sat. – Material inspection today, and we done good so no reveille for tomorrow.

Aug. 1, Sun. – Went to church and did my washing after I got back (oh, my back!).

Aug. 2, Mon. to Aug. 4, Wed. – Same thing each day, maintenance of material and went to see a show each nite at the 92nd. Going to a show tonite again, *Santa Fe Trail* is on.

Aug. 5, Thu. – Went to an airport and saw B-17, B-25, B-26, A-20, P-51, P-38, P-39, Beaufighter, and C-47's.

Aug. 6, Fri. – Hike, artillery drill, infantry drill, and map reading. Put on artillery drill show for the rest of the battalion officers. "C" Battery is always on top and way above the rest of the batteries. But that's because we don't get any breaks like the rest of the batteries. Boy, these officers sure do some funny things that make one so damn disgusted, he would like to throw in the towel and call it quits. Everything we do is done pretty good, but do you think they would tell us it's good? The time they tell you is when you make a mistake, and boy do they give you hell!

Aug. 7, Sat. – Inspection in ranks today, and Capt. Watts told me, "Your section was very good sergeant." Most of the fellows on my crew are a swell bunch of guys, and they are most of the time on the ball and ahead of the rest of the crews. Sent Carol's present to her.

Aug. 8, Sun. – Went to church in the morning. Washed clothes this afternoon and went swimming. Went to a show again tonite. Been to a show every nite this week. We usually take a watermelon, Joe Sokol, Curly Bluse, and myself, and we are the envy of all the guys around us.

Aug. 9, Mon. – Hike this morning. Went swimming just before dinner. Gun drill this afternoon. Show tonite.

Aug. 10, Tue. – Infantry drill, bayonet drill, and manual arms, then maintenance of material and gun drill. Went to town this afternoon with George.

Aug. 11, Wed. – Hike this morning (two hours), infantry drill, manual of arms. Went swimming before chow. Gun drill this afternoon. Going to a show tonite at the 67th.

Aug. 12, Thu. – Went on a field problem all day. It sure was a screwed up mess. My section was the only one that didn't screw up in the 1st Platoon. We were bestowed a special invitation to meet down at the officers tent. That is, all the section chiefs. I'm not worried though, as we were on the ball.

Aug. 13, Fri. – Lovely meeting last nite. They said my section (no. 2) and no. 5 were the only ones who knew what they were doing. This morning at 2:00 a.m. we were called out. We thought it was march orders, but it sure wasn't. No. 2 and no. 5 sections were allowed to go back to bed. The rest of them had to load up everything and do the field problem over. While loading up the trucks the officers set off smoke pots, so the men had to put on their gas masks. Good thing the wind didn't change as our tents were right close to the smoke pots. They tried to put tear gas in, but it burned up. They were sure a happy bunch of men?—ugh! Had the morning off. Practiced for review tomorrow.

Aug. 14, Sat. – We had inspection in ranks and then passed in review. We compete with the other batteries to see who was the best. The men were perfect, but you can't win with the officer giving orders screwing up the works. If we weren't first, it's entirely his fault. We should have had Sgt. Moore giving commands. We had the rest of the day off. I am sergeant of the guard starting at 6:00 tonite.

Aug. 15, Sun. – I'm on guard until 8:00 tonite yet.

Aug. 16, Mon. – Hike this morning. Cleaned guns and equipment. Gun drill.

Aug. 17, Tue. – Infantry drill, bayonet drill, maintenance of material, gun drill this afternoon. Class on "40" then went swimming. 7:00 tonite we were told to load everything to be ready to pull out tomorrow at 12:00.

Aug. 18, Wed. – Finished loading and striked tents. Left Port aux Poule at 12:30. Every section had to leave four men behind. It sure was a hard thing to do when I picked my men out. They are all good men and swell fellows. They were Ted Kapolanski, William Alexander, Francis Benoit, and Selmer Langaard. They are supposed to meet up with us at Algiers, but I'm pretty sure they won't as I'm sure we are going in on the next invasion, and we can only have a certain number of men which is less than our regular gun crew. We stopped at 9:10 p.m. and bivouacked for the nite.

Aug. 19, Thu. – Left at 8:00 a.m. and arrived at Algiers at 4:15 p.m. We went over some very high mountains, but I don't know yet what they are called. We are bivouacked just outside of Algiers with the 36th Division which we are connected with again. It sure is hot.

Aug. 20, Fri. – Reveille at 6:00 this morning. There sure are a bunch of men here, so we have to start eating early. Had to unload and reload our trucks and then took them down to waterproof the guns and trucks. We didn't finish today, so we have to finish tomorrow. After we are finished, we won't see our trucks again until we are on the boat. We are near an airport, so there are planes flying over all day. Went to a show tonite with Bluse and Millet. *Hi, Buddy* was on, it was pretty good. Bob Hope is supposed to be here in person tomorrow nite. I sure hope so as we aren't staying here long.

Aug. 21, Sat. – Went down to the 8th Ordnance and picked up my gun as it needed some fixing and then took it over to the waterproofing area to waterproof it. We stayed there all day and worked on the trucks and gun. Snuck into town and bought some grapes, tomatoes, and watermelon for dinner. Went to the show in field here tonite. Bob Hope wasn't here, but he is supposed to be here the 25th or Wednesday.

Aug. 22, Sun. – Got up at 5:30 a.m. for reveille and then went back to bed. Didn't eat breakfast, and I didn't miss much. The meals here are nothing to brag about. Slept most of the morning. Curly scalded himself pretty badly around his face and chest. He's in the hospital, and we're afraid we might lose him.

Aug. 23, Mon. – Still no word on how Curly is. Gee, I wish I knew if he's OK. Went to the airport with Federwitz. Boy there sure is a mess of planes there, and some of them are a mess, period. Those sure are shot up. Went to Algiers on pass with Spinnata, Spiezian, Kososki, Federwitz, Todd, and Cholette. It's the best city we've been in over here, but that's as far as it goes as there is nothing to do. We rode the trolley most of the day. Wee! Had fun with some Limeys. Some of them aren't a bad sort. Had to take care of Kip on the way back as he was slightly under.

Aug. 24, Tue. – First sergeant said there was no way for me to see Curly and that I couldn't go. Damn them! We'll see about that tomorrow. They don't even find out how he is getting along. Had a big mail call today, and I got the package from home with my camera. I also got three letters from my darling, which only made me all the more happier! Oh, how I wish I could be with her!— PX (post exchange) rations today also, so we had quite a day.

Aug. 25, Wed. – Went and asked Lt. Carey if I could see Bluse, and he said he told Lt. Hancock before that I could go. The son-of-a-gun never told me that. First sergeant and I tried to go with the ambulance as it's 23 miles away, but they were full. Going to try with Sgt. Moore tomorrow. Saw Bob Hope with Francis Langford and Jack Pepper in our area here. I just came back, and he sure was good! Francis L., um! Yum! She sure can sing too!

Aug. 26, Thu. – Went to the airport and saw General Eisenhower as he got out of his private B-17. Went and saw Curly with Sgt. Moore. Boy, he sure was a happy guy when he saw us. He thought we had gone and left him. He's much too valuable to leave behind. I think he will be out before we leave. I sure was relieved when I found out he was getting better. Guess my prayers were answered. Took another shower this afternoon and answered some letters. Had a campfire snack tonite with Spash and George.

Aug. 27, Fri. – The siren blew for an air raid this morning at 4:50 from the airport. We are right near there, so it sure didn't take us long to fall out. They got the searchlight on and we saw one go down, and they were supposed to have knocked another one down. They dropped flares which light everything up like daylight. We sure felt helpless just having to watch as our guns and equipment are all loaded on the boats. Shrapnel was dropping all around us from the "90's" as they flew right over our heads. I think they mostly came over with the idea of taking pictures which I'm sure they accomplished. Some new fellows from the States jumped in the latrine for protection, and boy did they stink. We expect them tonite or tomorrow nite to really give us the works as the docks are full of boats loaded with guns and equipment and a great troop concentration around us. We are ready to pull out soon. Wrote four letters today and didn't do much else. Went to a show tonite in the field, saw *Slightly Dangerous* with Lana Turner and Robert Young.

Aug. 28, Sat. – The *Stars and Stripes* this morning said that three planes were shot down, and a number of bombs were dropped. Damage was slight. Boy, I sure hope if they do come again they don't hit the boat we are going on. It has 100 octane gas, 1,500 pound bombs, and TNT. The name of the boat is *Ocean Valley*. It's a British freighter. It's just our luck to get stuck on a boat like that. Didn't do much today. Went and heard a war correspondent speak about the war in general. He was very interesting. When it got dark we saw the show *Sis Hopkins*. It was very good. In the usual "open air theater."

Aug. 29, Sun. – Reveille at 5:30 as it is every morning, breakfast at 6:00. The meals are getting better it seems, or maybe we were spoiled from before. Went to the airport this morning with George and Kip. MP chased us off after we saw all we cared to see though. The son-of-a-gun. Stopped in town and bought a watermelon each. They are about over with now. We sure ate our share while they were in season.

Aug. 30, Mon. – Was supposed to go on dock detail. That detail has to clean up the boat we are going on. The English might be good sailors, but they sure are dirty. The boat is filthy. In the morning and afternoon we have a spot of tea with the blighty blokes. Curly came here today as he got a pass. Lt. Carey went back with him to see if he could get him back now that he is better. We sure were happy to see him. Went or rather just got back from a stage show that really was tops! The name of it was *Three Women and a Man*. The guy weighed around 300 pounds, and he sure was crazy. One of the girls, around 16–17 I should guess and cute as doll, sang and danced. Boy, did she have the shape and cute, – – – wow! One played the accordion and the other one sang, danced, and gave imitations, and was she good! This show was on the order of Bob Hope's show, but even better. We enjoyed every minute of it!!

Aug. 31, Tue. – Had charge of the ration detail today. It's one detail that most of the fellows want to get on as they drink all the juices they can hold and eat about the same. There are crews there nite and day loading food rations on trucks which haul them down to the boats we are going on. Went to the open air theater tonite again.

Sep. 1, Wed. – Didn't do much today. It is awfully hot here and seems to be getting hotter. It sure is cold when we have to get up at 5:30 a.m. though. We take a shower every day in ice cold water that is stored in a big water tank which comes from a well. Boy but is it ever refreshing. Went to the show again tonite. We have to get there early in order to get a place to park ourselves so we sit two hours before show time. The ground isn't anything too soft either.

Sep. 2, Thu. – No passes today, and no one leaves the area. Don't know what's coming off. Maybe "blood and guts" is on the rampage again. Went and watched the 451st beat the 409th in a hardball game.

Sep. 3, Fri. – Italy was invaded. Someone claimed the radio said that Denmark and France were also invaded. It sure sounds good anyway. There is a bunch of Italian prisoners in the stockade right next to us. They sure look happy, and they sure are fed and treated good. Sergeant of the guard for 24 hours starting at 4:00 p.m. Going to the show tonite. Around 1,700 men just from the States pulled into our bivouac area. They sure look green. Some of them didn't even know how to set their pup tents up. They asked a lot of questions, and some pretty foolish, but they'll learn like we did that this is no picnic. Boy, I wish I were back where they were 14 days ago. Show tonite was *Spitfire* with Leslie Howard.

Playing ball

Sep. 4, Sat. – It's not much use going to breakfast as you don't get enough to fill a cavity. With 1,700 more men in the chow line, it's almost dinner time before you get breakfast. I sure hope we pull out of here p.d.q. There's nothing like gun positions. There we are our own boss, up to a certain extent, but it's a heck of a lot better than bivouac areas. The ordnance checked over our rifles this afternoon. We are supposed to get paid today. Going to see Abbott and Costello in *Ride 'Em Cowboy* tonite. Wrote a letter to Carol and home.

Sep. 5, Sun. – Got up for reveille, then Curly and I went back to bed and slept all morning. Got paid this afternoon and paid all my bills. Went to Algiers on pass with George and Ray. Got ice cream, cake, and lemonade at the Red Cross. Took some pictures, ate supper at restaurant in town. Had fried sweet potatoes, soup, tomatoes, French rye bread, and champagne. Bought some souvenirs. Had a swell time.

Sep. 6, Mon. – Washed clothes this morning. Went to a meeting where Major Cook lectured and reviewed things we had and what we are going into. We can't leave the area and have to have all letters to be sent in by tomorrow morning no later. Don't know when we can write again. Expect to pull out in one or two days. Going to the show tonite, I hope. Saw *To the Shores of Tripoli* with John Payne, Randolph Scott, and Maureen O'Hara. Very good picture.

Sep. 7, Tue. – Got last instructions today before we get on the boat. Part of the fellows are leaving at 1:30 this afternoon, 5:30, and the rest tomorrow. OD's are to be worn from now on.

Me in Casablanca, North Africa, 1943

Sep. 8, Wed. – Went to the airport this afternoon. Waited until the British canteen opened up, which is on the field. Had tea, sandwiches, cake, and pastries. It was a good supper and cheap. Came back and went to the show with Spash and George. *Two-Faced Woman* with Greta Garbo and Melvyn Douglas. Didn't care for it though. While at the show they announced that Italy had given up, under unconditional surrender. Italy gave up Sept. 3, but it was just let out today. After we got back, we were told to be ready to leave by 7:00 tomorrow morning.

Sep. 9, Thu. – Got up at 5:00 and left a little after 7:00 a.m. Took the dog to the boat but couldn't take him on. After we were all on, a British sailor ran down and got him for us. We are on the boat now, and they are still loading ammunition on. It is 11:50, so we should be eating dinner soon. The boat is a British coal burner with no sleeping quarters. George, Curly, and I are sleeping on deck, way up in the very front. Let's hope the waves don't get too high. No refrigeration facilities on this boat, so we can't have any perishables. They had meat and other good stuff for us but had to take it off on account of that. Boy! Good old canned stuff and "C" type biscuits for bread, ugh! We moved just to the other side of the docks. The name of the boat is *Empire Perdita*. It's only four months old, and this will be her second trip, but it looks like it's an old boat as it's plenty dirty.

Sep. 10, Fri. – Still parked by the docks. Boy, is this deck hard to sleep on! All nite long, depth charges are dropped to prevent subs from coming in and to stop sabotage such as swimmers swimming out to a boat and putting stick bombs on the hull of a boat. The concussion of the charge shakes all the boats around here, so you can imagine what it would do to a swimmer. We get up for breakfast, which is at 8:00, dinner at 12:00, and supper at 5:00. There are only 162 men on board, so it isn't so bad. We pass the time by reading or playing cards.

Sep. 11, Sat. – We were told we are going to pull out at noon today. Don't know if it will be out in the harbor or on our way across. We pulled out in the harbor this afternoon. Supposed to pull out at 5:00 a.m. tomorrow. Boy, does it get windy every nite up here. You stay awake for fear you'll be blown overboard.

Sep. 12, Sun. – They raised anchor at 5:00 this morning and that meant the end of our sleep. We sleep right along side of the winch, and it makes enough noise to raise the dead. We didn't go very far. We finally got under way at 11:00 noon. Went to church at 10:30. We are sailing along the coast of Africa. Saw some very old fish or whatever they were. The Mediterranean is very clear and blue. A sub must have been heard, as a corvette dropped a depth bomb just to the right of us. The sub was between our boat and the corvette, so if they had the same idea as we did, it sure wasn't good. This is the start of a so-called Mediterranean cruise. So far it's really beautiful. The shore all along is mountains, and the sun is setting behind them which sure is a beautiful sight.

Sep. 13, Mon. – Got up as usual at 8:00 and had breakfast. Was put in charge of a detail to swab the deck. There are over 50 ships in this convoy with corvettes as the only escort ships.

Sep. 14, Tue. – It is now 10:15 a.m., and we are heading into the harbor at Bizerta Lake. It is noted for its air raids, so we might have some excitement here. The harbor is full of boats. We didn't stop at Bizerte, but part of our convoy did. A launch came out with sealed orders for the captain of the ship. We just passed Cape Bon (4:40) also off the coast of Tunis. There are quite a few planes flying over head, but thank the Lord they're our own.

Sep. 15, Wed. – Came in sight of Sicily this morning. Been following the coast all morning. We have been at the head of the convoy since yesterday. Left the coast of Sicily this afternoon. Details were picked for each hatch to unload all the ammunition and supplies. We're told we would be under fire 90% of the time. We are supposed to load the stuff on LST's about a mile from shore.

Sep. 16, Thu. – Had an air raid at 3:40 this morning. One plane came over and dropped only one bomb which landed in the water one ship over on the port side of us. Everyone was pretty calm even though we thought there would be more.

George just sighted land thru the field glasses (8:40 a.m.). We have heard the distant rumble of guns, and they are getting louder as we get closer. We can now see land and the shore batteries firing. It is 2:30 p.m., and the front of our convoy is being bombed. I just saw two planes go down. The bombs came close but no hits. It is 2:50 p.m., and the firing has stopped. A number of P-38's above us now. It sure gives a fellow a better feeling. The hatches are being uncovered, ready to be unloaded. Just heard that we were here early this morning but had to go back a ways as it was all mined. They have been cleared out now. It is 6:30, and a barrage fire was sent up for six He 112's which hightailed out of here. We are in the Salerno Bay about 20 miles from Naples (my birthday today, 22 years old, no cake though) and about four miles from the front. We are in south Salerno. The poor dog is really scared when the fireworks are on.

Me with the dog we brought with us from North Africa

Sep. 17, Fri. – It is 10:20 a.m., and as I'm writing this subchasers are screening or setting an artificial fog, covering up all the boats as we were just alerted again. Last nite we were alerted off and on all nite. We didn't get much sleep. There sure was some terrific blasting not far from us. Those Jerries are really pests. The Germans must really be taking a pounding as all last nite we could see the flashes and feel the concussion of our own big field guns, and it is still going on. In today's news broadcast, the British 8th Army is only 18 miles from Salerno, and there is no stopping the 5th Army of which we are part of (ahem). Right now, I don't know as if I care so much for the honor though of being with the invasion forces. While the harbor was pretty clear of the fog, I saw where one ship is sunk and another one which is pretty much out of shape in the middle. An American subchaser just came along side of us and said our boat was a priority boat, and the barges are to get us unloaded first. It didn't make us mad as we are loaded with high octane gas, TNT, and ammunition, and the Jerries are pretty determined to stop these supplies from getting ashore. As soon as I get ashore, I can dig a slit trench, but I'll be darned if I can dig one in this deck. If we stay on board much longer we won't get anything to eat, as our food supply or what is left of it is hash, and my stomach doesn't agree with my appetite in that case. It is 11:50 a.m. and another red alert. They are setting off another smoke screen. It should taste good with our dinner, which is due now. I sure coughed last nite from it. Just finished chow and the Jerries came. This time they weren't fooling. They dive-bombed in and dropped their load but didn't hit anything. There sure is an awful racket when all the boats open upon them, but it's an awful sweet sound knowing they are your guns. The planes were Me 109's. They came from the mountains and out of the sun, so it was almost impossible to see them until they are on top of us. It seems funny with our planes overhead all the time that they don't see them until they are on top of us. It is now 7:20 p.m., and a battle wagon, which we can see pretty clearly, is shelling the German lines. We had alerts off and on all afternoon. A convoy waiting outside of the bay was bombed. There was heavy firing. We forced some Epsom salts down the dog's throat before as he is constipated. Tomorrow we'll have to send a detail around the boat to see if it worked. Hope he doesn't drop it in someone's bag. That would be jarring.

Sep. 18, Sat. – We slept a little longer last nite, that is up until 12:30, then the Germans came again. Hell really let loose then! We never knew they were around until a bomb landed in front of our boat, two more landed just in back of us. It seemed as though they were determined to get our boat, but lucky for us they missed. The Lord must have had a hand in that. George, Spash, Curly, and I sleep right under the gun turret of the 12 pounder in front, and when it went off we thought a bomb had hit us. Boy, it shakes the whole ship. If you don't believe me ask the dog, as he does everything but take off. He is rather gun shy, but we'll make him a front line dog yet. The British 8th Army and the 5th Army have met not far from here. The Germans are evacuating, and the heavy firing is a lot less. A few days ago, the bloodiest battle ever fought was on the beach here. As soon as the second wave hit the beach, the Germans opened up with all they had. There was no stopping our troops though. It is 4:00 p.m., and the usual alerts off and on all day but nothing dropped.

Sep. 19, Sun. – Had a pretty quiet nite last nite. Had two alerts, but we didn't see anything. We are still unloading the hatches. Yesterday a group of men from a work battalion came aboard to help unload. A good share of their outfit was wiped out a few days prior to our coming here. The radio today said that the Italians had driven the Germans out of Sardinia into Corsica, and heavy fighting yet around Salerno and Naples. The 2 ½ ton DUKW (duck) boats that come alongside and load up take their loads right from here to the front lines. 4:30 p.m. we were told to get ready to leave the boat. We ate supper, raided the kitchen of coffee, milk, and canned stuff. Left the boat at 6:00. The winch lowered Curly and I down as we had the dog. It was a good excuse for a free ride anyway. We didn't get on shore until 7:00 p.m. The LST was stuck a little ways offshore and couldn't get in any closer. We had to jump in the water and wade to shore. We went to the bivouac area where our gun and trucks were.

Sep. 20, Mon. – Had coffee and "C" rations for breakfast. Took the waterproofing off the gun and trucks and then had dinner. We are supposed to leave at 1:00. We were told we are going to guard the VI Army Corps headquarters up at the front.

Sep. 21, Tue. – Too much traffic on the road yesterday, so we didn't leave. Went swimming last nite and today in an ice cold creek which comes from the mountain. The rest of our men came today, that is the ones we left at Port aux Poule. We sure were glad to see them. It is 6:30 p.m., and we are all set to leave.

Sep. 22, Wed. – Left last nite at 7:30 to take up gun position around the VI Army Corps. We got to our assigned position at 10:00 p.m. We are in a field where a few days ago was occupied by the German tanks. The Americans bombed these tanks so there are bomb craters all over here. We worked until 3:30 a.m. digging one of these craters out which we rolled our gun into. We also put our machine gun in a crater. We have to dig our director in yet. General Star, our colonel, and our battery officers inspected our position this morning and said it was the best they saw yet. They really liked our dummy position also. The field around us is full of unexploded shells and a lot of German mines. The engineers haven't had time to clear out this area yet, so we have to watch our step. A large formation of German planes flew over this morning, but the orders were not to fire unless a hostile act was committed, so we are not to give the position away which we are guarding. It is 5:00 p.m., and Curly is busy making supper as he is acting cook today. We are using the stuff we put our gloms on before someone else did. Had spaghetti and meatballs for dinner and having roast beef tonite. Yep, it's all in cans.

Sep. 23, Thu. – Last nite we could see an awful lot of heavy firing. The front is around 12 miles away. The radio said this morning that the Germans are burning Naples and killing the civilians and also preparing to evacuate. The Germans sure left in hurry as they left a building full of mines which were still crated up and another house with a lot of German papers. These buildings are right near our position.

Sep. 24, Fri. – Last nite had to have four holes dug in our alternate position so we can blast our position with TNT, which we were issued if we have to leave this one in a hurry. Had a paratrooper alert last nite, so we were imagining all sorts of noises and things. Didn't see anything though. Had three alerts today so far. We are eating darn good now that we are in gun positions again. We get 5-in-1 rations now which can't be beat (except for home cooking)! There is an Italian soldier chopping wood for us now for something to eat. We have fed quite a few already. It is 5:00 p.m. and just saw a dog fight between a Spitfire and a Jerry. The Germans just bombed the bridge which "A" Battery is protecting. They were too far away for us to fire. Just came over the phone that a Fw 190 was knocked down.

Roger Air Dome with Spitfires, Italy, September 1943

Sep. 25, Sat. – Got up at 6:30 as usual as we have to take our mosquito nets down so as they won't be seen from the air. Got the battery radio tonite, so we got the news. Russians took Smolensk, 5th Army and 8th Army moving satisfactorily but getting heavy resistance in the hills of Salerno. We are in those hills, and there is heavy firing which starts at sunset and lasts thru the nite. We can see the big shells as they go thru the air toward the German lines. Glad I'm not at the receiving end.

Sep. 26, Sun. – Looks like rain today. The rainy season isn't far off. Didn't feel so hot today, had the G.I.'s laid down most of the afternoon. We are eating "C" rations again — ugh! The only thing that tastes good are the biscuits. They used to taste good, but they don't compare to the 5-in-1 rations.

Sep. 27, Mon. – Started raining just after we got up this morning, and boy did it come down. After everything and us were muddy and wet, we get march order. We had to take over no. 7's position as they are moving up to guard a bridge. Boy, this position is big enough to drive a tank in. Well, we might as well leave it, as I don't think we'll be here long.

Sep. 28, Tue. – Well, here we go again. Just get set and we get march order today. Todd brought over some 150 German shells to make a gas stove out of. They sure work swell. You fill them half full of sand and then put gasoline in. We moved to a new airport in which the first two Spitfires just landed. We had to dig our "40" down so it wouldn't depress any lower than seven degrees and the same with the "50." We had to blast for the "50" as the ground was almost solid rock. We had to quit blasting though as a bunch of Spits landed and dispersed all around us.

Sep. 29, Wed. – Boy did it rain last nite! We had pup tents up, and I was on guard when it just started. Kapp and I took cover under the gun, and a little while later George hightails it thru the mud to get under the cover as our pup tent might as well not have been up. Everything and everybody was soaked thru. It rained almost all nite, and this morning the pit had seven inches of sticky clay. Kapp and Benoit set their tent over a bees' nest. After they got stung, I guess the bees kept dry 'cause they were the only ones left in it. We dried our equipment out most of the day and blasted the rest of the "50" pit out. Just had supper and the CP (command post) called and said to get set to pull out tonite or tomorrow. I wonder what we did to have this done to us. We moved dug down three times in three days. This is, or was, a beautiful spot. The Germans occupied this air dome, and there are quite a few Fw 190's which crashed and some self destroyed by the Germans so the Allies couldn't get them. We set up our two pyramidal tents also, expecting to stay here awhile. Well, such is the life of a Soldier.

Bridge we were protecting with a tank, Italy, September 1943

Sep. 30, Thu. – Packed everything up today and moved to a spot to wait for the rest of the 1st Platoon. We left about 3:00 p.m. to move 17 miles up the mountains to guard a bridge. These are the Apennine Mountains and a lot higher and more beautiful than those in Africa. It took us three hours to get here as the road was very narrow and snaky. We went thru the town of Battipaglia, which was a very good railway center. Every building was in ruins. It sure was a terrible sight. We set our "40" next to the bridge and the "50" on the next curve. We had to set both guns right next to the edge of the cliff as the road is very narrow.

Oct. 1, Fri. – Boy, was it cold last nite. It is plenty warm now after the sun gets to us. This is a very important bridge. It isn't very long, but it's the only way across. The Germans blew it up, but the engineers put another one up. The 5th and 7th Armies have been moving up past us all day. Every time a tank goes by, there's a dust storm. There are a bunch of tank destroyers going by now. We get our water from a hole in the cliff, and is it cold and good. It hasn't got that medicine taste like we've been getting from the mess truck. George is peeling apples now for apple sauce. Well, we had the sauce for supper, but those who only tasted it feel OK now. Ed and I ate a little more, and we had to call the medics as we sure felt like heaving. The 10 gallon pail they used sure sparkled on the inside from the acid in the apples. It sure was a shame to have to throw it out.

Spash Esposito and me with a Focke-Wulf Fw 190 German plane, Italy

31

Oct. 2, Sat. – A large number of 155 howitzers and "Long Toms" went thru yesterday and today. As long as the tanks and 155's are ahead of us, I feel much better. It rained this morning, and did it come down! It's 10:15 p.m., and I'm on guard, and it's raining like the dickens again but with Federwitz's truck right next to my "50" it makes it just perfect. I also have my radio hooked up in here. I have a German station on with some very popular American dance music, and boy does it sound good. The Germans must like our music. I got the news a bit ago and the 5th Army has got control of Naples and is well beyond. The Germans left the city in ruins. The Germans better not let the Russians get to Berlin before the Allies or they'll burn and kill the civilians like the Germans did at Smolensk and such. George and I made fish hooks and tried to catch some fish, but the rain made the stream below us too swift. We are right up in the clouds, and the thunder and lightning is deafening. There isn't any of the rain that gets by us either. A fellow from the engineers, while walking on the side of the road next to the cliff, was forced over by an ambulance. He fell down on some rocks about 30 feet. We made a litter and carried him up. He had internal injuries and sure was in tough shape. No doctors near either, but someone went to see if they could get an ambulance. The one that forced him off the road didn't see him as the road is so narrow.

Oct. 3, Sun. – Got march order and left at noon. We moved up about 17 miles to a bivouac area next to a field hospital which was just set up. There are plenty of nurses, but they have no time for us, too busy with the wounded. We put up pup tents and just in time too as it started raining and lasted all nite. Every place we bumped against it started leaking.

Oct. 4, Mon. – We repacked our trucks today to be ready to move up as soon as the officers get back from a reconnaissance. A young Italian priest was here today and gave us pins with Christ on or some of the saints. We also picked a bunch of walnuts and apples. The officers came back and said we would pull out tomorrow. The battalion headquarters has a movie projector so we saw a movie tonite *Palm Beach Story* and the news. It was rather old news though.

Oct. 5, Tue. – We pull out at 9:30 this morning. We drove until 3:00 this afternoon over the mountains yet, and the way the Germans have wrecked the roads and bridges it's a wonder a truck can get thru. All section chiefs and officers are supposed to go on a reconnaissance to pick out our positions and pull in tonite or tomorrow. We can hear the Germans shelling the town before us. The only thing ahead of us is the infantry. We have to guard a pass so the tanks can get thru. On the way down here the people cheered and threw apples and nuts and gave us wine when we stopped or were moving along slow. The wine here is a lot better than that which we got in Africa. The Germans took most of it though. Boy I've ate so many figs, apples, grapes, nuts, and "C" rations today that I feel sick. We've all got foxholes dug, ready to pile in if the Jerries start shelling us. Our infantry is only about 1,000 to 7,000 yards ahead of us, and the artillery is just below us in the valley.

Oct. 6, Wed. – Still here today yet. The Germans are still shelling the town of Benevento, the place we are to take positions in as soon as the Jerries let up a bit. The place is full of dead Americans and Germans. We cooked some potatoes which the Italians gave us, and threw in some hash, stew, beans, and onions, and boy was it good! There goes our artillery giving the Germans hell again. We are no longer the Coast Artillery Anti-Aircraft (CAAA), we are Anti-Aircraft Artillery (AAA). We are connected with the VI Corps under General Star (*) and the 45th Brigade under General Clark (**) 5th Army. In Africa, we were with the 7th Army under General Patton (***). All of the section chiefs went on a reconnaissance to find our gun positions. We pulled out as soon as we got back and pulled into our position. We used a bomb crater so we didn't have to dig so much. We had it dug out enough by 10:30 p.m. so knocked off until tomorrow.

Oct. 7, Thu. – We finished lining the sides with sand bags today. Boy, this position is one of the best we ever made. It is the perfect shape of a spearhead. This town of Benevento is really in ruins. It is still burning yet. The 105th are just a ways in back of us and around us, and when they start shelling the German lines there really is some racket. We are right next to a huge tobacco factory and an airplane factory. We got some good tobacco to smoke now. There are a lot of planes not finished and loads of wings, tails, and other parts. We sleep and eat in a house just across the road. We have deluxe beds to sleep in and there are beautiful boudoir sets in each bedroom. This town was shelled 48 hours ago, and the people started to come back today. When the people who lived here came back today (this is a modern apartment house), they sobbed on each other's shoulders. It sure was pitiful. The people back home can thank their lucky stars they don't have to go thru this. It'll take years to build this place up and there are many more towns and cities like this. War sure is a horrible thing! The people asked us to watch what was left of their belongings as they weren't going to come back and live here just yet. They have hardly any food left. We give almost half of our day's rations to them almost every day. We don't starve and can't see them starve.

Oct. 8, Fri. – Well we are quite comfortable here now. This is the best place we've been in yet. Boy, the 2nd Platoon sure is jealous 'cause we are set up so sweet. We have all the frying pans and kettles we want now. We made gas stoves from German shells and set the stove in the house, but they could be better. We found two gas stoves but need a pressure tank.

Oct. 9, Sat. – Slept till 8:00 this morning, and boy did that feel good. Just like home with a brand new bed and double mattress. I sure would like to stay here for the duration. It's the closest to home we've been to yet. I got two letters today. The first in Lord knows when. I got one from Margaret and one from Art. Most of us have an Italian rifle and ammunition. We've got so much junk or stuff we want which we've picked up that I don't know where we'll have room for them.

Italian family going back to their bombed home, Italy, 1943

Oct. 10, Sun. – I've been so busy since we got here that I haven't had time to wash. We found two rural district phones, which are run on dry cells. They were made in the USA. We put one at the gun and one here in the house. They work better than our field phones. Talking about phones, well we were caught with our britches down. We got a call from our CP that the colonel was on his way around, so I told Spash to call the house and get some more men over at the gun. Sgt. Moore and I were working on the axle tree lock. Spash called the house and told them the colonel was on his way and to send some men over. Sgt. Moore happened to look up and who was standing on the edge of the pit but the colonel. Boy, we certainly froze and did we feel foolish, 'cause the colonel heard Spash calling the house. He didn't say much, but boy he sure could have. We had a raid about 5:00 p.m. About 10 planes were over the objective but didn't drop any. Two more came from around, right over our heads but too high to make sure whether they were ours or not. Then these two pulled off and dropped their loads. They were just out of our range, otherwise we could have gotten at them. (The other 10 planes were drawing our attention while the other two snuck around to come in unexpected.) Hooked up lights from CP power plant so we have every convenience you could think of. 2nd Platoon moved up to guard the engineers as a big push is coming off tonite.

Oct. 11, Mon. – Fixed the Victrola and tried to get the radio to work, which we picked up. Most of the crew have wrist watches which I went and bought from an Italian. They keep pretty good time. Going to send one to Carol and Bert I think. Our gas stove works beautiful but it leaks, so Curly and Sam are fixing it. Got paid today in Allied Military Currency. It's in Italian lire with each lira one cent. It's a lot better than francs.

Oct. 12, Tue. – Took a bath and washed clothes. Boy, they sure were filthy, and I felt about the same. Got four turkeys today for $1.50 a piece. Killed two of them tonite. We felt pretty sick, most of us, from eating something.

Oct. 13, Wed. – Bill and I went over to the airplane factory and picked up a brand new Italian machine gun. We cleaned it up, but now we have to find some ammo for it. We have an Italian lady fixing the turkey and whole meal. It's almost supper time, so I can't wait. We are getting "B" rations now and cooking it ourselves. We get fresh bread, which tastes darn good.

Oct. 14, Thu. – Had an air raid around 8:00 this morning just after the alert hour, but it didn't take long for the whole crew to get out to the gun and put it in action. We are pretty sure we got some hits with the 50 cal. We drove them away anyway, so the colonel was well pleased for that. They couldn't carry out their mission, so that's almost as good as a hit. It rained nearly all day, and all the mosquitoes really reproduced on it. There are a number of malaria cases in our battery 'cause those men didn't take their Atabrine pills regularly. The mosquitoes are pretty bad, so we have to take one a day.

Oct. 15, Fri. – Got march order at 11:30 last nite. We have only one truck, and all the stuff we had and wanted, well there just wasn't room for any more. The truck was so loaded that it was top heavy. We left to move up about 30 miles to hold and protect a bridge which the Americans were supposed to have taken. We went about 10 miles and Major Cook met us and told us the bridge was still in German hands. He told us we could dig in where we were until the bridge was taken. It didn't make us mad as we would probably have gotten caught in the artillery fire, which goes off at dawn. It was 4:00 a.m. when we pulled in here, and we are still digging at 10:00 a.m. The ground is all sticky clay, and it won't leave the shovel. There was an awful barrage of anti-aircraft fire not far over the hill, but they were out of our range. Boy, was it cold last nite! Enemy planes flew over a little while ago, and we opened up on them.

Oct. 16, Sat. – March order at 4:30 p.m. We moved up at dark and pulled into a field about five miles from the bridge. It was about 10:30 p.m., so we dug foxholes and slept in them up until 2:00 a.m. when we up and moved into positions about a few hundred yards from the bridge. We are right up with the infantry. We were supposed to go across the bridge into the town right with the 2nd Infantry Battalion and help take the town, but the 88's were shelling all around us, and they blew up the bridge. We took up positions where we are and made darn sure we dug foxholes first which was a darn good thing. We can hear our shells going over our heads and landing just the other side of the river into the Jerry lines. Between the machine gun fire from our lines and our long guns, which are a ways behind us, they make quite a display of fireworks, but I'd sooner see it in a news reel. You can tell the 88's coming as they have a more whining sound than the 155's. The first one that came toward us, we dove for the slit trenches. I dove in one and Spash dove right on top of me. My whole face went in the dirt and I was eating dirt the rest of the day. There have been quite a few prisoners taken, and there are still some running loose. Our officers caught one yesterday, and another one was taken close to us by an infantry patrol. Our artillery is trying to knock out the battery of 88's and boy what a barrage. Every time I get tired a shell goes whizzing by and then see me dig. Todd had to leave everything and get out. After, he went back and had to pull out again.

Oct. 17, Sun. – We made our beds in slit trenches last nite. It was the first sleep since Wednesday nite that amounted to something. We were so dead tired we slept thru a barrage of 88 fire on the bridge. George was on guard at the time and said it was terrific. Our other truck came back today. We got march order at 11:30 a.m. and were set to move in 20 minutes. It's the fastest we ever moved. We had to beat the artillery across the river to protect them as they went thru the bypass the engineers made last nite.

Oct. 18, Mon. – Finished our pit, and Curly and I took a walk over the ravine. The Germans sure left in a hurry as they left a lot of valuable equipment. We got an infantry machine gun (zipper gun) and lots of ammo, an automatic rifle, and hand grenades. We had to watch out for personnel mines, and most of the stuff left was booby-trapped. It rained again last nite as usual. Gee, what a mess again. Note: This is an incident that happened at this time. The battalion dentist and his assistant came to our gun to check our teeth. The assistant pedals a stationary bike to drive the drill. While he was working on one of the guys, the Germans started shelling again. The Dr. and his assistant both dove for a foxhole leaving the guy with his mouth open sitting on a stool. After the shelling stopped, which wasn't that close, the Dr. wouldn't finish and said we would have to come to the battalion headquarters to get our teeth fixed. He wanted no part of that front line stuff.

Oct. 19, Tue. – The 88's opened up above and around us last nite again. Boy, when they start whistling, everybody makes one dive altogether. We got a bunch of mail yesterday. Boy, I was so happy I didn't care how many 88's came over, just so I would have time to read them.

Oct. 20, Wed. – We slept in our slit trenches again last nite, and boy was it damp as it rained during the day. Took some pictures in our trenches and of our "40."

Oct. 21, Thu. – Fired our German machine gun, and boy does it zip. Spash and I bought us each a 38 revolver, and boy are they neat. Built our pit wider so it is a good yard wide all the way around. Had pancakes for breakfast and turkey for supper.

Oct. 22, Fri. – Naples was bombed last nite, and boy did we see the fireworks. Wave after wave of German bombers flew over our position toward Naples. We didn't fire as we would have given away our position, and we couldn't see them. General Eisenhower and General Clark were around today. Boy, were we busy cleaning up. Wrote 11 letters today. I don't think I'll ever get them all answered.

Oct. 23, Sat. – Naples was bombed again last nite, and they put up the biggest barrage I ever saw. The Germans circled over us quite awhile, but didn't drop anything. We saw a flamer go down.

Oct. 24, Sun. – Naples bombed again last nite. They sure dropped a lot of flares. Don't know what damage they did as of yet. Going to services this morning. Big mail call today. Hurrah!

Oct. 25, Mon. – An inspecting party came around. A major really put everybody thru the mill. Everybody was wrong but him. Boy, if many more come around, we might as well go back to the States.

Oct. 26, Tue. – Last nite we thought the Jerries had dropped flares over Naples again, but Mount Vesuvius started erupting again. It sure is interesting.

Oct. 27, Wed. – General Star brought our power plant back today (damn it). Now we have to dig a director pit. We got the director in, and we did a pretty neat job. We checked for zero deflection, but our director is off. We can see Mount Vesuvius good thru the field glasses, and there is a steady stream of smoke coming from it. We got another large bunch of mail today but no packages yet. The officers are really keeping track of what we do since the major gave them hell. Been raining off and on all day. It sure is miserable.

Oct. 28, Thu. – We have to be clean shaven everyday and clean fatigues. Boy, right up near the front lines and they pull that stuff. An inspecting captain was around today and went over everything he could think of with me. I think he was pretty satisfied. Had two apple pies for supper. Bought a neat combination watch and stop watch from a guy from Naples. "Joe" the old fellow who used to drive stage coach for "Buffalo Bill" when he was in the States. He bought it for me and a lot cheaper than I could have gotten it. He wanted $50, but the old man got it for $32. I'm going to send it home to Dad.

Oct. 29, Fri. – Oriented today, but the director is out of phase. An officer was around today to checkup on our aircraft identification. He couldn't catch us though. Had pork chops for supper. We enjoyed them in the rain and mud. Got march order at 6:00. Moved up to guard an ammunition dump.

2nd Edition

October 30, 1943 to February 11, 1944

Our campaign in Italy continued

By September 1943, the German army occupied Italy and established a new fascist regime. The Allies landed in Italy focused on taking back the Italian Peninsula. During their campaign in Italy, the 451st Anti-Aircraft Artillery seemed to move constantly, digging in their 40 mm gun pit at each stop. Jack's frustration with this movement, inspections, and even some of the English and French soldiers is apparent through some of his entries. While there were times of intense battle, they were also able to see the sights of Italy including Pompeii and Rome.

Oct. 30, Sat. – Went to bed at 3:00 this morning and got up at 6:00 for the morning alert. Finished our "40" and "50" pits and set up the pyramidal tents — and not a second too soon as it started to rain, and it came down in torrents, then it started hailing. We couldn't get all our blankets and things in soon enough, so everything and us are pretty well waterlogged. Part of our pit caved in on our ammo boxes. Boy, I hope it stops, or we'll have to dig a new pit. It sure seemed queer. The sun was shining just as bright as could be but rain! Boy, I never saw it rain so much before.

This morning I smashed my thumb between the trailer hitch and truck while trying to hook it on. I'm having one heck of a time writing this.

Oct. 31, Sun. – We were supposed to dig our director in today, but we haven't a field of fire for it. We could see the 2nd Platoon firing on planes. Halloween but we can't shove our latrine over.

Nov. 1, Mon. – Sent two packages home today. I drove Sokel's German motorcycle this afternoon. Boy, was it fun. It is 8:00 p.m., and the Jerries just got thru bombing Naples again. We are northwest of Naples, but the planes circled over our heads to keep away from the barrage fire, and it sure was thick. We got a blanket and our winter clothing today. Boy, and it doesn't make us mad as it's plenty cold. An Italian fellow came over scared and excited as heck. Some drunken soldiers were swiping his chickens and beating him and his wife and daughter. Spash, George, Ed, and I went along with him, and the Yankees took hand of things. Those guys don't care what side they are on.

I'm in camouflage

Nov. 2, Tue. – Got march order this afternoon. Boy, we had a nice setup. The people near us cried when we left. They did our washing and ironed every bit of it and wouldn't take hardly anything for it. They gave us all the wine we wanted. We pulled out at 4:45 p.m. to go guard a bridge that was just taken yesterday which is about 20 miles from here.

Nov. 3, Wed. – Last nite we pulled in and started digging our emplacement at 7:30 p.m. We finished the whole "40" pit and machine gun pit by 10:30 p.m. and had the guns, director, and power plant in by 12:00. Boy, we sure had some nice digging. We set up our big tent and camouflaged everything. Sgt. Moore brought the motorcycle around, so Curly and I took it for a spin on the main road. Boy, was it fun and go! Boy, oh boy!

Nov. 4, Thu. – Some American planes came over and some other anti-aircraft outfit opened upon them. I don't see why, 'cause we could see plain as day that they were our A-36's. Quite a few Jerry observation planes came over, but there was a haze so we couldn't see them.

Nov. 5, Fri. – Got some more mail from Mother. Wrote some letters. Got some long johns and shirts today. Boy, and do they fit too. We are only 90 miles from Rome. I hope we get to see it.

Nov. 6, Sat. – Naples was bombed again last nite. The Germans have been driven out to the plains. We watched waves of A-36's go over us to strafe and bomb the German lines. We could see the German ack-ack firing on them, but they couldn't hit the side of a barn.

Nov. 7, Sun. – (10:00 a.m.) 12 German Me 109's just finished a raid on us. We were the first to open fire, and boy did they come down. As the gun followed them down, it was just above the pit, and boy did the pad of the pit start jumping around and dirt, gee we couldn't see anything. We got two possible planes out of it. Last nite was the big drive. Boy, there was so much shooting it sounded like anti-aircraft firing. Not far from here a big tank battle was going on and still is. Gee, the racket.

Nov. 8, Mon. – It started raining early last nite, and it's still raining today. Boy, and does it come down. Good thing we put the pyramidal tent up or everything would be soaked. The Germans have put three new divisions to make a last stand before we take Rome. The hills just before us are the last ones between here and the plains which extend all the way to Rome. Once we get the Germans on the plains, they won't have a chance to dig in. The field hospital close by needed blood for transfusions so all the fellows with type "O" blood were asked to donate. Benoit and Williamson and George went from here. I am type "A."

41

Nov. 9, Tue. – It's cold as the dickens today. Had a raid close by, but we didn't get a chance to fire. Another one this afternoon. Naples was bombed last nite again and 90's opened up on planes right over our heads.

Nov. 10, Wed. – Gee, was it cold last nite, and it's getting colder with a north wind blowing. Had pancakes for breakfast. Lt. Hedricks told us that the Germans were given until tomorrow to surrender otherwise thousands of bombs were going to hit Germany and not sparing nobody. Rommel is in full charge of the Germans here, and they have brought up two more divisions. George Hemminger gave a pint of blood yesterday as our boys are being hit pretty hard and a lot of Germans taken need transfusions also. The fighting is at a standstill, and the Germans counter-attacked five times but gained nothing. We watched our A-36's and P-40's dive bomb some German railway guns which are dropping shells up the road a ways. They must have knocked out the German anti-aircraft as they never fired at all on our planes. Boy, it sure is a thrilling sight watching them dive down and knowing the Germans are catching hell. They must be catching more hell as an artillery barrage is going on now. Got paid today $38.35 (that's for one month plus $35.00 went for war bonds).

Nov. 11, Thu. – Armistice Day today. I sure would like to know how the M&M game turned out. Tonite around 4:00 p.m. a flight of P-40's went over, and on the way back as they came over again one of them started to dive. We couldn't imagine what the heck was up. Then the pilot bailed out, and the plane continued its screaming dive down and hit not far from our emplacement. There wasn't much of an explosion, but when Curly and I ran over to it, it was scattered all over and there was a hole about 15 feet deep where the nose and gasoline were burning. We couldn't find much even for a souvenir. Good thing the pilot wasn't in it 'cause there wouldn't be anything left of him.

Nov. 12, Fri. – Got march order today at 12:30 p.m. It is now 4:00 p.m., and we pulled the trucks off the road into a grove of trees and dove for some slit trenches the infantry was so kind to leave us. I am in a slit trench now writing this. The 88's spotted us on the road from the hill and opened up on us. Boy was there hell popping just a minute ago. Shrapnel was flying all over us, but no one was hurt. I see George is digging his hole deeper. It happened too quick to get scared.

Nov. 13, Sat. – We lost George and the "40" truck as they took the wrong turn and were heading for the front yesterday. They turned around after they couldn't find us. My section had to cross the Volturno River, and we are setup on the other side of the rest of the gun section. Boy, was it hard digging. All gravel and rock. It was a full moon, so it was nice and light out. The field artillery is all around us, and the 88's started shelling at 2:00 a.m. until 7:00 this morning. The shells were short of us and over our heads. The Germans were shelling the town of Venafro, for about 30 minutes this afternoon, which is right near us. Lucky for us they didn't land close. Two fellows from "B" Battery were killed when an 88 made a direct hit on their gun emplacement, and two were seriously wounded. One officer from our battalion headquarters was killed also. Every time the Germans send over one shell, our Long Toms reply back with about 25. The Jerries came over at breakfast time with about 25 planes trying to bomb out the Long Toms. They were just out of our range to fire on them. They came over at noon again just as I was opening three Christmas packages I received from home. We fired on them and got one. Boy, this is just like duck hunting, we wait for them to come over and then let them have it. Only thing, these birds shoot back. It is 4:15 p.m., and the Germans are shelling the town of Venafro about a half mile from here. We have been watching the artillery fire on the hill and the Germans lobbing their mortars back over. Boy, they are dug in back of this hill, and it's going to be a heck of a job getting them out. We have cavalry and mules here to get up on the mountain in order to drive the Germans out. Boy, I'm crazy about the things I got from home, and boy, did I get a dandy pen from Mom and Dad. I sure didn't want them to pay so much for it, but being they are the best parents in the world accounts for it!

Frank, Louie, and Mustafa (standing). Gun pit and 40 mm shell casings are from this morning when we fired on Jerry Me 109's. Got credit for one our platoon did. November 1943

Nov. 14, Sun. – It started raining last nite, and it's been raining all day. We got march order at 12:15 p.m. this noon. It was raining like the dickens and was it miserable.

It's still raining to beat heck. We sergeants have to go on reconnaissance now to pick out our new positions.

Nov. 15, Mon. – We moved up eight miles to guard a bridge the engineers are making. We aren't far from the infantry, and we went by their mortar guns and boy, were they letting loose last nite. We pulled into positions at 6:00 last nite and had to ford a river, which came over the running boards on the truck. Major Cook wanted my section set up on a knoll, but we couldn't get up there. Lt. Hedricks saw a knoll quite a ways back and said to set it up there. When the trucks arrived I took them up to the spot, but it was a lot different after we got there. It was so dark and talk about rain, gee it sure was coming down. After picking a spot which we thought was a pretty good field of fire, we commenced to dig our pit. Every time we took a shovel of dirt, it filled up with rain so we got disgusted and quit. We were all soaked to the skin and piled in the truck the best we could. I squeezed into the trailer, and boy was I frozen and cramped. I managed to get my shoes and socks off, so I put my wool cap and one I found on each foot and then shoved my feet in a barracks bag. It was raining so hard and I was shivering so much I couldn't sleep. We just left our gun pit go today as it's still raining. We put our tent up and rigged a stove up in it and dried out a bit. I opened up my bed roll tonite, and every blanket is soaked. I guess I'll freeze again tonite. The river is too high to cross so if the Germans open up on us, we'll sure get caught like rats if we have to retreat. They can't even get our food rations to us, but we have some "C" rations we saved but don't know how long it will last. I can hear shells landing now, and they sound pretty close. I hope and pray they don't get any closer.

Nov. 16, Tue. – We set the stove up in the tent yesterday, and last nite at 1:30 a.m. Spash and I were froze so we got up and made some coffee and warmed up. It's 6:30 now, and it's still raining. At 8:00 tonite it will have rained 72 hours. We put the tent up in the rain and it got wet inside, so the tent is leaking pretty bad. We haven't been dry for four days now. They floated our rations across the river to us on a pontoon. The paratroopers were pushed back last nite, and they are setup in our area here. A bunch of infantry walked past us this afternoon going up to fight tonite. Boy, you really have to give those boys credit. They looked like a happy bunch of fellows, soaked to the skin, but still smiling. I just hope the Germans don't come any closer as we'll never get our trucks and gun out of this mud, and we'll never cross the river with this rain coming down the way it is. The roads are all rivers now.

Nov. 17, Wed. – Rained till 10:00 this morning, and the sun was out a little while this afternoon. There is snow on top of the mountains just to our right. We moved the gun three times to try to get out of the mud. We didn't dig it in and are making a wall of rocks around it for the emplacement. Our rations didn't come today as the pontoon broke away last nite. The 88's started dropping close again this evening.

We can hear the gun as it goes off and then the unmistakable whistle and then, well we don't wait to see it hit. We make one dive for a foxhole and what goes thru your mind waiting for it to land, you'll sure be surprised 'cause you wouldn't believe so many things could go thru your mind so fast.

Nov. 18, Thu. – Esposito and I were picked from my crew to go to a rest camp at Naples on the 20th of this month. It's more or less a pass as we don't need a rest anymore than the rest of the fellows. After we get back, two more from each crew will go. It rained most of the day again. There go the 88's again. The airborne captured some German prisoners about a mile from here, and they said the 88's are setup in caves and very hard to get at. No wonder our artillery can't get at them.

Nov. 19, Fri. – They are getting our rations, gas, and mail across the river on a trailer rack which is run on a cable stretched across. We are supposed to get march order in a day or so to guard another bridge up where the 88's are landing. Boy, is that going to be fun. The Germans really have been shelling the valley over there. We can hear every one coming thru the air, but a lot of them are duds. We can thank the French working in German munitions plants for that. They slip a piece of cardboard between the striker and percussion cap, which makes the dud. We fired on the Jerries this morning and one was hit, but we don't know if we hit it or one of the other crews as it was very cloudy and hard to see.

The "40" is trained on planes, but they were friendly. Close up can be seen some of the mud we had to contend with. This is the Volturno Valley. The Germans' front line is just on the other side of the mountains in the background. A German 88 explosion can be seen on the side of the mountain closest to our position.

Nov. 20, Sat. – Left for Naples this morning at 6:30. It rained from 5:30 this morning until we got there at 1:00 p.m. It sure is a relief to get away from the mud and the 88's. When we got here, they said we weren't scheduled to come, so they had to put us up in an old garrison. They gave us cots and three blankets apiece. We got a meal of spaghetti first thing and an hour later got another one. Boy, we were hungry. It's 8:30 now, and I'm hitting the hay. Boy, we sure are tired.

Nov. 21, Sun. – Got up at 7:30 this morning. Boy did I sleep good. Spash, Kip, and I went window shopping for awhile this morning and bought a few things. We are waiting till noon now when they are going to let us know if we can stay or not. Boy they sure do screw things up in the Army. The officer in charge of us told us to clear out and when the trucks came he couldn't find us. Boy, we sure cleared out in a hurry and didn't come back until bedtime. We went to the Red Cross Theater and saw a good stage show and then saw the movie *Thank Your Lucky Stars*. After the show, it was so darn dark and so many people on the streets. Boy we were bumping into everyone 'cause the city of Naples is blacked out.

Nov. 22, Mon. – Got up and ate breakfast and hit for the main section. Boy, the people. It's just like the loop in Chicago. We are sitting in a small restaurant waiting for our dinner of spaghetti, meat, and potatoes. Had an air raid here last nite. Saw Mount Vesuvius this morning, and boy is it active. We are going to try to see the isle of Capri. Went to the show and saw *Crazy House* with Olsen and Johnson. Went over to a private house for spaghetti supper and met two swell fellows from the infantry. They are fighting just ahead of us on the snow-capped mountain.

Nov. 23, Tue. – It rained off and on all day today. Went to the Red Cross Theater and saw *The Sky's the Limit* with Fred Astaire and Joan Leslie. Did some more window shopping. Boy, I sure am tired of walking. Boy, there sure are a lot of beautiful girls here.

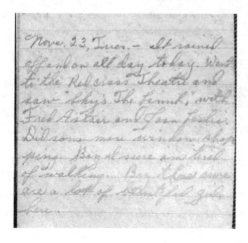

Nov. 24, Wed. – Got our pictures today. They sure have to be touched up. Went to the theater again and saw the first U.S.O. show to be put on in Italy. Ella Logan and her show. It consisted of only three, but it sure was good. After that the 337th Eng. put on a stage show, which was also tops. Came back for supper tonite for the first time. We were late but they fixed us steaks, and boy were they good. We are supposed to go back tomorrow. We don't mind though as we are pretty tired, and our money is all gone. This was supposed to be a rest, but I think we'll go back to the front and rest. Had a good time though, and sure am glad I got to see Naples. Saw Mount Vesuvius and took a picture of it. Had an air raid a little while ago.

Nov. 25, Thu. – Today is Thanksgiving, and we also leave here at 11:00 a.m. to return to our gun positions. We got back to our gun positions tonite at 7:00. The old familiar booming again. It sure was good not to hear it for a week. When we got to the river just before our position, we found the river too high for the trucks to cross. The rope for the ferry was broke at the other end, and the trailer was hanging in the water from the cable out in the middle of the river. There were seven of us who had to get across, so we pulled it in and Kip and I worked our way across the cable to the other side where Sgt. Moore was with a truck to connect the winch cable onto it. We got 20 feet from shore and couldn't go any further as we were pulling up hill. So Paul J. Meyers wrapped the cable around himself and scaled out to us. Just as he got to us, he dropped the cable so all three of us were stranded out there, and boy was it raining and blowing. Sgt. Moore finally worked it out to us on a snatch block and pulled us in. The other fellows pulled it back, and then we winched them back over. Boy the mud. It rained all the while we were gone to Naples.

Nov. 26, Fri. – The colonel came across on the ferry and visited us for the first time since we came here. He was well pleased with everything and said we should keep as dry as possible so we wouldn't get sick. There's an artillery duel going on right now between our 155's and the Germans. The Jerries are coming plenty close to us. Sending a box home and one to Carol today. We can hear the infantry pound away with machine guns and rifles in the hills just before us. Both of our trucks are broke down, so I sure hope we won't have to retreat 'cause we'll have to hoof it if we have to. Eight of our P-51's came over and dove on the Jerry artillery positions. German shrapnel and explosive shells from German anti-aircraft guns fell all around us. General Star informed us that the 451st is the best anti-aircraft battalion up here, and that we have the best record. He said that we could have had gun positions back guarding a big airport in Foggia, but we have a good outfit and are needed up here. We just had our turkey for supper, and boy it sure was good. All of the fellows overseas are supposed to have turkey for Thanksgiving.

47

Nov. 27, Sat. – It rained last nite and also rained 88's. Boy you never get used to them damn things. The sun was out for awhile today, and it sure felt nice. Mailed two packages today.

Nov. 28, Sun. – The sun was out all day today again. The Germans started throwing 175 shells last nite and today. Spitfires strafed the Jerries and boy did the Jerries throw up the ack-ack. You'd think it was ours as it was so close. As soon as the airports dry up a bit, our planes can take off and bomb and strafe the hell out of the Jerries, and we can move up. From reports, Berlin is really catching it. Boy, that don't make us mad.

Nov. 29, Mon. – A flight of 40 B-24 liberators with an escort of P-38's flew over us a little while ago. The Jerries are surely going to catch heck someplace. I got four boxes today. One from Carol, Grandpa, Aunt Anna, and Mr. and Mrs. Krutz. Boy, I'll need another barracks bag to put all the things in soon. It's been raining off and on, so maybe the rainy season is close to an end. The good thing about this place is that the only officers we see are our platoon officers. The CP is on this side of the river, but they are swell officers and don't bother us. The rest are afraid to cross the river except the colonel who was across once but came just to see how we were. Lt. (or Capt. Carey now) wanted us to string a rope across the river so we could cross hand over hand. Boy is he balmy!

Nov. 30, Tue. – Boy, the mornings and nites are really cold. There was an extra heavy artillery duel all last nite, and it's still going on. Only thing, the Germans aren't returning them as heavy as we are sending over. They start at about the same time with their heavy shelling every nite, and we always call them the bowling allies as the sound rolls along the hills like a bowing ball and then hits. Only thing, it is a lot noisier.

Dec. 1, Wed. – The days are getting shorter and colder. It rained for a while today just to keep everything nice and muddy. A flight of 15 B-25's came over today and circled the lines and came back over our Long Toms to the left of us here. I was watching them thru the field glasses, and just as they got over the guns there was a barrage of ack-ack thrown up around them and then some big explosions around the Long Toms. I couldn't figure it out, our own planes dropping bombs on our guns. Then the report came over the phone that four Me 109's had snuck in under them and dive bombed our guns. Boy them damn Jerries are pretty smart. But I still think our own planes did it as I was watching them the whole time.

Dec. 2, Thu. – It's been cold as the dickens all day today. The Jerries are short on planes or else this rainy weather has kept them grounded as they don't come around like they used to. Flights of our bombers go over every day.

Dec. 3, Fri. – It rained nearly all day again. Four Germans were caught trying to blow up the bridge we are protecting last nite. This is the Volturno Valley, and there are big artillery pieces all along it, and they fire constantly day and nite. The Germans haven't been returning so many lately.

Dec. 4, Sat. – It's been raining all day today and last nite. The Volturno River is raging again and is up 4 to 5 feet higher already. The Germans are firing air bursts at us right now, and gun crew no. 3 can't be gotten on the phone. It's raining pitchforks out now, and our director is almost in the water, and it's standing on a three foot tripod. Our ammo in the "40" pit is covered by water, and our slit trenches are all bath tubs. I don't know what's worse, to drown in a slit trench or dodge 175's and 88's.

Dec. 5, Sun. – It stopped raining, and the sun came out today. The water was up even with the outriggers, and the ammo chests were completely covered. We bailed all morning to get the water out. It rained about a foot and a half in 36 hours. Five men over 38 from our platoon left today to go back to the States. Boy, those guys were sure happy, and I don't blame them. I gave two films to Anker Larson to give to the folks back home. There's a rumor going around that we won't be in this theater long. We are supposed to get four-barreled "50's" and go in on the next invasion. Hope it isn't true.

Dec. 6, Mon. – It rained most of the morning again. We got paid today. George and I fried pancakes for breakfast, and we've been eating them all day. We are supposed to evacuate this area tomorrow but have to wait until the bridge is put back up as it was washed away.

George making breakfast outside of Salerno, Italy

Dec. 7, Tue. – Got march order at noon today. All the trucks had to be winched up the hill by us as the mud is terrible. It started raining this noon, and we finally got under way at 2:30. We pulled in at the battery CP where we are staying overnite and then pulling out at 6:45 to a bivouac area where we have to clean up all our equipment and get re-equipped. We are going to get four-barreled 50 calipers and get rid of our water-cooled machine gun and trailer. Later on we are supposed to get twin "40's" mounted on full tracks. The barrel broke away from the gunstay on the way here, and it hit two poles and swung to the other side of the road and forced a jeep and a weapons carrier into the ditch. Boy the old gun is covered with four inches of solid mud. I can just see the fun we are in for cleaning our equipment. Got a package from Minerva today, and boy was it full of swell surprises.

Dec. 8, Wed. – Capt. Carey couldn't get a convoy permit because it was too dangerous to travel in convoy, so each gun section left at 15-minute intervals. We left at 7:15, and it started raining just as we left. It rained so hard we had a hard time keeping on the right road. We went about 10 miles and are now in position waiting for the rest of the battalion to come, and then we are going back to a bivouac area to start cleaning up.

Dec. 9, Thu. – We sure didn't get much sleep last nite. The Jerries were landing their shells right in here. Gee but you get the most awful feeling in the pit of your stomach when you hear them things whistling in at you. Boy, are our planes giving them hell this morning. Wave after wave of P-40's and B-25's keep going over us at the German lines. We can see them dive down as the front line of the Germans are just the other side of the mountains. I've got to get out to the gun as the colonel is coming around. We finished cleaning the gun and carriage and ran the trucks in the crick near by to clean the mud off as our new divisional commander, General Bradshaw, is coming around tomorrow to inspect. French troops relieved us up where we were, and there still is a bunch going up. They have everything of ours except our helmets. I heard they are supposed to relieve all of our troops in this theater.

Dec. 10, Fri. – We've been all setup for the general, but he didn't come today. Our infantry must have made an attack today as our artillery were landing a lot of smoke shells on the other side of the hill just ahead of us. Got a box of cookies from Mother today. Good? Well I guess! Also got a honey of a letter from Carol.

Dec. 11, Sat. – The colonel and major were to inspect today. We got orders from the 5th Group to dig our guns and director in. We took our time and got the guns in but have the director to put in yet. Had two raids today. This dry weather has brought the Jerries back in the air again. Today was the swellest day we had for a long time. The sun was out all day.

Dec. 12, Sun. – Rained most of this morning. We are preparing for General Bradshaw who is coming tomorrow. Saw a dog fight between a Spit and an Me 109. The Spit came out on top. Today was Kip's birthday.

Dec. 13, Mon. – Had to bail out the "40" and "50" pits this morning as we dug in next to a creek, and the water seeps into the pits. The general is on his way around but hasn't been here yet. Hope he comes 'cause we're all set for him. We were commended thru the colonel today on the large number of planes shot down and the least ammo used of any other AAA group.

Dec. 14, Tue. – The big shot didn't come around yesterday. Our officers are out on reconnaissance, so we expect march order today or tomorrow. Our fighter planes, A-36's and P-40's, have been going over all morning. Some Jerry planes came over and boy the ack-ack thrown up at them. Awhile after there was a dog fight. A P-40 and a Jerry. A shell from a cannon on one of the planes hit and exploded close to us. The Jerry must have been hit as the plane was smoking and kept going around in a circle like a chicken with its head cut off. He finally went down behind the hill. Bill's truck got stuck in the mud and broke another front axle. Kip was scrubbing the mud from his shoes by the crick when I went over there as he fell in the mud last nite. Boy, did I laugh.

Dec. 15, Wed. – Boy, did we see the pretty fireworks this morning when we got up for the morning alert which is before sunrise. We could see the flash of our artillery going off and then the big flash when the shell hit. We could see the machine gun tracer fire of the infantry. In one way it was a pretty sight, but I sure wouldn't want to see the sight it made. We got march order at 11:30 this morning. We had to winch Bill's truck all the way to the road and had to cut a road across the river and go thru Kip's position. We were holding the whole bunch up, and the colonel and Carey were there blowing their tops. Boy, were they mad! The whole battalion got relieved, so we all went back and bivouacked outside of Santa Maria, which is about 15 miles from Naples.

Dec. 16, Thu. – We started to clean all our equipment today. We finished working at 2:30 p.m. and have the rest of the time to ourselves. Passes for Naples start tomorrow. 25% (or 40 men) from the battery go. They have a guard list again and boy that Spizzan sure is screwing things up again. I'd sooner be back in gun position dodging 88's.

Dec. 17, Fri. – Still cleaning our equipment. Boy, and have we a job ahead of us. Kip and I fixed it so we both go out together Monday. I'm sergeant of the guard tonite.

Dec. 18, Sat. – Cloudy and cold today. It rained a little while this noon. All wet equipment, rifles, and cooking utensils have to be spic and span as we are having an inspection Monday. Boy, I picked the right day for my pass. Rommel said if he could hold General Clark's 5th Army for eight weeks he could hold any army in the world. Eight weeks was up yesterday. They held, but who could advance in this mud and rain.

Dec. 19, Sun. – Repacked the wheel bearings on the gun and went on gun guard at 12:00 noon until tomorrow noon. "40" went to the ordnance.

Dec. 20, Mon. – Went on pass to Naples with Kip, Spash, and Curly. Had to stand inspection in ranks at the battalion area, so we didn't get to Naples until 12:00 noon. Had a swell time. Last nite took my first hot shower since we were on the boat coming to Salerno, at University at Santa Maria.

Yud's, Spash, and me

Dec. 21, Tue. – Had a memorial service for the fellows in our battalion who were killed or wounded. It was held in a beautiful theater in Santa Maria. Played football this afternoon. Since we left the front, we are no longer connected with the 5th Group. We got a letter from Col. Hennigen, who is the head of the 5th Group, and he said when we come back to the front he hopes we all get connected up with him again. He commanded us and said we were a very good outfit.

Dec. 22, Wed. – Went to the ordnance to get the "40," but it wasn't ready yet. Capt. Carey had a chief of section meeting today. He said if all our equipment is cleaned and ready that just after Christmas we will take up gun positions near Naples. He said we would get buildings to sleep in. Boy I sure hope so. We are supposed to stay there for two weeks or so and get the four-barreled "50's" and then go back to the front. We were all issued overshoes the other day so we won't have wet feet so often anyway. We are under a new TVA and are going to be re-equipped.

Dec. 23, Thu. – It's been raining nearly all week, so we haven't been able to do much on our equipment. Went to the ordnance and got the "40." It's about 15 miles away and raining, and the road is all mud. Boy, is it a mess again, and we have the whole thing to paint yet.

Dec. 24, Fri. – Went on pass today with Kip, Moore, and Ray. Lt. Hedricks couldn't go but he let us have the jeep, so we had a swell time in Naples. Saw a stage show at the Red Cross Theater. An Italian orchestra played and boy, was there a neat looking dancer. Rained part of the day. Sang Christmas songs tonite. Got a letter from Mom saying she got her ear-phones. Boy was that a swell Christmas present knowing she has the chance to hear like the rest of us again.

Dec. 25, Sat. – Christmas Day. Went to services at Santa Maria in a beautiful theater. Took communion. Had the best meal today I believe we ever had in the Army!!! Ralph, Kip, Ray, and I got a special pass from Lt. Hedricks for Santa Maria this afternoon. Going on a reconnaissance at 7:30 tomorrow morning.

Dec. 26, Sun. – Went on reconnaissance to Castellammare. It's at the foot of Mount Vesuvius and about three miles outside Naples. We will be right next to the water and the town on the other side of us. We are taking over from the Limeys. It should be a pretty good setup. Breakfast at 4:30 a.m. tomorrow.

Dec. 27, Mon. – Left at 6:00 this morning. Halfway there we thought the truck was on fire. We stopped and found the brake drums on every wheel red hot and the lugs nearly off on one wheel. Boy, were we lucky we stopped. We finally got here, and the "40" truck wasn't here yet. The rest of the battalion had gotten lost. We have a pretty good setup but didn't get a house to stay in. We have a Limey and a French soldier sleeping with us tonite.

Dec. 28, Tue. – Boy, this is the best place we've setup in yet outside of Benavento. We have an Italian fellow who comes every day from Sacramento. He comes by train about 7:00 every morning and leaves at 2:30 p.m. to catch the train back. He makes all of our beds, cleans up the tent, chops wood, washes our mess kits, and anything else that needs being done. Boy, he sure is a good worker and honest as the day is long.

Dec. 29, Wed. – Passes started today. Got a typhus shot and a smallpox vaccination this noon. Had my picture taken with needles in both arms.

Vaccinations, December 1943

Dec. 30, Thu. – Went to the dentist and had two cavities filled. Kip, Spash, and I went to town and took a bath in a bathtub. Boy, it was swell. They were sulfur baths.

Dec. 31, Fri. – New Year's Eve tonite. Going over to see Kip.

Jan. 1, 1944, Sat. – Boy, what a time we had last nite. We went to Kip's position and then to Chapman's. Spash and I went and we sure celebrated. Had a swell supper tonite. The Italian working for us had some homemade spaghetti made for us with sauce, turkey, chocolate, etc. Spash is cook now, and boy it was good. Rained most of yesterday, and today the wind is blowing like a gale. Have to hold down the tent. Curly and some of the fellows went over to a warehouse and got some lumber and stoves, so we made a kitchen today. Boy the way we have this place fixed up now it's the next best place to home. Wouldn't mind staying for the duration, but the Limeys were here to look the position over, so we won't be here long. Have alerts almost everyday and red alerts nearly every nite. Nothing dropped though.

Jan. 2, Sun. – Spash and I went on pass this afternoon. Were invited over to a girl's house, so we spent most of the time there.

Jan. 3, Mon. – Curly and I took two girls for a boat ride in our German lifeboat which the Limeys gave us when they left here. The Jerries were over Naples last nite, and a barrage was sent up. Passes for Pompeii start tomorrow.

Jan. 4, Tue. – It's raining again tonite. A British officer and a sergeant who is going to take over this position were here today to look it over. We will be here about a week yet as most of their guns are still on the boat. They just came from Africa. Spash and I are going to Pompeii tomorrow.

Jan. 5, Wed. – It rained all morning, so we didn't go to Pompeii. We almost had snow last nite as the mountains at the end of town were 3/4 covered with snow, as was Mount Vesuvius.

Jan. 6, Thu. – Spash and I went to Pompeii this morning. It sure was an interesting place. We also saw the most beautiful church I've ever seen in my life in Pompeii. It has a million dollar altar which I don't doubt at all. Today is more or less the Italian Christmas. They exchange gifts today as the wise men were supposed to have reached Bethlehem on the 6th and given their gifts to Mary and Joseph.

Jan. 7, Fri. – George went to Pompeii today. Weiden is our battery commander now. Capt. Carey went to "A" Battery. Spash, Moe, and I went to the show in town tonite. We saw *You Were Never Lovelier* with Rita Hayworth and Fred Astaire. We only saw part of the picture. There was so much smoke, and the lights would go dim and then get brighter and finally went out completely.

Pompeii, Italy, destroyed by Mount Vesuvius in 79 AD

Jan. 8, Sat. – Some Limey officers and sergeants were here today again to look the place over. They said they were going to take over this coming Monday. Spash and I went out and had a picture taken. While here we are under the P.B.S. (peninsula base section), and the English are the higher-ups. A British general came and inspected us this afternoon. Gee, and was he a goofy son-of-a-gun. I thought our inspecting officers were bad but, boy, he sure took the cake. I'm pretty sure we made the best showing of all the gun sections though. The British are practicing landing invasions from barges next to us here. They are probably getting set for the invasion of France, which I'm sure isn't very far off.

Jan. 9, Sun. – I think Mount Vesuvius might have some funny ideas as all day yesterday and last nite we could hear her rumble. Quite a few bombs have been dropped in the crater which might have started something. I just hope we can have clear sailing if it does. Pete went thru the trailer this morning trying to find his bag. He couldn't find it, so we checked thru it and found six bags missing and one was mine with all my clothes and a lot of personal stuff. How they got by us and swiped them I don't know, but I know that if I ever catch the guilty party they'll wish they were never born!!

Mount Vesuvius, Italy before it erupted, January 1944

Jan. 10, Mon. – It rained last nite and part of this morning. All section chiefs went on a reconnaissance this morning to pick out our new positions. Gee are they in a godforsaken territory. They are situated at the floor of Mount Vesuvius on lava beds. Just got word from CP that we won't occupy those positions, but they will be near there anyway. They can't be any worse. Loaded our power plant, director, and spare barrel this evening. We have to be ready to leave Castellammare at nine tomorrow morning, that's if the Limeys relieve us on time. Boy, is the surf making the noise this evening. The mail is being held up somewhere as I haven't heard from Carol or home for quite awhile.

Jan. 11, Tue. – Left at 10:15 this morning. Pulled in at the port of Torre Annunziata to wait for the officers to pick out our positions. We pulled into position at 12:10 this noon. We are in a field next to the track of the electric train. We dug our "40," "50," and director in and were thru by supper time. It was swell digging, but the ground is almost too soft. It caves in too easy.

Jan. 12, Wed. – Put our shack or kitchen up today. The officers came and inspected our position today, and they said we had a very fine position. We are setup close to Mount Vesuvius and near the Pompeii airport. Vesuvius flows up every little while. Flames shoot way up, and you can see the red hot lava flow over the side. In the daytime all you can see is smoke, but it sure is an awesome and thrilling sight to see at nite. There is a cauliflower patch next to us, so guess we'll have some tomorrow. There is also an orange grove, which we plan to take advantage of.

Jan. 13, Thu. – Another swell day today. Over 200 B-17's flew over our heads today to give the Germans hell someplace. There might have been more, but that's just what we counted. It's really a thrill to see that many go over at a time. There is a rumor that the invasion of France was started. Could be. Going to the show tonite with George, Spash, and Louie.

Jan. 14, Fri. – Saw *The Pride of the Yankees* with Gary Cooper. I always wanted to see that and boy, I'm glad I did 'cause it sure was a good show. Alert last nite at 11:30. Major Cook was around to inspect, and all the crews were gigged so no passes.

Jan. 15, Sat. – Went to church this morning with George and Sam over at the battery CP. The pit for our "40" caved in again on one side, so we worked all afternoon re-enforcing it. Alert again last nite. There was a barrage put up over Naples, but they never came over by us — darn it!

Jan. 16, Sun. – Capt. Lossen came around and inspected this noon. We had the coffee on for dinner so he and Lt. Hedricks had a cup. Boy, he sure is a sharp article yet. We got no. 1's power plant as Kip's gun is out of order and boy is Kip blowing his top as he was using it for lights. Our power plant was out of order.

Jan. 17, Mon. – George and I went on pass to Torre Annunziata this afternoon.

Jan. 18, Tue. – "Old fighting Jim" was around to inspect today and was well satisfied. I'd much rather have the colonel come around than the major or any of the captains.

Jan. 19, Wed. – Boy, did it turn cold early this morning. The gun was all white this morning when we went out for alert.

Jan. 20, Thu. – The English brigadier general was supposed to be here, but he didn't come. Spash and I went on pass to Torre Annunziata. Boy, that sure is a dirty town.

Jan. 21, Fri. – Some English officers were around today to look at our positions as they are going to take over tomorrow, and I guess we are going to dig new positions near the port. Boy, we sure take a screwing from those damn Limeys. We dig the positions and sit for awhile and then the Limeys take over. I guess Alabam will be in the invasion as we heard they loaded the trucks onto the LST's. We will have to have some other outfit move us tomorrow as eight of our trucks went to move the 400th today. I sure can't understand how they do some things in this Army.

Jan. 22, Sat. – The Limeys relieved us at 3:00 this afternoon. Went on a recon. to look over our position this morning. Boy, this pit is the crummiest I've ever seen. How "A" Battery passed inspection on it is beyond me. We had one heck of a time getting the gun in. We are between Torre Annunziata and Castellammare.

Mustafa, Dudgil, our gun position in Castellammare, Italy

Jan. 23, Sun. – We rebuilt the pit today, and it sure looks a hundred percent better. Started raining tonite.

Jan. 24, Mon. – Rained most of last nite. The rain sank into the ground almost as fast as it came down, so there wasn't any mud to contend with. We can see the ruins of Pompeii pretty good from here. The rangers were supposed to have landed above Rome sometime yesterday. From this position I guess we are going back to Salerno, and then I think we will get on boats again move up above Rome. I hope so, 'cause I would just as soon be up there fighting and take my chances of getting killed as to go crazy from all the inspections around here. The Jerries were over Naples last nite.

Four planes were shot down. The Jerries must have been stirred up from the invasion as we had three red alerts last nite, so we didn't get much sleep.

Jan. 25, Tue. – Went to Castellammare with Kip and George and took a nice hot bath. It's been a swell day today. Lt. Weiden has been around every day to inspect and not once has he found anything wrong. If he stays as nice as he is, he's going to be the best battery commander we've had yet.

Jan. 26, Wed. – Had another alert last nite. The British G.O.R. ordered gun positions to open fire, that is those near the planes. After firing a barrage, they found out the planes were ours. It rained just as Ed and I went on guard at 1:15 this morning. Boy, did it come down! I went and got the truck and parked it next to the gun pit, so we didn't get wet.

Jan. 27, Thu. – The Jerries were over Naples again last nite. Went to the show at Castellammare but didn't see hardly any of it as the lights would go off and on. The ordnance came and took my gun this afternoon. We had to tear half the pit down to get it out. Got a package from Aunt Elsie and Uncle Guy this evening. I haven't received a letter from Carol since before Christmas. I don't want to admit it, but who is getting her mail now.

Jan. 28, Fri. – Another red alert last nite. Boy, were there the fireworks over Naples. Played horseshoes most of the day. Sgt. Moore came over last nite to say goodbye as he is leaving for the States tomorrow on a 30-day furlough from which he will go to whatever camp he wishes. Gee we sure hated to see him go. He didn't have much to say. After he shook hands with Curly and I he said, "well—" and two big tears came rolling out of his eyes. He left in a hurry then 'cause his emotions were getting the best of him. We all felt the same way. They also called up and said to have Ed Mustafa ready in the morning 'cause he was being transferred to the 2nd Platoon. I put up a big kick, but it didn't do any good.

Jan. 29, Sat. – Buck and Hagen went up on Vesuvius this morning. Ed left at 8:30 a.m. Gee, he sure is a swell kid, and I hated like hell to lose him. Went over to Kip's this afternoon to watch Kapp and Frank take his two best men on in horseshoes. Then went over to a house with Kip where five sisters live. They invited us over for a dance tomorrow nite. Went to Or, am at the show now with Spash. *Moontide* is on. We're waiting for it to start now. These seats are too darn close together, and we tried pushing them apart but just broke the seat in front of us trying. Our trucks that left a week or so ago were in on the invasion, and tonite we heard that five drivers from "C" Battery were wounded and two killed from a different battery. Gee, I hope nothing happened to Alabam.

Jan. 30, Sun. – Kip came over today so we played some horseshoes.

Jan. 31, Mon. – Got march order this afternoon. We had to leave Philip and a lot of stuff as we expect to catch a boat this time. We left at 3:30 p.m. and are bivouacked between Naples and Caserta. We saw Alabam going the other way, and boy was I glad to see him. Got paid tonite.

Feb. 1, Tue. – Philip sure hated to see us go yesterday. He ran all the way home to bring his wife and kids to say goodbye. He was crying when we left. We got a truck today, so we repacked both trucks. We just had supper, and we're waiting around to pull out. We got more ammo this morning. I got my gun this morning also. We are going to board boats and guard a port near Rome. Alabam was here today, and boy did he bring the tails back. He was hauling ammo in the invasion. Our truck is full of shrapnel holes. He's got to go back again, so we'll probably see him there.

Ammo trucks

Feb. 2, Wed. – We were supposed to go a staging area yesterday but stayed here instead. Played football against the 2nd Platoon this morning. Just before dinner, the battalion formed into mass formation where General Ruttlidge decorated the men who had the Silver Star or Purple Heart coming to them from our battalion. It's 2:00 p.m., and we are just starting to pull out for Puzzoli staging area no. 3. We just finished eating supper and were told we would stay here for the nite. We went along the coast of Naples and went thru some beautiful parts of it to get here. George and I leveled out the ground and made a bed.

Feb. 3, Thu. – Boy, was that ground hard to sleep on, and it sure was cold last nite. Played the second platoon in football this afternoon. We've been ready to pull out all day, but our boats are being taken by tanks as they are needed badly up there. The Germans have been counterattacking with tanks, and we haven't enough up there to stop them yet. We are going to sleep here again tonite.

Feb. 4, Fri. – Gee, but am I stiff this morning from playing football. It's starting to rain a little. It's 8:45 a.m., and the trucks are starting to leave now. It is 2:30 p.m. and the boats are all loaded. We are the last ones on, but Kip will get off first and then my section.

Group picture, February 1944

Feb. 5, Sat. – We stayed tied to the dock last nite and pulled out in the harbor at 8:30 a.m. We started out at 10:00 a.m. It's been raining part of the morning. We are on a British LST and boy, is this thing rocking. Went by the isle of Capri a little while ago. I felt funny in the stomach this afternoon, so I laid down most of the time. Some of the fellows are pretty sick.

Feb. 6, Sun. – Dropped anchor outside of Anzio about 1:30 last nite. Had a raid at 3:00 a.m. and another one at 5:00 a.m. They dropped about 25 flares, and everything lit up like day. Gee, I never saw so much ack-ack in all my life. The Jerries dropped bombs and were trying to get us, but there was too much ack-ack for them to get in close. Pulled into Anzio at 9:00 a.m. and got off the boat. Boy, we were all glad to get off the boat 'cause it sure was a jarring and rocky trip. We are dispersed in an area just outside of Anzio waiting for further orders. I think we are going to protect field artillery. It is 11:30 a.m., and we just had another raid. Saw a plane go down and boy was he going. There's a dog fight up there now. The Jerries must have some big guns up there 'cause two shells just went screaming over. This is just like old times again, only I sure don't like it. Went on a recon. to pick out our positions. Boy, we sure are in the thick of it this time. Our job is to protect a battalion of 155 howitzers. Our positions are in between the 2nd and 3rd infantry lines. The Jerry lines are about 6,000 yards away, and we can see our front line from our position. On the way back from recon., a shell landed just to the side of us. Boy, did Lt. Hedricks step on it then.

Feb. 7, Mon. – We finished our "40" and "50" pits about 11:30 p.m. last nite and dug the wheels of our truck down and put up the camouflage net. Boy, was it cold, and it still is. Didn't sleep much as our guns and the Jerries and the cold sure put the clamp on a little shut-eye. We watched the machine gun fire of both sides last nite. Gee, it sure gives you a funny feeling. We are expecting a big counter attack, and we were told the Jerries outnumber us six to one. Kip is just to the right of me and is next to a canal which is heavily mined and booby trapped in case the Jerries break thru. Had a raid and fired on Fw 190's this afternoon. Also got our first casualty. Tommy Carisa stepped in front of the "50" as it fired and it cut his head off. He was from no. 7 gun crew. Went on recon. to pick out our alternate positions in case the field artillery has to retreat. Shells have been dropping all around us all day, and shrapnel has been coming plenty close. The Jerries are in the hills, and we are on the flats so they can see every move we make. George and I dug sleeping quarters and stretched our sheet halves over it. It's not bad at all. Saw two Jerry planes go down this evening. All day long the air is full of planes, most of them ours.

Spash digging my dugout, Anzio beachhead

Feb. 8, Tue. – Had orders to put half the crew on a relief last nite for guard, as we put on a big drive, and they were afraid the Germans might retaliate. The tracer fire from our infantry and the Jerries was almost like ack-ack as there was so much of it. Naval guns, tanks, and everything around here opened up all nite on the Germans. The ground shakes like a leaf. Three Me 109's strafed the infantry, and they were so close to the ground we couldn't fire until they pulled up; otherwise we would have hit our own men. We all had pretty good shots after they pulled up, and Kip claims he got one. Two were shot down, and our shots came awfully close, but I wasn't sure as I didn't put any claim in. The Jerries have been throwing up quite a bit of ack-ack at our bombers which dropped their loads on the Jerry lines. In "D" Battery, one man was killed and five wounded from German artillery. We froze on guard duty last nite.

Feb. 9, Wed. – Boy, what a miserable nite. It was cold as the dickens and then it started to rain, and it rained most of the nite. The wind started blowing so strong this morning that our little gas burners wouldn't burn, so we had a cold breakfast. Cold! Man-o-man! A mortar outfit is setting up in back of us. I'd rather see them in front of us though. Got orders to put our director in, and we have to go get it tonite and put it in while it's dark. Boy, did I rave when I heard that. I'm going to set it facing the Jerry artillery so they can get a good shot at it. Boy what a headache that thing is. A gas tank fell off a plane going over us and just missed our truck and George's and my tent. It wasn't bad enough, now we have to watch out for gas tanks falling on us. Formations of B-25's and A-20's have been bombing the Jerries' lines all day. Our P-40's just got done bombing and strafing and not a German shot fired at them.

Feb. 10, Thu. – Heavy shelling and ack-ack last nite. Gee, what a show we had this morning. Waves of B-17's and B-24's came over and dropped their loads on the Jerries just below the hill ahead of us. I watched the bombs fall (thru the field glasses) on a town, and boy did it go up in smoke. The Jerries really threw up a lot of ack-ack, and two B-17's went down in flames. They tried to get back over our lines but couldn't. One exploded in midair, and the crew must have gone with it. The other one the crew bailed out, and the plane exploded as it hit the ground. It sure was a devastating site to see. There's a dog fight going on over us now. Seven killed in our battalion since we landed here and quite a few casualties. It's been raining off and on all day today. The ground is red clay, and gee is it sticky. George and I are in our dugout, and the ground shakes and is it ever hard on the ears from our artillery and the Jerries. They really made kindling out of a building close by a little while ago. Our officers got direct orders to have our directors in tonite, rain or not, as they went down to 35th Brigade headquarters to try and talk them out of it, but they only stepped into the fire then.

Feb. 11, Fri. – We put the director and power plant in last nite, and boy was it raining and blowing. We dug our pits and filled sand bags and had to fill them by hand as the mud wouldn't leave the shovel. Gee I was never so disgusted in all my life. It was so dark, the only time we could see what we were doing was when the flares from the Very pistols over the infantry lines went up. The Jerries were staging a big counterattack, but we still had to get the director in. Our "40" pit was caved in on both sides from the concussion and heavy clay. It blew and rained all day today.

3rd Edition

February 12 to June 6, 1944

Anzio: Our campaign in Italy continued

Some of the most intense fighting in World War II happened on the Anzio beachhead. According to multiple sources, the Battle of Anzio resulted in an estimated 30,000 Allied VI Corps casualties including 4,000 killed. By June 5, 1944, the Allies had liberated Rome, and about 1,000 miles northwest the Allies were planning their D-Day invasion in Normandy. Jack highlights the intensity of these experiences including shelling from the Germans and his gun crew firing back at their planes. Some of his crew were injured during the battles receiving Purple Hearts for minor injuries, while others in nearby gun crews were killed in action.

Feb. 12, Sat. – The ground shook so much last nite we hardly got any sleep as the German barrage of artillery fire was landing all around us. One of Kip's men had to be taken away this morning as his nerves were shot. We got orders the other day that the German Army was expected to desert and to disarm them and treat them good if any came this way. So far we haven't seen any. Our B-24's and B-25's bombed the hell out of the Jerries just ahead of us again today. Two of our planes were shot down, but that's little compared to the damage the bombs do to the Jerries. A large formation of Fw 190's went over us this morning, but were too high for us. They bombed the harbor in Anzio again. They've been pulling sneak attacks every day there. Just before sundown tonite Stukas came over, and two were shot down. There are two Jerry planes that come over every nite and drop personnel mines. They follow radio beams in, and if they see any light they drop them. "A" and "B" Batteries got it the last two nites from these planes. This is the "Anzio beachhead," and we are holding our own but can't get much further until the relief (which is supposed to be coming) arrives. It looks like we'll be in this spot for quite awhile as there is no place in the harbor to dock big boats. They are going pretty slow on the front we left as Cassino is surrounded on three sides but still isn't in Allied hands yet. It's really a job trying to drive the Jerries out of the mountains, but I don't see how they can stand much more of bombing and shelling they are getting. It's 8:00 p.m., and Jerry bombers are flying over. Boy, the ack-ack going up at them. One just went down in flames.

Feb. 13, Sun. – Boy, did we have the excitement last nite. Jerry planes were flying over all nite dropping flares and personnel mines. Just when George and I went on guard at 3:00 a.m., they dropped a flare which landed just outside the "40" pit. Boy, there were some tense moments. A mine landed a few feet from the pit and sprayed shrapnel all over, but nobody was hurt. We fired on Fw 190's this morning and knocked part of a wing off of one. Our bombers came over again this morning, and a B-25 went down behind our lines. One of our ration dumps was bombed a little while ago, and boy is it blazing.

Feb. 14, Mon. – Jerry planes flew over again all last nite dropping flares and personnel mines. First one plane drops a flare, and then a second one dives down and drops a package with around a hundred personnel mines which scatter all over and go off. Boy, they can sure think up the fiendish things to keep a guy's nerves on edge. We made our sleeping quarters bomb proof today, so maybe now we can get some sleep without so much fear of personnel mines and 88's. It's been a beautiful day today.

Feb. 15, Tue. – Me 109's just strafed our lines. We couldn't get the gun on them as our pit is built up a little too high. Got some mail today. I finally got one from Carol, the first one since December 2nd. Another nice day today, but the nites sure get cold. We had a paratrooper alert last nite, and three were captured between us and the field artillery. One fellow from gun crew no. 5 was hit by the strafing planes. Three Me 109's just zoomed over our lines strafing. The tail of the last one was shot off, and boy he came down like he fell off a ledge . He didn't burn or explode, but there isn't much left of the plane or pilot. Just after the sun went down, two formations of Me 110's came over and dropped what looked to us like rocket bombs. We fired on them and got two of them. Just after it got dark they came over again and dropped flares first which lit everything like day and then dropped their bombs. George and

I were in our dugout and boy, are we glad we reinforced it and put a heavy roof on 'cause shrapnel was flying all over. I believe our Beaufighters are up there after them 'cause we could see tracer fire coming from planes. They must have gone back after another load 'cause we can't hear them anymore.

Feb. 16, Wed. – Spent another nite on edge again. The Jerries staged a big counterattack on our right flank at dawn this morning, and boy what an artillery duel by both sides. Boy, planes were over all day, that is Jerry planes, as ours are over all the time. We fired on them, but they came and went so fast we didn't get many shots at them. We got quite a bit of mail the last two days.

Feb. 17, Thu. – Boy what an exciting day today. First of all this morning the Jerries got our range with their artillery and opened up on us and the field artillery we are guarding. Shells were screaming over our heads and dropping all around us. Boy, did we hug the side of the pit. Two fellows from the field artillery were hit when a shell landed next to the foxhole they were in. We could hear them screaming for help. One man from no. 8 gun crew was hit also. Our bombers started their mass bombing at about 9:30 a.m., and there was a continuous formation going over until after dinner. It's now 1:30, and here they come again. It sure is a beautiful sight in our minds to see them go over and drop their loads and to see what looks like half the mountain taking off. We saw a B-17 and a B-26 go down in flames. Four men jumped out of the B-17, but nobody got out of the B-26. Three bombers went down behind our lines here and landed in the water. Some jumped and the rest were picked up. The Jerries might be knocking a few of our planes down, but they sure are paying for it when our bombs drop on them. The Jerries found our range again this afternoon, and we have some nice garbage pits by our kitchen now. We picked up some shrapnel in front of our dugout, and boy I sure wouldn't want to get hit by it. It must have been a 170.

German plane we shot down

Feb. 18, Fri. – Shells were flying again today. One landed near the pit. Curly and Hagan were standing outside, and it knocked Curly's helmet, but nobody was hurt. We heard tonite that 150 men from our battalion have to go up and help the infantry. Boy, it certainly has everyone on edge.

Feb. 19, Sat. – Thirty-four men were picked from our battery, and I was one of four sergeants who have to go. Well, anything just so this war will end soon.

Feb. 20, Sun. to Feb. 28, Mon. – Came back last nite after seven days and nites of hell! We had to lay barbed wire, dig trenches, build machine gun emplacements, and be ready to take over the trenches if the Jerries broke thru. Most of the work had to be done at nite as it was right up near the Jerry lines. We were constantly being shelled by mortar and artillery fire. Nearly every nite planes came over dropping flares, then anti-personnel mines and bombs. Two fellows from our battery were killed. One of the fellows was on my squad. Dack was his name. Three of "B" Battery men were seriously injured, and a bomb landed directly on a "D" Battery truck. Sgt. Chapman and I slept together, but we didn't get much sleep as we were sweating it out nearly every nite with Jerry planes overhead or their artillery. We sure were glad to get back here and can thank the Lord that we did. A bomb landed about 50 yards from the gun pit one nite while we were gone. It made a big crater and shattered the range dial on the director. Outside of that it didn't do much else. It sure had the fellows scared though, and I don't blame them.

Feb. 29, Tue. – The Jerries started throwing shells early this morning and have kept it up all day. We've been hugging the side of the gun pit or when off guard the side of our dugouts. It's a terrific and terrifying feeling. This is the worst we've been shelled yet, and oh God, please watch over us!

German artillary fire, one landed right next to our water cans

Mar. 1, Wed. – Boy, March really came in with a roar starting, and it's still going on today. They cut our communication line to the CP four times with direct hits. When we looked by the pit this morning, there were five holes where the shells went in and exploded about five feet under ground, making a sort of cavern under the ground. The mud and soft ground really help a lot as it is too soft so the shell doesn't go off until it hits the hard ground. The fellows are holding up pretty good, but it sure is an awful strain on a guy's nerves! It's been raining all last nite and all day today, so there has been hardly any air activity at all. Our bombers can't get off the ground, so that's why they've been shelling the heck out of us. Fellows have been going everyday on that infantry detail, and it sure raises heck with the guard. The Jerries were over again last nite dropping personnel bombs. This beachhead is so small and crowded that all the Germans have to do is shoot at random and hit something of ours. (The beachhead is approx. seven miles wide by 10 miles deep). P-40's and Spits just went over and strafed the Jerry lines.

Mar. 2, Thu. – There wasn't so much shelling last nite and today, but every now and then they send over a barrage which sets your heart up in your throat again. It stopped raining, and it's been a pretty nice day. The airports must have dried up some 'cause hundreds of B-24's and B-25's came over and bombed the Jerries. Boy, we sure were glad to see them come. We saw three of them go down, but I think they all had a chance to bail out. The Germans had 10 divisions in here fighting us, but they have more now. They even have the Gestapo's (storm troopers) S.S. troops in here. We just hope we can hold on here until the big invasion takes place, which we think will be pretty soon. After that takes place, then there will be hopes of this war being over soon. The Jerries sure have the range on the 155 howitzers we are protecting. They are throwing them in there left and right about 200 yards from us. They just dropped a few real close ones by us today. It sure was a relief. Guess I talked too soon 'cause boy, did they just pour a barrage in here! They dropped glider bombs over the port. Damn those Jerries, they are shooting air bursts at us now. Two Me's just came over strafing.

Mar. 3, Fri. – The Jerries were over again last nite. We have to fire a barrage at nite now, but they didn't give us the order, and I know the first time we fire they'll shift their load over on us. Rained most of the day. The Jerries are using remote-controlled midget tanks filled with high explosives which are set off when desired. They are using them on this front here.

Mar. 4, Sat. – Rained all nite, but otherwise it was pretty quiet with an occasional shell going over our heads. Kip, Spash, and Gordon went on the infantry detail all last nite. Our battalion shot down the most planes this week out of all the ack-ack outfits on the beach head. Col. Sexton left for the States yesterday on the rotating system. Major Cook is our new commander. The news today said this beachhead is secure and that the Germans are cracking. One thing I do know is that their shells are cracking and not to our comfort either.

Mar. 5, Sun. – I got another man yesterday, and so I have 16 men now. As the weather man would say 'continued rain and shelling for today.' Not much air activity. We are now under a new group (the 9th Group). They are some brass hats just from the States with some crazy ideas. The officers have to sleep with the gun sections now. Our director box is full of holes, and a piece of shrapnel went thru the gun tarp and then thru an ammo chest. A piece also went thru a chest on the 50 caliber.

Mar. 6, Mon. – Got another man tonite. Don't know why we are getting so many. Didn't rain today, so things are drying up pretty good. A bunch of mail is supposed to be in.

Mar. 7, Tue. – A dog fight just took place over us, and a Spitfire and an Fw 190 came screaming down and crashed near the lines. One pilot bailed out, but I don't know which one. Our artillery was rather quiet today, but the Jerries were throwing in quite a few shells. They hit a house directly in back of us this morning, and some outfit had their CP in there. This afternoon they were shelling the Bailey bridge in back of us and hit a huge haystack which is really going up in smoke. There is a stockade with German prisoners in nearby. I wonder how they like to be at the receiving end of their own artillery. The Jerries must have moved up some guns or their Tiger tanks as we can hear the guns very plain as the shell goes over our heads. Been a pretty swell day, weather wise.

Mar. 8, Wed. – The Jerries came over three times last nite and dropped bombs. This was the first nite for about three days. We fired at some Fw 190's this morning. One was smoking, but he must have made it to their lines. First time we fired in about a week. The haystack was burning bright all nite long and is still burning today. They threw a lot of shells around it as they know the bridge is close to it.

Curtiss P-40 Warhawk plane

Mar. 9, Thu. – Our P-40's have been dive bombing most of the day. Saw one go down. The Jerries have plenty of ack-ack yet and are throwing just as much artillery shells around us. We don't seem to be returning so many. Air bursts have come awfully close today. Our bombers haven't been over for awhile now. There are rumors that the second front has started, but I think it's a lot of bologna. When the Jerries come over at nite, they drop what is called "windows." It's strips of silver-coated paper to throw the radar off. There are tanks that move up here at nite, and boy do the Jerries ever try to knock them out. They are tank destroyers, which they use for artillery pieces at nite.

Mar. 10, Fri. – It's full moon now, and the nites are really beautiful. That is, not talking about the artillery shells coming in. Took pictures of the Mussolini Canal with Kip today. The Jerries' OP's should have a field day today as it is so clear today; the mountains they are on seem right next to us. When we hear their guns going off and the shells screaming over and around us, well, they're just too damn close. Our battalion tied with another ack-ack outfit for the most planes shot down last week.

Mar. 11, Sat. – Jerry was over about four times last nite, and each time an awful heavy barrage was put up. A 105 howitzer and a half-track ack-ack outfit pulled into the same field with us last nite. This morning the half-tracks fired at Spitfires which came over low. There was a big dog fight over us, and a Jerry Fw 190 came by trailing over us with a Spitfire right on its tail. They fired at them also. Boy they sure are a bunch of dumb clucks. They fire at anything. We fired on friendly aircraft once, and that was when we were green at it yet. The Jerries have been throwing the shells over, boy! They threw two right inside the CP and all around no. 3's and no. 4's "40" and "50." Nobody was hurt though.

Mar. 12, Sun. – It started raining last nite and rained all day today. Gee, is it awful again. The water seeped thru the ground into our dugout. I had four inches of water in mine before I found out, and I've been bailing out water all afternoon. It looks like we'll have to work in shifts tonite bailing water. A fella wouldn't mind this half so much if it wasn't for the rain. George, it's your turn to bail.

Mar. 13, Mon. – It started out as a beautiful day this morning. Then the Jerries started throwing heavy barrages one after another around 300 yards from us. At 11:30 a.m. they changed their course a bit and all hell broke loose. We didn't hear the first one come in, nor the ones that followed, until they cracked. One lit right in front of our kitchen and one on the side of the truck. Our truck, trailer, kitchen (with dinner just about ready), and shelter halves over our dugouts were just perforated. Our mess kits, personnel equipment, water cans, and gas cans all have to be salvaged. One shell landed about five feet in front of Kip, Frank, and Gordon, and Kip got a piece of shrapnel thru the finger. Moe was on the floor in the kitchen and got a slight cut on the side. It was just an act of God that nobody else was hurt. Each and every man was praying and all say it was just thru God that we are here yet. One man on no. 4 was killed, and a man on no. 6 wounded pretty bad. That field artillery that moved in by us the other nite is what is drawing their fire so close. Just before each barrage, there is a sad-sack that flies around over us with American markings on which we think might be directing the Jerry fire. I'm going to find out about him or else open up on him. We can't figure out why our bombers haven't been over lately. Must be that they are using them for the big invasion, which we are wondering whether it's going to take place or not. A major from the 5th Army was here today. He went around to the battalions which were being shelled the heaviest. He sure picked a good day for it 'cause this day, March 13th, sure was an unlucky day for us. This major took a plane back to Naples this afternoon and told our officers that we probably will be back there soon. A big drive is expected by our troops here, and I don't doubt it 'cause supplies have been coming in every day, and we haven't been doing much in general just hollering. So we don't doubt that something will pop up soon. They came and took our truck back to CP as shrapnel went thru the radiator. Alabam and six other truck drivers left on another detail. They are back in Naples now. It is 9:30 p.m., and Jerry planes are over head. The 90's are opening up at them. Our Navy guns are firing over at the Jerries, and boy they really are throwing it to them.

Shrapnel holes in our truck. One piece lodged in a rolled up pair of my socks in a carrier bag I had in the truck. Anzio, Italy, 1944

Mar. 14, Tue. – Rained a bit last nite, both shells and rain. It's really windy as heck today and hard to hear the shells coming in. The sky was full of Jerry planes about 6:30 this morning but our ack-ack drove them off. Between 4:30 and 5:00 p.m. the Jerries threw in two heavy barrages all around us again. They threw shrapnel all over the place, cut our communication lines, riddled our kitchen again, and ruined another water can. Spash got hit on the leg, but it just left a welt. Boy when those barrages come in you never expect to see tomorrow.

George Hemminger. Water can on the left was damaged when a German shell landed just in front of it. Ted Kapalanski and Augie Stanek were hit by schrapnel and both received the Purple Heart.

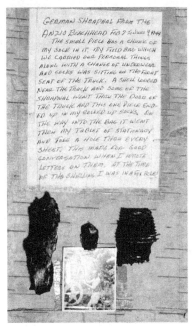

Anzio Beachhead shrapnel

Mar. 15, Wed. – A mess of Jerry planes were over again last nite. Some of our planes must have been up there also as there was a lot of tracer fire coming from some planes. This tracer fire was red, the Jerries have white. Our 90's were bursting right over our heads so we were showered by shrapnel. Our battery is going to be relieved tonite. Four gun crews are going back in position, and the other four are going to bivouac. We are going on a reconnaissance in a half hour to pick the place out. They haven't thrown any "too close" shells in here yet, although they threw some in on the CP while I was there this morning. Came back from recon. at 5:30. We got march order as soon as it got dark. It started raining late this afternoon.

Anzio Beachhead

Mar. 16, Thu. – Just had dinner, and boy are we all dead tired. We started taking down our sandbags at 6:30 last nite. When it got dark last nite, it really got dark. It was pitch black, and you couldn't see a thing. The wind was blowing strong, and it was pouring rain. We had to feel for everything we did, and boy was it a nitemare. After we got the trucks loaded, we had about 175 yards of soft red clay to go thru to get to the road. We started winching the gun and trailer and didn't get very far when the winch broke on us. Boy we were in a fix then. The trucks just dug themselves down, so we had to pole the trucks out. We moved inches at a time. Dug the poles out in under the wheels and lay them in front. Had to put the chains on the trucks in about a foot of mud. Everybody was soaked and mud from head to foot. We started at sunset and got to the road at daybreak this morning. Twelve hours to move 175 yards. To make matters worse, the Jerries put in a heavy artillery barrage at about 1:30. Part of the "50" pit was up yet, so most of us piled in it and laid right in the mud. We sure have a relieved feeling being here. There's an occasional shell which goes over into Anzio which has a booster charge. It's a second charge which goes off about halfway and sends the shell farther. About 15 Jerry planes bombed Anzio this morning, but we didn't fire as our guns are still hooked to the trucks which are stuck, and we left them until after breakfast.

Mar. 17, Fri. – The Jerries were over again last nite or rather most of the nite. First they came and strafed, and then they dropped flares and bombs. George and I were sleeping in the open and shrapnel was dropping all over. I don't know how it was missing us. They came over this morning, but couldn't get set on the target as the ack-ack was too heavy. We finished all our pits and put a pyramidal tent up. The major was around yesterday and gave me hell for not having the gun's pit all dug. They just don't realize the nitemare we went thru this morning. He told me my men are expendable, the equipment isn't.

Mar. 18, Sat. – The Jerries were over last nite and a daylight raid again this morning. They dropped a flare last nite right over the pyramidal tent, or rather it almost landed on it. They dropped personnel bombs close by, but none near enough to do any damage to us. Our position is right near a B-24 which we saw go down while we were up on the front. It's the one that circled the Jerry lines and ours and finally crashed. We heard the pilot is supposed to get court martialed as they say he could have saved the plane (don't know how he could have saved the plane 'cause it was full of shrapnel holes). George and I built part of our bed today. Beautiful day today.

B-24 Bomber, Anzio

Mar. 19, Sun. – Rained last nite, but I never heard it and thought we had an extra heavy dew until I looked again and saw my blankets laying in a pool of water.

Beautiful day again as everything dried up pretty good. Curly, Hagen, George, and I built up sandbags in the big tent for our beds. Just hope the walls don't cave in on us.

Mar. 20, Mon. – Twenty Fw 190's came over and bombed the port at dawn today. We fired on them, but they ran into heavy clouds over the port, so we lost sight of them. Quite a few barrage balloons came down from the ack-ack. It started to rain a bit this morning, but didn't last long. Went to services at the CP this afternoon. The chaplain said he tried to get to us while on the front, but he couldn't as the Jerries were shelling us too heavy. He held services in the gun pit while we were up there, but I was on the infantry detail at the time. Capt. Weiden and Lt. Hancock came over today with the rest of the sergeants to show them my pit. We really have a beautiful pit, and its four feet wide at the tops in most places, to six feet at the base.

B-24 shot down on Anzio. This was the tail section full of shrapnel holes.

Mar. 21, Tue. – It's cloudy today so it looks like rain. It turned out to be a perfect day after all. Capt. Lossen and Capt. Cortney came around to inspect today. Everything was in tip-top shape. He put excellent in our inspection sheet. The radio said Vesuvius erupted last nite. For the past week every once in awhile we could feel the earth tremor, and there was no explosion so we couldn't figure it out. We know it must have come from Mount Vesuvius now. When we had gun position at the base of it, every nite the flames got bigger and you could see the lava flow down the sides. I thought then that it would take off one of those days. Two cities were evacuated.

Mar. 22, Wed. – The Jerries were over last nite. Our code word came over to fire, so we did. There sure was a barrage put up. We felt the earth tremble again last nite. It's a beautiful day today. Went to Anzio with Kip, Chap, and Federwitz. Took a shower there. A major and lieutenant colonel came around to inspect this morning. Boy they went through everything. That's the trouble with being back here. The brass hats aren't afraid to come here, but you didn't see much of them up on the front.

Mar. 23, Thu. – Started raining last nite, and it's still raining this morning. Old Vesuvius is still belching lava. We could feel tremors in the earth again last nite. The 34th Division is here now. There's going to be a big push one of these days. Our gun position is right next to an infantry CP from the 45th Division. Quite a few new recruits have come in here and gone up to the lines.

George and Kip in Anzio

Mar. 24, Fri. – The Jerries were over last nite again. They dropped quite a few bombs. There are smoke generators all over the beachhead, and they keep almost a constant fog in the area as the Jerries' railway guns are still shooting into Anzio. Our P-40's will knock them out, but they just bring up more. Our bombers bombed the hell out of Cassino and took most of it, but the Jerries are back in again. It is really discouraging when we don't make any headway.

Mar. 25, Sat. – The Jerries were over again last nite. They dropped a bunch of flares, and we saw a flamer go down. Rained hard and blew like the devil for awhile today. Conners, from our battalion, went home on the rotating system today. He went back on a hospital ship.

Mar. 26, Sun. – Major Cooper came around to inspect this morning and caught us with our pants down. He didn't look at our gun at all, just our personal equipment that was laying in the trailer which still had mud on from our last move. The fellows make me so damn mad at times when they leave their stuff lying around and dirty. I've still got the best damn section Uncle Sam's got tho! The Jerries were over again last nite. A grasshopper (observation plane) was blown to pieces this afternoon when it was hit by an artillery shell. Pieces flew all over. It was probably a shell from a Jerry's big railway gun that he's shelling Anzio with. We hear the booster charge go off above us and look toward the water and usually see a big column of water go up as it lands in the water. They don't always land in the water tho.

L-5 observation planes over Anzio

Mar. 27, Mon. – Jerry was over again last nite and dropped incendiary bombs on our battery CP. Willy Taylor was killed while he was on the switchboard. Gee he sure was a swell kid. Sgt. Oliver got some pretty bad burns from it.

Mar. 28, Tue. – The Jerries hit an ammo dump with their railway guns near us. They sure were poppin' all over. Went to services with Kip and George this afternoon. The Jerries came over on a sneak raid at sunset yesterday and bombed the port. We never got a red alert on them, but were all set and let them have it. We got off 27 rounds and Bill claimed hits with the 50 caliber.

Mar. 29, Wed. – It is 3:45 p.m., and the Jerries just made another sneak raid on the port. Buck and I were in the seats, and if I say so myself it was damn good shooting we did. They were Fw 190's, and three of them were shot down. I know we got one of them. We never got the red alert again. We saw the 90's firing so we knew something was up. Some outfit opened up on a Spitfire just after the raid yesterday and knocked it down. It hit the water after the pilot bailed out, but his chute never opened up. He was falling right behind the plane and sank with it. Another Spit a little while ago came over in formation, and then we saw it nose dive into the water. Don't know what made him go down and never saw the pilot get out.

Mar. 30, Thu. – The 90's opened up this morning and then the rest of the ack-ack did. We held our fire 'cause they were Spitfires. Boy some of those outfits are really trigger-happy. The deputy commander is supposed to come around to inspect on cleanliness and sanitation.

Mar. 31, Fri. – Capt. Lossen came around today with a hat full of catchy questions. Rained part of the day. The Anzio Express has been coming closer to us for the last few nites. They also must run tanks up 'cause you can hear them shoot, and they were landing between my position and Kip's. They hit an ammo dump to the right of us.

Apr. 1, Sat. – Jerry was over last nite raising hell again. They dropped some signal flares so everyone stopped firing thinking they were ours; then they dropped their own flares and bombs. Boy, they really threw the ack-ack up at them then. Went down to the CP with Curly where we all had a big debate on the oil gears. Then went over to no. 3 where Capt. Cortney and Capt. Lossen fired two rounds to prove you can adjust the recoil cylinder for recoil as well as counter-recoil. Didn't prove much, but he said he would be back tomorrow and prove it. Boy, those oil gears are really a headache when getting down to the technical points about them.

Apr. 2, Sun. – Jerry was over again last nite. They dropped personnel mines on our battery CP and hit no. 8's truck. Capt. Weiden was around and gave us a different theory on the oil gears. Don't know what to think now. Boy, we really have arguments on the gun and director. The Anzio Express has been sailing thru all day.

Apr. 3, Mon. – Kip came over for awhile yesterday. The officers were around with some more questions on the oil gears. The Italian people are all going to be evacuated to Naples in the next few days. They caught some Italians sending information to the Germans by radio. They also caught an Italian with a cart load of ammo covered up with vino bottles. There are so many things crowded on this beachhead, and a lot of vital information is leaking out, so that's why they all have to leave.

Apr. 4, Tue. – The Jerries were over again twice last nite at 8:30 and 12:30. We got our code word to fire. Fired three barrages. There really were some nice barrages put up, and Jerry couldn't get in at all. Major Cooper came around to inspect this afternoon. The only thing he can do is find fault, he won't give you any credit whatsoever. Well he couldn't find much wrong here. The Italians have been around trying to sell us vino as they can't take it with them. (The wine they couldn't sell they buried the bottles in the animal manure piles, thinking we wouldn't find it.) It's been a beautiful day today. Starting to take Atabrine pills again as the mosquitoes look as big as hornets. We are right in the big marshes (Pontini Marsh) which is an ideal place for mosquitoes to breed. Got mosquito bars today.

Apr. 5, Wed. – Went over to Kip's last nite. We went and sang in a wishing well with a girl. You'd sing into it and then your voice would come back to you. We also had some wine and spaghetti at these Italians' shack. Three Italian girls came by this morning crying like everything. Gee, they sure hate to leave. Lt. Hancock came around on a donkey this afternoon which the Italians left. The old Anzio Express landed pretty short of Anzio and dropped just to the left of Kip's position. It's a wonderful day today except for the shelling. A truck from no. 7 gun crew got a direct hit by a shell last nite. The wrecker came and got it this morning.

Here I am on one of the horses we had. All animals were left on the beachhead when all the civilians were evacuated. Anzio beachhead, 1944

Apr. 6, Thu. – The Jerries shelled the Long Toms pretty hard last nite. Our 1st sergeant and a cook left today for the States on the rotation system. A second cook from "B" Battery was scheduled to go home today also but was killed last nite by a shell. We haven't heard from Sgt. Moore yet whether he got home or not. Bill and Charlie rounded up three horses which the Italians left and also a cart. Been riding them all evening. One was never broke in yet and bucked to beat heck. More fun!

Apr. 7, Fri. – The Jerries shelled the Long Toms terrifically all last nite. They set off a big ammo dump which was exploding all nite. It was just like a huge fireworks display about 300 feet in the air. Tracers and shrapnel flying all over. The Luftwaffe must be pretty well thinned out as we haven't seen any planes for the last three days and nites. Our planes patrol from the break of dawn until sunset. Another beautiful warm day. The flies are getting pretty bad. Good Friday today.

Apr. 8, Sat. – Jerries came over again last nite. They sneaked in someway 'cause the first anybody knew they were here was when they started strafing the 90 outfit just below us. How they got by our radars. They must have come in on a long glide. They must have something new up their sleeve as they dropped something which looked like a bunch of flares from way up. When it hit the ground it just lit everything up. We saw one plane go down. George and I dug our hole down so part of us is below the ground anyway.

Apr. 9, Sun. – Easter Sunday. Rained all day. We were supposed to go on a recon. but didn't. Going tomorrow tho. We are connected up with the 240 mm's. They are an 8-inch gun throwing a 360 pound shell. Rode horses after supper.

Kip and I on "Whirl-a-Way," Anzio beachhead

Apr. 10, Mon. – The Jerries were over again last nite. Every time we get a card game going, the damn Jerries come over. Major Cook, Capt. Lossen, Capt. Gestuch, and

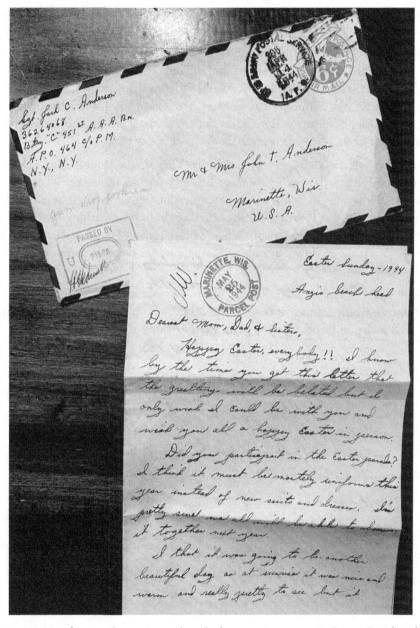

Easter 1944 letter to home. Note that the letter was written on Easter Sunday, but it wasn't received until May 25 as shown by the postmark.

Capt. Cortney came around to inspect on everything. They were pretty well satisfied and put excellence in the inspection book. Kip and I went on a recon. with Lt. Hedricks this afternoon. The area where we have to set up in, in case we move, is just loaded with ammo of all sort. Every nite the Jerries shell in that area and knock out numbers of piles. They threw some close ones in here last nite and today, and a few air bursts. The Jerries are using a 280 mm to shell Anzio, and some don't get that far. Kip and I rode double on our stallion down to take a shower.

Apr. 11, Tue. – Jerry was over again last nite dropping bombs and personnels (a.p.'s). One bomb dropped awfully close to us. I thought our house was going to fall down. We rode the donkeys and horses again this evening. We have a little ranch started here already. Picked up Kip with my stud, and we went over to the CP where they were raising particular heck, and having a good time. Kip and I sure had fun on that horse. He got away on us after I had him tied up. When I came back here to the gun pit, there he was.

Apr. 12, Wed. – Jerry was over again last nite, and we fired two barrages on our code. The Germans shelled heavy again. Blew up some more ammo piles, which sure went sky high. Infantry have been coming in by boat all nite and day. I think the big invasion is going to take place soon and that they are going to put on drives from all points at the same time. The Jerries came over about 6:15 this evening. There were about 30 planes which dropped bombs. The smoke generators had the beachhead all fogged up so it was hard to see them, but we got off 30 some rounds at them. Pete and I were in the seats. I don't know how many went down, but we saw four of them go down. They were Fw 190s and boy the ack-ack thrown at them. Nine were confirmed to have gone down.

Apr. 13, Thu. – The Jerries were over last nite again, and we got our code word six different times. Saw one of them go down. Spash and I each got letters from home saying they got the pictures. They must have been the ones I sent with Sgt. Moore. Still haven't heard about the ones I sent with Anker Larson back in November. Got a new barrage data, which I think will be more effective. I'm supposed to be getting some packages, and we haven't received much mail lately either. Two merchant or liberty ships were sunk in the Mediterranean last month, so our mail probably was on it. Gee I hope not.

Apr. 14, Fri. – Jerry was over again last nite and they really caught the G.O.R. sleeping. They dropped a big load of personnel and bombs before we got the order to fire on them. We fired six barrages.

Apr. 15, Sat. – Jerries were over again last nite. Headquarters drew names out of a hat today for those going home on rotation. An ammo pile blew up next to the 90's this afternoon, and was poppin' all afternoon. Shrapnel was flying all around us. I got a picture of it.

Apr. 16, Sun. – Jerry was over again last nite. They usually come over 3–4 times a nite or early morning. We fired six barrages at them on our code word. During the day our P-47 and P-40 bombed and strafed the Jerry lines. They shot 88's at them as they reach almost up to us here. The Anzio Express comes over all day long. Capt. Weiden came around blowing his top today.

Apr. 17, Mon. – Jerry was over again all nite. Shrapnel from the 90's hit our tent, and Spash and Gordon almost got hit in the "40" pit. Five planes were brought down nite before last from the barrage fire. Two beach crafts with a Spitfire escort landed at the airport this morning, and P-40's and P-51's have been flying around here all morning. I wonder who the big shots are that came in. A big drive was supposed to come off last nite, and this morning we heard that we advanced three miles on this front. There goes the Anzio Express overhead. It's very windy today, and sand is blowing all over.

Apr. 18, Tue. – It rained all day today. Jerries came over again last nite, but the 90's were the only ones who fired. Played poker to pass the time. Frank and I have been giving out on the bass viol we originated and the banjo. (Made the bass viol from an ammo box with a string and stick attached to the center of the box.)

Apr. 19, Wed. – Rained a little today. Our platoon CP has been quarantined as Pee Wee Harris was taken to the hospital with spinal meningitis. Got a letter from Carol today, first for quite awhile. Nobody was getting any, but it is starting to come now. We can see the Navy firing again. Just saw a dog fight above us. One plane went down, but we couldn't make out what kind.

Apr. 20, Thu. – The Jerries really threw in a barrage of shells last nite. When they came whistling in they sounded louder than ever. They set off two ammo dumps. Just got word that our battery is going to relieve "D" Battery as they can't take the shelling they got last nite. One killed and an officer wounded. Now the rumor is that we are going to move between the forest and Anzio near the hospital. The damn Germans have been shelling the hell out of the hospital. They have a 240 howitzer set up near it, and are just waiting for the Jerries to shell it again and if they do, they are going to shell the German hospitals right back. I hope they do shell the Jerries' hospitals 'cause they've been doing it all along since the landing here, and our hospitals are over half a mile away from any military installations. Went for a horseback ride with Kip this evening.

Apr. 21, Fri. – The Jerries came over at three this morning and again at 4:15 dropping flares, bombs, and personnel mines. There must have been a bunch of them 'cause they were diving all over. Saw one go down. Had another raid at sunrise this morning.

Nine Fw 190s came over, but we stopped them before they could do any damage. We are going to go and dig our pits now and move into them in a day or so. We have to move in at nite. I'm glad we can dig them now and just pull into them.

Apr. 22, Sat. – We dug our two pits yesterday, but boy what a swamp hole it is. We got stuck with our truck in there and went to get someone to help us get out and had three trucks stuck. We finally got ours out, but one truck broke his winch and had to get a wrecker to get him out and all on account of our truck. I told Capt. Weiden we would never get the gun in there, so we might look for a different spot. I hope so 'cause it's full of snakes and mosquitoes there. Now we might take over the 441st A.A. positions in Anzio. I went on a recon. with Capt. Weiden and Lt. Hancock about 9:30 this evening to find a different spot. It was dark so couldn't see much but have picked the location out.

Apr. 23, Sun. – Got march order at dawn this morning. We had to double the guard last nite as the Germans broke thru this side of the factory area. The infantry has them cut off from their main line now, so it didn't do them any good to break thru. Finished most of the pits today and our shelters. They blew up some duds nearby, and boy the big pieces that fell around us.

Apr. 24, Mon. – Rained a bit last nite. Finished putting sod all around the pit for our camouflage. Got two boxes from home. One today and one yesterday. It sure was hot this afternoon. Spash and I took Dan (the horse) and went for a shower. We needed another one after we got back. Played cards this evening, but we had to break it up as Jerry came over as usual.

Apr. 25, Tue. – Another hot day today. Lanie Kockler came back this morning to stay, and we sure were glad to see him. My section has to move again as we are too close to no. 1 and no. 3. Boy, if this Army could ever do the right thing at the right time, this war would be over a long time ago. The CP is right next to us, and Lt. Hancock made a place for the horses to jump over. We were jumping them all evening—more fun!

Apr. 26, Wed. – We were having a nice poker game until a shell landed too darn close. It shook everything and all the mess kits came down which made it sound that much worse. The Jerries set off another ammo dump which was throwing shrapnel all over. Went on a recon. with Capt Weiden, Lt. Hedrick, and Lt. Hancock. They are still undecided, so we are going after dinner again. Finally found a spot. It's been raining all day as Capt. Weiden got permission from the major to let us dig our pits tomorrow and move in the next day. It's one consolation anyway. Boy, I really felt like blowing my top today when I heard we had to move. The major and five captains came around to inspect this afternoon. He said we had a very good pit, and it was a shame to have to move. Well, I sure as hell agreed with him on that. There's a rumor out that our tanks penetrated 10 miles in Jerry territory, and all they came across were anti-aircraft guns.

Apr. 27, Thu. – Dug out pits and shelters today. A bunch of infantry in trucks and tanks went by going to the front this evening. Rode horses again this evening. The CP, who are right next to us, called over and told us to get in the gun pit for the evening alert. Boy, they sure burn me up. Work and pull guard day and nite, and they deprive us of a little fun.

Apr. 28, Fri. – Pulled out after breakfast this morning, got the guns in, and then finished building our shelter. Boy, we really did work today. After supper Lt. Curtis came around with the PX and a bottle of beer or Coca-Cola. Boy, were we glad to get that! I read in the *Stars and Stripes* the other day that the combat troops were going to get beer, but I didn't believe it. Frank got a call today, asking if he would like to run a movie projector in Naples. He told them no 'cause he wanted to stay with us fellows. I sure hope he doesn't go to Naples.

Apr. 29, Sat. – Jerry was over last nite, and boy he dropped some personnel mines and bombs awfully close. The dirt really came down in our shelter. We camouflaged our pit all with sod, and boy it really is a good job. You couldn't tell there was a gun and director there if it wasn't for the stiffkey stick. The first sergeant called up Frank and told him to pack up and be ready to leave. They must have turned his name in anyway. He hated to go just as much as we hated to see him go. He was really the life of the crew. Now that we are away from CP, we can have a little fun for a change. Hagen hauled water to no. 3 being as they are set up next to a ration dump. Hagen threw six boxes of 10-in-1's on and brought back. The G.I.'s are guarding it, but they don't care. Dixon brought eggs around today, and we had four apiece for supper, and boy were they good!

Apr. 30, Sun. – Capt. Weiden was around blowing his top today. We got a bulldozer to dig truck, trailer, and ammo down. George was transferred to Todd's crew and Cholette came over here. Boy, they sure are screwing things up proper around here. Kip couldn't get along with Cholette, so I have to.

May 1, Mon. – Last nite Cholette, Louie, Hagan, and myself were playing poker in the big tent. It was 9:30, and all of a sudden the tent almost took off with shrapnel and dirt flying all over. All four of us went out the door at the same time into a slit trench. Just got down and another one comes in. We waited awhile and were just going to get out, and this time it really hit close. We couldn't hear any of them coming in, but we sure saw the last one. We were covered with dirt. One landed next to the trailer, one close to the truck, and the other one in back of the latrine. It blew our shelf we made on the trailer off and knocked 10 pounds of sugar all over the ground. The truck is full of new holes, and we'll have to salvage the pyramidal tent. Got paid today.

May 2, Tue. – Played cards in the dugout last nite as we don't take any more chances in the tent. Washed clothes this morning and boy what a pile.

May 3, Wed. – Oh what a nite we had last nite! The Jerries came over last nite and all hell broke loose all around us. They dropped 17 flares right over our position, then came in and dropped 250-pound bombs and personnel bombs. One landed three feet from Kip's and my dugout and a 250-pound landed 20 feet from the "40" pit. The 25th Division is bivouacked in the grapes right next to us. Two 250-pound bombs landed direct on two of their dugouts, killing seven men. Gee, it was an awful sight when they dug them out this morning. King, our stud, was killed also. The other two were OK. Seven planes were shot down. They really were out to get us. Axis Sally says that the Jerries are out to get the ack-ack guns and the Long Toms. Last nite really looked like she was right. A big push is supposed to take place soon up here as they can't wait any longer as the ground is dry and just right for tanks. 500 tanks came in the other day and are bivouacked by the battery CP boy, and do the Jerries shell them. Reinforced our dugouts and camouflaged them. The nites are really terrifying, and all you can do is sweat them out. There were 40 bombers which did the dirty work, and seven were shot down.

May 4, Thu. – A quiet nite last nite except for a few shells. Rode horses this evening.

May 5, Fri. – A large number of tanks went up last nite. A push is supposed to come off the 7th, 8th, or 9th of this month. I sure hope something is done. Everybody is getting jittery wondering when we will push up or get off this beachhead. It'll be three months tomorrow that we've been on this beachhead under constant shell fire and bombing raids.

May 6, Sat. – A first sergeant from the 45th Division was at my pit this morning. He wanted us to show him the parts and nomenclature of the "40" as he is in charge of one that is going up to the front tonite and shell a Jerry supply road and to draw fire so as to spot the Jerry artillery. They are trying to cut the supplies down for the push. A P-51 landed, or crashed I mean, around 300 yards from my pit. Five minutes more, and he would have made the airport. He had just come back from his 32nd mission and was strafing the Jerry lines when he was hit by flak. He was pretty low when he bailed out, and his chute opened up just in time. He was burned a bit but that's all. Kapp and I are on guard now, and I'm writing this by moonlight. The Jerries are throwing in some shells and just hit an ammo dump. Boy, is it going up.

May 7, Sun. – Went to services this morning with George and Kip. We were interrupted a little while when a few shells landed pretty close.

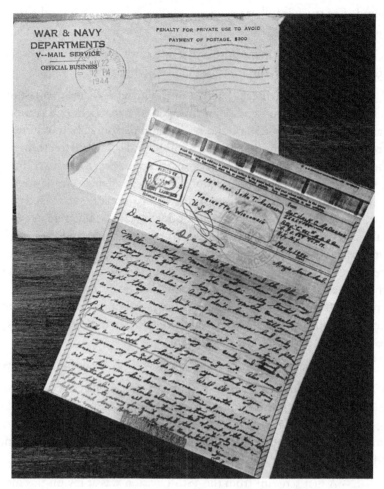

Before there was e-mail, there was v mail (or Victory mail) where letters were photographed and transferred onto microfilm and then blown back up to a readable size and printed.

May 8, Mon. – All section chiefs and gunners went over to no. 4 where we took a recoil cylinder all apart. There really is a mess of tanks around in this area. German recon. planes just went over. They were so high you could hardly see them. Got a package from home this evening.

May 9, Tue. – Jerry was over last nite. First time in 4–5 days. A bunch of tanks went up this evening. Looks as though the push might come off. Someone stole our two horses last nite. Hangover and Zipper. The latter was small, but he could go.

May 10, Wed. – They say the push didn't come off last nite as everybody from here to Naples knew about it. It's probably a lot of b.s. Been making rings all day from pieces of an Fw 190.

May 11, Thu. – Jerry threw in quite a barrage last nite. Went to a horse race today near the 2nd Platoon. Murph entered his horse, and it really was a good race. They had a track all taped off, band, judges, and a loud speaker. For the elimination prizes they got a can of stew, can of meatballs and spaghetti, and a can of "C" ration. For the derby prize it was a two-pound box of chocolates. Those really were some pretty horses. Played pinochle all evening.

May 12, Fri. – Jerry was really throwing her artillery around here last nite. Three flights of B-17's just went overhead toward Jerry territory. Boy, it sure was good to see them again. First time in two months. Washed clothes this morning. Two fellows from each gun section went to fire the new bazookas this afternoon down by the beach. Major Cook and Capt. Lossen went down a little ahead of them. There are a bunch of Jerry mines in there yet but were taped off. They walked around the top and all of a sudden heard a click. They both stopped and wondered what it was. In five seconds the mine went off and Major Cook caught the full force right in the stomach. He was killed instantly and Capt. Lossen standing right next to him got a little scratch. He was going to get his lieutenant colonel rating this month too. One minute he was laughing and joking and the next minute—dead.

May 13, Sat. – The Jerries threw in a terrific barrage all nite long. Then at 5:00 this morning every gun on the beachhead opened up for about two hours straight. More flights of bombers went over today. Wonder if the invasion has taken place or is about to. If something doesn't happen pretty soon, we'll all be heading for a Section 8. Charlie swiped another horse this afternoon. She's a bay mare and think she's going to be alright.

May 14, Sun. – The Jerries threw in another terrific artillery barrage again last nite and this morning. They were over our heads or short. Went to no. 4 where we took an oil gear all apart. It isn't such a mystery now. Our new colonel came around this afternoon. His name is Snider and a pretty swell guy. Got our ration of beer again tonite.

May 15, Mon. – Beautiful day today. Our artillery really threw a barrage at Jerry this morning.

May 16, Tue. – Rumors that the invasion took place were heard today, but the information is coming from other than Allied sources. A big push started on the Cassino front tho.

May 17, Wed. – We traded horses today for a beautiful sorrel. Boy, is she a beaut and really can step. Played an infantry team from the 34th Division this evening and beat them in baseball.

May 18, Thu. – Jerry planes were over again last nite dropping personnels. Heard over the radio that Cassino was taken. Things are beginning to look brighter now. Played the infantry again and lost. Charlie and Bill came back with another stud this evening. Boy, and is he fast. The Jerries shelled a Long Tom going down the road, and they almost got caught in it with the horses.

May 19, Fri. – Pushed 17 miles in two days on the Cassino front. As soon as they get to a certain point, we are going to make a drive here to try and get between the two mountains just ahead of us (near Cisterna) and cut off Highway 6, and trapping those between here and Cassino. We counted over 500 B-17's which flew over us coming from a bombing raid just a minute ago. There are still more coming. Boy, what a thrilling sight! It started raining this afternoon. The Anzio Express was dropping rather close this evening.

Our family car while on the Anzio beachhead. L to R: me, Inar, Mitch, Carlie, and Kip. There's still room for three more. Want to come along?

May 20, Sat. – Rained most of the morning. The colonel is coming around to inspect today, so they have me busting my hump getting things the way they want them. We have our positions all picked out up front to protect the eight-inch howitzers when the push comes off. They have Long Toms and 240's dug in up on the lines, camouflaged and ready to let loose as soon as the push takes place. Our artillery just threw a 15-minute barrage over at the Jerries. Boy, what sweet music that is! Here comes Jerry answering it. If our shells have the same moral effect on them as theirs have on us, well I'm sure they ain't feeling so good. 16th Division came in today.

May 21, Sun. – Went to church with Kip and George this morning over at the 45th Division headquarters. Heard from a pretty good source that the push was going to take place tomorrow morning but isn't going to as the Cassino bunch is supposed to have come all the way down Highway 7 and are up in the first ridge of mountains just ahead of us. I sure hope it's true 'cause it means there are hopes of this war coming to an end as long as we can keep pushing. From reports, the Germans are evacuating so fast they are leaving behind a lot of guns and equipment. The Cassino bunch is shelling the objective of our boys, so the push had to be called off.

May 22, Mon. – An order came out today that everybody has to wear their gas mask wherever they go as the Germans are expected to use gas to stop the push. They altered their planes a bit to a different objective. The push is going to take off tomorrow morning. They said we wouldn't get much sleep tonite as our artillery is going to throw over a terrific barrage all nite long. We all have that tense feeling now that the big push is going to take place.

May 23, Tue. – Our artillery was going strong all nite long and still is. The roads were one-way traffic last nite going up. All the tanks went up. The push took off this morning between four and six. The air support has been going over and coming back since dawn. Medium, heavy bombers, and dive bombers. The 90's in back of us are firing field artillery now. They just threw 50 rounds over in one minute. The Navy has been throwing a lot over all day. Truck loads of prisoners have been going by all day. Our troops were almost to Cisterna this morning at 8:00. They will cut off Highway 7 there, and their next objective is Highway 6. The Jerries threw some shells in this evening. Traded our stud off for a mare.

May 24, Wed. – Heard we are going to get march order today. Went to services this afternoon with Kip and George. Got march order at 6:30 this evening. Went on recon. at seven. We are moving up with the eight-inchers, two miles on the other side of the Bailey bridge.

May 25, Thu. – Left about 9:00 last nite. There was so much traffic and so darn dark we didn't get here until 12:00 midnite. Once I thought I was lost, but we finally got here. (Once we started moving up, the traffic was terrible. A column of half-tracks followed us to our position. A lieutenant came over and asked me where we were. I said, "At my gun position." He said, "God, I'm lost!") We dug all nite and day today just on the gun pits. It is just like rock. On the way down here, the artillery was really opening up all along the way. We almost hit a couple of tanks as the flashes from the guns was blinding. The colonel came around this morning. He sure is a swell guy. The eight-inchers have been blasting away all day. Just got word that we are going

91

to move tonite or tomorrow about five miles up with the eight-inchers. Boy, the front is really moving up.

May 26, Fri. – Jerry came over last nite and really had us sweating. They must have been after the eight-inchers as they dropped their loads pretty close. Went and took some pictures of the eight-incher or 240 mm. We stayed (Spash and I) for a few fire missions and boy, the concussion when they go off. We took some pictures of a bunch of tanks in the field next to us. Went to CP to go on recon. but didn't go so are staying overnite.

May 27, Sat. – Old Jerry was over again last nite. Went on recon. at 4:30 this morning. We are going about six miles up. Saw dead Jerries and G.I.'s. It really is an awful smell up there. A lot of tanks were knocked out up there, most of them ours. We really have a hell of a spot for our position. The battalion of tank destroyers is pulling out now. They are going to make a drive tonite in the same sector we are going in. There are mine fields all over up there.

May 28, Sun. – We didn't get march order so are staying. Going to pull out 4:30 tomorrow morning. Been sleeping in the pit every nite. Gun crews no. 3 and no. 4 left to go up with "C" Battery of the eight-inchers. Todd and my crew are going up to protect "B" Battery.

May 29, Mon. – Jerry was over again last nite. We are too far up forward to fire barrage fire. Left this morning to move up with the eight-inchers. Went on recon. after we got here. The roads are all a powdery dust and sure is dusty and dirty. They put me on a hill in plain view of the mountain, which our troops are fighting for at the base of it. When I brought the trucks up there, they threw an air burst right above us. Didn't stay there. Pulled down the slope next to a ridge which isn't so much under observation. Boy, talk about hard digging. We put 24 half-pound charges of TNT to blast a hole, but we had to pick most of it anyway. The eight-inchers are firing from the base of the hill we are on. The shells going not far above our heads. The concussion is really great.

May 30, Tue. – The 90's knocked a Jerry plane down last nite after they dropped bombs and personnels. Kip, Cholette, and myself were playing cards next to the "40" pit. All of a sudden we heard a shell come screaming toward us. We were so startled we couldn't move, so just sat and watched it come in. It landed about two feet in front of Bill's truck and about 15 yards from us. If it was 15 yards further it would have hit us as it was right in line with us. We watched a Jerry tank dodging our artillery shells on the mountain ahead of us. We can see everything that's going on thru the glasses when it is clear.

May 31, Wed. – Jerry was over again last nite. Our planes started to bomb the Jerries at 5:00 this morning and have been coming and going all day. We can see every load that is dropped. Boy, how the Jerries can stand it and not a bit of ack-ack. Our troops are fighting for Velletri, the big town on the side of the mountain. The 36th Division is going to make a push tomorrow to get on the other side of the mountain to cut the Jerries off.

Jun. 1, Thu. – Kapp and I were on the last relief this morning, and the push must have taken off 'cause at the crack of dawn all hell broke loose. Jerry was doing an awful lot of strafing last nite. We watched them strike our lines and then they started back toward us so we didn't watch any longer. Major Huff came around today from the 9th Group and raised heck about our director not being in, but we got orders we didn't have to. Imagine they will be changed now tho. Our troops have Velletri now, and the British 8th Army has Frosinone on Highway 6. General Clark said in a speech on Memorial Day that we would be in Rome in three days. I sure hope he's right. Got our beer ration today.

Leaving the Anzio beachhead. The town is Velletri.

Jun. 2, Fri. – Jerry came over again last nite, and we got orders to fire. Sure don't care to as he generally turns around and comes back strafing. He dropped three bombs near our 50 caliber. There are usually six or seven planes that come over all nite long. Our Beaufighters go after them, but they can't do it all. Heard we are going to get march order this evening. The eight-inchers have to fire over the mountains, and the range is too great from where they are.

Jun. 3, Sat. – Went on recon. this morning. We are going to take up position about 3,000 yards from the mountains and about parallel to Velletri. Got march order about 1:30 this afternoon. Got a pretty good spot this time. Got our guns in by 7:00 and made our shelters in German trenches. Found about 100 gallons of nice white wine back in a cave. No more morning alerts. Boy, it doesn't make us mad. I'll have to pull the evening alert tho.

Jun. 4, Sun. – Our troops were in Rome at 6:00 yesterday evening. Going to get march order this evening and are supposed to convoy to the outskirts of Rome. Gee, it sure is peaceful not having any shells coming in. The eight-inchers fired only a few rounds here. The Jerries are going back so fast our infantry is moving up in trucks.

Men from Kip Todd's gun crew standing by a German 88 mm gun moving up through Rome

Jun. 5, Mon. – Left about 1:00 p.m. today. We stopped just outside of Rome, which was declared an open city so no troops or equipment can go through it. Got our first look at it from the hill we are on. Pulled into position on the left flank of Rome. McCarthy's crew and mine are guarding "B" Battery of the 194th Field Artillery. Don't expect to be here long as the eight-inchers only have a radius of 400 yards to shoot in. We have a swell home to stay in here. The Jerries were in here yesterday, so we found quite a lot of stuff they left behind. Got a bunch of fresh potatoes and cabbage from a patch next to our pit.

Jun. 6, Tue. – Jerry was over strifing last nite. Saw one go down. Got march order at 5:30 this morning. We have to pass our IP at 10:00. We are going to set up on the other side of the Tiber River. Beautiful country around here. Went thru Albano yesterday, and it sure was wrecked. Took a picture of it. We are set up about 2,000 yards on the other side of the Tiber River. We crossed it on a pontoon bridge at the outskirts of Rome. Heard the invasion took place and am pretty sure it did this time.

4th Edition

June 7 to December 11, 1944

Our campaign in Italy continued and France

The Allies invaded southern France in August 1944. The 451st headed in that direction, landing in Saint Tropez, France and setting up their gun positions nearby, although the fighting had already been over with the liberation of Paris by late August. During this period of time, they occupied a medieval fort which was a luxurious setting compared to what they were used to over the past year in Italy. This is where Jack obtained the piano he is pictured playing on the cover which provided an additional opportunity to entertain and bring music into their experience when they weren't in battle. Their time in France offered a bit of respite, but the war was not over.

Jun. 7, Wed. – Jerry or "barracks bag Joe" came over again last nite. Didn't get much sleep last nite as they were over all nite dropping personnels and strafing. Dropped some big bombs just over the side of the hill which jarred everything around here. We explored a huge cave in the hill which had shafts running all over. We thought we could find some Jerries but no luck. Left about 10:00. Went about four miles north of Rome and six miles west. Saw a bunch of Jerry 88's, trucks, and tanks knocked out along the road. Boy this is the life. We move every day or so, set our guns down, but don't have to dig any pits. The Jerries are really on the run. Saw some Jerry prisoners down the road, and when they heard the invasion of France took place, they said it would all be over in three months. Gee I sure hope so.

Jun. 8, Thu. – Jerry came over again with his barracks bag full as usual. They came from all directions at once it seemed. No caves or holes to get into, so we just had to sweat it out. Expected to move up today, but didn't.

Jun. 9, Fri. – Jerry was over again last nite. The moon was so bright we could see the planes; a two engine plane just skimmed over our heads. We could have possibly knocked it down but have orders not to fire unless they commit a hostile act in the area we are protecting. We are supposed to convoy to Civitavecchia today, but the plans were changed, so we had to dig our guns in. The 194-F (8") might go to Corsica but don't know if we will go with them if they do. Kip came over today, and we are going to take off for Rome regardless.

Jun. 10, Sat. – Went to Rome this morning with Kip. Boy and did we have the walk to get there and come back. We stayed all day and just walked around. We had some drinks but couldn't get any dinner as food is very scarce there. Went to St. Peter's Cathedral. It's beautiful, and huge isn't the word for it 'cause it's bigger than that. Saw where the remains of St. Peter are entombed, which are inside of the Cathedral. Met an Italian who spoke English, so he showed us the place where Mussolini lived and spoke or made his speeches and went and saw the Coliseum. It's one of the seven wonders of the world, and boy I don't doubt it. We got screwed up on the road back, so here we sit waiting for a ride still 10 miles from our sections. Got back just before dark then went on a recon. Bill and Louie took off for Rome this noon and aren't back yet.

Kip and I are at St. Peter's Cathedral, Italy

Jun. 11, Sun. – Got march orders at 8:30. Moved up about five miles to a deep grove of pines. All of the VI Corps artillery is assembling here also. Looks like another boat ride as VI Corps has been relieved.

Coliseum, Rome, Italy

Outskirts of Rome, Italy

Jun. 12, Mon. – Have to clean up all equipment, inspection tomorrow. Got march order this noon. Have to move 75 yards down the runway. We are set up next to an airport. Finished our pits in record time.

Jun. 13, Tue. – Right after breakfast we went on recon. about 50 miles up near Tarquinia, other side of Civitavecchia. The rest of the guns and crews came up about 2:00. We are guarding another airport of Spitfires. We just got here, and another outfit has come to relieve us already. Something is screwed up someplace. Expect to pull out this evening.

Jun. 14, Wed. – The 898th pulled in last nite, but we didn't pull out until this morning. Went back about 25 miles to Santa Marinella. We are set in a grove of trees. Capt. Weiden said we would be here about two weeks for a rest. We were told to unload our trucks which we did, and then the order came thru we are pulling out tonite or tomorrow. We went on a recon. to Tarquinia to relieve the 898th guarding a bridge. We got there and the 425th was in there yet. The 898th hadn't relieved them yet. Boy what a screwed up mess. It seems that the ack-ack are all being shifted around. Dig in one day, move the next.

Jun. 15, Thu. – Left about 7:00 this morning. Boy what a pit we got. A tank and two trucks would fit in it. How some outfits get away with such pits is beyond me. We wrapped our stiffkey stick around a tree, and it sure as heck won't be used any more. We are supposed to stay here three days and go back for a rest. This will be the third time we are going back for a rest and something turns up to send us back up. I'd just as soon stay in position as go back in bivouacked. We are living in a house with Italians. We use two rooms upstairs. They are really clean people, this family.

Jun. 16, Fri. – Really slept good last nite. Have to fix the pit over and put the director on. Heard that Tokyo was bombed by our B-29's. First time they were used. Flights of B-26's have been going over all morning. The dawn patrol took off from the airport about a quarter mile from here at 4:30 this morning. It gets light at 4:30 and gets dark at 9:30. Doesn't give one much sleep as he is pulling guard most of the time. We are pulling out tomorrow. Supposed to go up 70 miles to guard tank destroyers.

Jun. 17, Sat. – We aren't going up now, going to guard an airport near here. Boy they sure do screw things around, but this time it sure didn't make us mad. Pulled into the airport about 10:30 a.m. Have our positions picked out but can't work on them as there are two German magnetic mines about 200 yards from my position. They have never encountered anything like it before and claim dog tags might set them off. We were right up next to them taking pictures but didn't know at the time how sensitive they were. Experts are coming down here to try and neutralize them. We had to move to a spot 600 yards away in order to be safe in case some vibration sets them off. The experts just came in on a B-25, and we have to get out of here as they are more powerful than 6,000 pounds of TNT. It took about four hours for them to make them safe. We made our pits out of bails of hay.

Jun. 18, Sun. – Rained last nite. Charley and Spash got a young pig last nite, so we'll have some swell chops now. Got march order this noon. Man, all we do is move. Going back to Santa Marinella for a rest. Got here, set up our pyramidal tents and just in time as it started raining. They don't hold out much rain as they are full of shrapnel holes. I am sergeant of the guard tonite.

Jun. 19, Mon. – We unloaded all our equipment this morning, had the afternoon off. My section played Kip's in a ball game after supper. We were issued pamphlets for France. Looks like we are in for another boat ride.

Jun. 20, Tue. – Got typhoid and typhus shots today. Boy did the last one sting. Went swimming with Kip at the beach in town. Went to see the show *Two Girls and a Sailor*. It really was tops! We are getting passes to Rome and passes to see the stage show *This is the Army*.

No. 2 gun crew

Jun. 22, Thu. – We have a training schedule in the mornings and have the afternoons off. The battalion assembled in our area where Lt. Col. Snyder gave a talk on our outfit and the record we have made for ourselves. Then Col. Hennigen gave a talk. We are back with the 15th Group again. Went swimming in the Tyrrhenian Sea again this afternoon.

Jun. 23, Fri. – Each gun section got five gallons of wine today. It's really good stuff. Getting ready for inspection tomorrow. Went swimming this afternoon.

Jun. 24, Sat. – Had a full field inspection this morning. Major Lossen came around to inspect. Boy he's one of the best officers I know! Went swimming this afternoon, played ball this evening.

Jun. 25, Sun. – Went to services this morning with Kip and George. Went swimming this afternoon. Had a raid last nite. They didn't drop anything around us tho.

Jun. 26, Mon. – We started the week out by a mile run this morning. Going to be every morning along with the training schedule. Went swimming this afternoon, played ball this evening.

Jun. 27, Tue. – It's really a hot one today. Went swimming this afternoon. Went over to an Italian's with Kip about 8:30 p.m. and had a spaghetti supper. Boy was it good!

Jun. 28, Wed. – Kip, Spash, and I went on pass to Rome today.

Jun. 29, Thu. – Loaded our truck and went to the 5th Army firing point. It's about six miles from Santa Marinella. We set our gun and director up and then our tents.

Jun. 30, Fri. – Took the mile run this morning as usual. Did artillery drill orientation, and fired a number of trial shots also with the 50 caliber this morning. Fired at rockets this afternoon. At 3:00 the plane came with a towed target. We are with no. 8. They fired today, we fire tomorrow. The 289th Army band, the "Griffens" put on a show after supper for us. Boy and were they good.

Jul. 1, Sat. – We fired 35 rounds this morning. The gun and director wouldn't stay in faize so had to track off. Didn't get any hits, but had some awful close shots. We finished our firing this afternoon and got a hit. My crew, no. 3, no. 5, and no. 7 were the only ones who got hits in our battery. I think we tied for the record on the firing point. Got paid after supper.

Jul. 2, Sun. – We struck our tents this morning getting ready to go back to Santa Marinella. Just before we were going swimming, a call came that we had to go back and police up our area, so three men and the sergeant from each crew had to go. There wasn't a bit of paper there, but some Major Moody from the 5th Group was putting the blame on us for it being nowhere near us.

Jul. 3, Mon. – This morning my section and no. 8. were restricted from getting passes 'cause we were the closest to the place where the paper was. Then to top that off, men from both crews had to dig a big hole. Boy I blew my top then. But what good does it do when our pit officers are afraid to open their yap for fear they might lose 10 points. Boy if ever I felt like smashing in a big nose it's now. Went swimming this afternoon. Went to an Italian stage show this evening. Boy was it good. Two girls were really good lookers. One sang and talked English and danced. Man, oh, man was she nice! Played "B" Battery in a ball game and lost.

Jul. 4, Tue. – No passes for us today either. We are supposed to get them tomorrow. Went swimming this afternoon and really had fun. Played "A" Battery after supper and won. Kip does the pitching for us and really does OK.

Jul. 5, Wed. – No passes as we are alerted. We have to load our trucks today, expect to leave tomorrow. Went to a stage show this afternoon. We are going to leave tomorrow morning at 6:15 and coming to Naples. The 7th Army is assembling there, and I'm pretty sure we will be in it as we had to remove all 5th Army insignias and cover our unit numbers on our trucks. This is going to be a secret move. Sergeant of the guard tonite.

Jul. 6, Thu. – Had breakfast at 4:30 this morning, hit the main highway at 6:15. Went through Rome on Highway 1, then took 6 and 7. Went through Terracina, Vittoria, Velletri, Albano, and the Pontine Marshes, which the Germans flooded to stop our advance while we were driving on the beachhead. Houses were covered with water above the doors. Every town this side of Rome was almost all in ruins. We pulled into an area just outside of Sparanise. We are still about 20 miles from Naples.

Jul. 7, Fri. – We are going to stay here for awhile. Had a full field inspection this morning. We are sure we are going in on another invasion as each chief of section had to turn in a list of the men in order of their value. We will each have nine men with us, no director or power plant, and one truck. According to the news, England is catching hell from radio bombs. It's hot as hell around here. We have most of the day off. There's a corn field next to us, so we've boiled corn every evening, and it really is good.

Jul. 8, Sat. – Had a rifle inspection this morning. Passes for Naples start tomorrow.

Jul. 9, Sun. – Rained most of the day. Went to church and took communion with George.

Jul. 10, Mon. – Some of the guys in both platoons screwed up by getting drunk and causing trouble, so the whole bunch of us have to suffer for it by drilling all morning and some passes cut out. Got a package of cookies from Mrs. Krutz.

Jul. 11, Tue. – Had an inspection of our equipment this morning. Went through the gas chamber. We were issued combat shoes this evening. Went to a show last nite at the 11th evac. hospital *Thousands Cheer* with Kathryn Grayson. Went to another show this evening in our battery area. *His Butler's Sister* was playing with Deanna Durbin, Franchot Tone, and Pat O'Brien. Didn't see it all as the transformer burned out.

Jul. 12, Wed. – Close order drill this morning as usual. It rained hard this afternoon. We all got a bottle of beer for supper. Went to the 11th evac. to see the show *The Adventures of Mark Twain*.

Jul. 13, Thu. – Went to Naples on pass with Spash and Kip. Had a swell time and better than at Rome. The same show with Deanna D. was shown in our area tonite. After the machine broke down every little while, we finally saw the finish. It was good though.

Jul. 14, Fri. – Sergeant of the guard today as I don't do anything all day, which sure makes me mad. Ordnance was around checking our equipment this morning. Went to the show with George and Kip, saw *It Happened Tomorrow* with Dick Powell, Linda Darnell, and Jack Oakie.

Jul. 15, Sat. – Had inspection in ranks and field inspection laid out on our bunks. I was in charge of a group of guys to Cassino this afternoon on a sightseeing tour. Boy it really is in ruins and will never be built up again. The monastery is really leveled off. Went over to the field artillery where we saw a stage show after which the Red Cross passed out all the doughnuts and coffee we wanted and then a movie. Danny Kaye in *Up in Arms* was showing. It was really good.

Cassino

Jul. 16, Sun. – Went to the Red Cross at Santa Maria this afternoon with Spash. Had a lot of fun. Went to a stage show at the field artillery this evening.

Jul. 17, Mon. – Went for a shower this morning. Went swimming this afternoon out to a beach about 10 miles from here. It really was swell. Went to the show this evening with Kip, Spash, and George. We played pinochle until the show started.

Jul. 18, Tue. – We went on a 12-mile hike this morning, which we did in two hours. We were doing 132 steps a minute, that is almost double time. Boy we were all pretty well petered out after we got back. Went swimming again this afternoon. Went to a show in our area this evening. *See Here, Private Hargrove* was playing.

Jul. 19, Wed. – Hot as heck today. Took a shower this afternoon. Our PX was handed out this evening. It's the biggest we've ever got. They managed to get the P.B.S. rations. We got orange juice, tomato, pineapple, tidbits, cookies, cigarettes, candy bars, cigars, and other misc. Our battery officers arranged a dance for us tonite at the Red Cross in Santa Maria with a 10-piece band and about 100 women consisting of Italians and WAACs. Don't know how these big G.I. shoes will work.

Jul. 20, Thu. – We had a pretty good time at the dance last nite. The only girls that came were Italians, but some were really nice and swell dancers. The WAACs didn't come at all. They have boyfriends in the P.B.S., and I guess they have an impartial feeling toward the combat Soldier. Went swimming this afternoon again. Went to a movie in our area this evening.

Jul. 21, Fri. – Spash and I went on pass to Torre Annunziata today. That town really stinks. The first sergeant was along too, so we talked him into going to Sorrento. That really is a pretty town. Hardly any Soldiers and beautiful swimming beaches. Heard in town that Hitler was injured by an assassin and that a revolution was started in Germany.

Jul. 22, Sat. – Today we heard that Hitler arrested 5,000 of his officers and executed the assassin which was a lieutenant colonel in the German army. Guess they are afraid of the Russians getting to Germany first. Frank is making stencils for our barracks bags, A & B, and 5698 K for our code number. It's the same as when we left the States. There are rumors that we are going back to the States. I know that's too good to be true tho. We are supposed to waterproof also which looks like another invasion soon. Some outfits have already loaded on boats, and we've had priority on everything since we came in this area which is only given to those who are going into something. The *Stars and Stripes* today said "general's conspiracy shakes Hitler's Germany" which sure sounds good. We had inspection this morning. A few crews got gigged, so we had to stand another one at 11:30. We all got a beer and two bottles of Coke for dinner. Went swimming this afternoon. Went to a show this evening.

Jul. 23, Sun. – Didn't do much today. Went swimming this afternoon with Kip. Boy we really had fun. The waves were about 10 feet high. Went to a show at the 10th evac. Just as we got there some French and a Canadian brought a man from our battery in. The pass truck coming back from Torri Annunziata hit a tree then a wall, and then turned over. Six men were hurt. They were taken to the hospital.

Jul. 24, Mon. – Had rifle practice this morning. Going to the firing range this afternoon. Fired the M-1, got a score of 178. Not so good. Went to a show at the 11th evac. Saw *Dangerous Blood*.

Jul. 25, Tue. – Went out to the range again all day. Fired the carbine this afternoon, shot 180. We were told to forget about the 7th Army and put our 5th Army insignias back on. It might be just for a protective measure. The revolt in Germany is still going strong, but there aren't many confirmed statements about it. Went to a show at the 10th evac. this evening with Kip, George, and Spash. Saw *The Hairy Ape*. It wasn't bad.

Jul. 26, Wed. – We stenciled our bags today. We have the same training schedule every morning. Calisthenics, infantry drill, and class until noon. Went swimming this afternoon with Kip and George. Went to a show in our area this evening. *Coney Island* was playing with Betty Grable, George Montgomery, and Cesar Romero. It was in Technicolor and sure was good!

Jul. 27, Thu. – Went on a hike this morning. We had a meeting with the captain and got our checklist on loading our equipment. Yesterday we were going to take 14 men with us, but it's down to 10 again which I think is definite. We should know in a couple of days whether we are going in on another invasion or not. An M.P. in town said that German planes are landing on our airports giving themselves up. Sounds logical. Went to the Red Cross with Curly this afternoon, another movie in our area this evening but saw it before.

Jul. 28, Fri. – Went on a hike this morning. Went swimming with Kip this afternoon, show this evening.

Jul. 29, Sat. – Inspection in ranks and bunks this morning by the colonel. Everything OK. Went swimming this afternoon. Kip was sergeant of the guard so couldn't go.

Jul. 30, Sun. – Sergeant of the guard today. Went to the show this evening, saw a double feature. *Lassie Come Home* and *Bathing Beauty* with Red Skelton and Esther Williams. They both were tops.

Jul. 31, Mon. – Got our beer ration today, four cans. Got our PX which really was the biggest yet, over $100 worth for every crew. We also got paid today. According to the news the Russians are just outside of Warsaw, and we are advancing on the Normandy front and also on the Italian front. Went to the Red Cross with Kip this afternoon. Flights of bombers went over all morning.

Aug. 1, Tue. – We were issued gas impregnite and other gas equipment this morning. Went on pass to Santa Maria with Spash. Saw the show *Top Man* with Donald O'Connor, Peggy Ryan, and Susanna Foster. It really was good. Each crew loaded their one truck today as we're only taking one. Went to a U.S.O. show at battalion headquarters. They sure were good.

Aug. 2, Wed. – Cleaned all our equipment this morning. Went to another U.S.O. show this evening at headquarters. It was pretty good.

Aug. 3, Thu. – Went on a hike this morning. Went to the Red Cross this afternoon with Kip, George, and Spash. Went to the show there, saw *Government Girl* with Olivia de Havilland. Went to a show in our area this evening. *Madame Curie* was on with Greer Garson and Walter Pidgeon. It was all about the discovery of radium and was very good.

Aug. 4, Fri. – From the news this morning, we gained 40 miles in France and the English 20. Things are looking good, but there are too many rumors going around to put much faith in anything unless its heard direct from a good source. Went swimming this afternoon with Kip and George.

Aug. 5, Sat. – Usual Saturday inspection this morning. Went to the Red Cross with Kip and Spash this afternoon. Went to the 108th this evening to see the show *Broadway Rhythm*. It was in Technicolor and was really good.

Aug. 6, Sun. – The news really sounded good this morning. The American armored division took Brest last nite. They have almost the whole peninsula now. The Russians have flanked Warsaw and are about 50 miles from German soil. Flights of B-17s have been going over all morning bombing the southern coast of France. Went swimming at the King's Palace in Caserta this afternoon. It's a pool about 500 yards long, and boy is it nice. A lot of WAACs swimming there also which really caught our interest. Stopped at the Red Cross at Santa Maria on the way back. The show was in our area this evening. *Once Upon a Time* with Cary Grant and Janet Blair.

Aug. 7, Mon. – Sergeant of the guard today. Kip and I went to see about a three-day pass yesterday starting tomorrow. We got the pass, but today all passes and details were canceled, nobody leaves the area. "C" and "B" Batteries are the alert batteries. So I expect we'll be pulling out soon. They let us go swimming this afternoon, so we took the truck to Caserta again. I made contact with the cement bottom and left some of my face down there. I look like I tangled with some Jerry.

Aug. 8, Tue. – Went to the Red Cross with Kip and Spash this afternoon. "B" Battery got march order at 7:00 this evening. They are going to be attached to the 45th Division.

Aug. 9, Wed. – Went to the Red Cross with Kip and Spash this afternoon. Hike this morning. Major Lossen came over and said we had to get ready to pull out. Two hours later, the orders were changed and "D" Battery is going instead.

Aug. 10, Thu. – Rained this morning. All passes are cancelled. We are expecting to move this afternoon or tomorrow morning at 7:00. If we leave this afternoon we are going right on the boat, otherwise we are going to a bivouac area just outside of Naples. This invasion force is going to be a big one and the last one. Boats are going to leave from Italy, Africa, Corsica, and Sardinia.

Aug. 11, Fri. – Went to a movie in our area last nite. *Wintertime* was shown with Sonja Henie and Cesar Romero. Reveille at 5:00 this morning. Left at 8:00. It is now 10:30 a.m., and we just pulled into a bivouac area about 12 kilometers outside of Naples. We set up our pyramidals the first thing. Kip and my tents are about two feet apart. All around us we have apple, pear, peach, and plum trees. Kip and I went to town, which is about a block away, and got us a supper of two eggs and a plate of french fries for $1.00.

Aug. 12, Sat. – Didn't do anything all day. Went with Kip over to get our laundry and stayed all evening talking and drinking some good white wine.

Aug. 13, Sun. – Went on pass to Naples with Kip and Spash today. Boy there sure are a bunch of boats in the harbor. In the news last nite the Germans were said to have evacuated Florence.

Aug. 14, Mon. – Cleaned up our equipment this morning. George, Pete, Louie, and myself played pinochle all afternoon. Kip, the first sergeant, Curly, and I went over to the Italian gal's house and had a meal of eggs and potatoes.

Aug. 15, Tue. – Sergeant of the guard today. Just heard that southern France was invaded. Went to a movie at the 109th this evening. *Lost Angel* was playing with Margaret O'Brien and James Craig. It sure was a wonderful picture.

Aug. 16, Wed. – Oiled the inside of our tent this morning. The ground all over has about two inches of powdered dust on top. The news said we are meeting with little opposition in southern France. The Nazi radio report said the Allies are fighting for Paris already. Went to a U.S.O. show at the 6th chemical outfit. Really was swell.

Aug. 17, Thu. – Last nite around midnite we had an air raid. Been quite awhile since we've had one. The searchlights picked them up over Pozzuoli where the 40's and 90's opened up on them and followed them over Naples. Don't know if any damage was done. Went to Santa Maria with Sgt. Michleson this morning. Kip and I went to see about our three-day pass. We intend to catch a plane at Naples and go to Rome. A number of ack-ack outfits are being turned into infantry. I don't think we'll have to worry as we are supposed to be the best Bofors (40 mm) outfit in this theatre and rank 2nd in all ack-ack. Two half-track outfits are ahead of us.

Aug. 18, Fri. – Didn't do much all day. Our battery had a dance this evening in Naples. It was held on a terrace overlooking the sea and sure was a pretty spot. We had the 45th Division orchestra which is the best around here. Helen Young, who is with a U.S.O. unit, came and sang a few numbers. I did quite a bit of dancing with a girl from Minneapolis, Minnesota. Boy was I surprised when she spoke to me. Elaine Thurson was her name.

Aug. 19, Sat. – Inspection this morning. Played horseshoes all afternoon. The news sounds damn good lately. The southern front is supposed to have 100 square miles which sure is going some. An unconfirmed report said we're 12 miles from Paris. The Normandy front and southern front are only about 300 miles apart and are expected to link in two weeks. It sure is tiresome laying around here. Most of us would like to go to France as the old man is really busting our hump around here, and this waiting works on a guy's nerves too much.

Aug. 20, Sun. – Carol's birthday. Another day of nothing to do. Went to a show at the 108th. *Guadalcanal Diary* was shown with Preston Foster and Lloyd Nolan.

Aug. 21, Mon. – Started the week out with the usual schedule. Hike, classes, and cleaning of equipment. Went swimming with Kip and George at the King's Palace in Caserta this afternoon.

Aug. 22, Tue. – Went on pass to Naples today with Spash. Went to the Garrison Theater and saw *Best Foot Forward* with Lucille Ball, Tommy Dix, and Harry James. The harbor at Naples is full of ships again. 2–4 heavy Italian cruisers out there also. The news tonite was very encouraging; the Allies are moving forward on all fronts.

Aug. 23, Wed. – Had an air raid about 12:20 last nite. The Navy must have opened up with their big guns as there were some awful big flashes which I know weren't from 90's. Got reports about "B" and "D" Batteries today. They landed on D-Day and haven't had any casualties as yet. They captured 16 prisoners. Over the news today they said that from an unconfirmed report we made another landing near

Spain, south of Bourdeaux. General Patton, who is in charge of 3rd Army in France, has made a big drive flanking Paris to cut off all German retreat. They are on both sides of the Seine River. All those who want to go swimming at the pool at Bagnoli had to take a physical this afternoon. It wasn't much of one. The news this evening said that Paris was liberated by about 50,000 French. There are no American troops in there as yet. Romania has made peace terms with the Russians, and Bulgaria I believe will also as they are having a peace conference with Russia now. Florence is completely free of all Germans. Everybody got 12 bottles of beer this evening.

Aug. 24, Thu. – Sergeant of the guard today. Went to the show at the 108th. Saw *Four Jills in a Jeep* with Kay Francis, Carole Landis, Martha Raye, and Mitzi Mayfair.

Aug. 25, Fri. – Went swimming today but couldn't get in the pool so took a ride all around Naples. Went to a show at 108th *Old Acquaintance* was playing with Betty Davis. Our A.P.O. was changed to 512.

Aug. 26, Sat. – Inspection this morning. Half the battery got gigged. The news this noon said that southern France is all liberated. General Patton's armored forces are 130 miles from German soil. Romania has declared war against the Germans, and the Russians have 12 German divisions trapped in Romania.

Aug. 27, Sun. – Went swimming this morning at the pool in Bagnoli, and we stayed all day. It sure is a beautiful pool. Went to a show at 108th. Saw Spencer Tracy in *A Guy Named Joe*.

Aug. 28, Mon. – Had another air raid last nite. There was a lot of ack-ack thrown up, but I believe they came over to take pictures as they dropped flares that didn't last long. Played cribbage this afternoon. Went to Naples with Kip and met Danell Anderson at the Red Cross.

Aug. 29, Tue. – Expect to move out of here soon. Went to a U.S.O. show at the 403rd. The 45th Division band was there and Helen Young and Pettie Brien. The news said the Russians are two miles into Hungary, and all fronts are moving up. Went to the 108th saw *Up in Mable's Room*.

Aug. 30, Wed. – Played badminton with George all afternoon. The news this evening said General Patton's Army is near the Belgium border.

Aug. 31, Thu. – Went on a two-hour hike this morning. Went swimming at the pool in the medical center this afternoon. Sergeant of the guard tonite. News said the Russians took Bucharest.

Sep. 1, Fri. – Sergeant of the guard all day today. Learned how to play chess this afternoon. The news this evening said that the fronts are moving so fast that by the time reports from General Patton get to General Eisenhower's headquarters, it is old news.

Sep. 2, Sat. – Went on pass to Naples with Kip, Spash, and George. We looked at the large war maps in the orientation building in the morning, where we were 50 miles from Germany. This evening just before going back we looked again, and they were 40 miles only. The German retreats are disorderly.

Sep. 3, Sun. – The news this morning said the 5th and 8th Armies in Italy drove six miles into the Gothic Line. German reports say we are three miles from Luxembourg. Went swimming at the pool in Bagnoli most of the day with Kip and George. The news this noon said we are 11 miles from Germany, and the Germans are threatening to use gas. Rocket bombs haven't dropped on England since Friday, but some were reported dropped in Paris.

Sep. 4, Mon. – The morning news said the Finns have quit fighting. The Germans are evacuating Brussels. Kip and I went to Naples this afternoon. They had a sort of fair at the Red Cross to celebrate Labor Day with everything on-the-house.

Sep. 5, Tue. – Went swimming at Bagnoli this afternoon.

Sep. 6, Wed. – Went to the Red Cross with Kip this afternoon. The *Stars and Stripes* today said the Yanks are in Germany. While in town next to our area here, an Italian news broadcast came over, and the people started yelling and jumping and gave wine and champagne to us. They said the Germans were finished, the war was over. Nobody heard anything about it back here.

Sep. 7, Thu. – Went on a four-hour hike this morning. Went swimming this afternoon. We were supposed to leave for France today, but they can't get the boats.

Sep. 8, Fri. – Went on another all-morning hike. Just for a few guys screwing up, they take it out on everybody. It looks as though we'll be going to the Pacific after the war is over here. Anything just to get the whole thing over with and soon. It's two years today we were sworn into the Army.

Sep. 9, Sat. – Inspection in ranks, tents, and equipment this morning. Sergeant of the guard tonite. The news commentator said no definite news would be given for four or five days.

Sep. 10, Sun. – Sergeant of the guard all day. Kip and I developed pictures this evening.

Sep. 11, Mon. – Cleaned our guns and loaded our other trucks this morning. Expect to pull out of here by Wednesday. Went to the Red Cross this afternoon with George. The news this evening said the 2nd Army is six miles in Germany.

Sep. 12, Tue. – Didn't do anything all day. Battalion headquarters. Went down to the staging area this morning. We are going on the same boat so expect to leave tomorrow. The news this evening said we are 10 miles in Germany. All fronts are moving up.

Sep. 13, Wed. – Got orders to pack this morning, going to leave at 12:30 noon. The first truck is taking off now. We convoyed to the staging area Texas and boarded the LST–655 at 5:30 this evening.

Sep. 14, Thu. – We are still in the docks yet. Expect to pull out tonite or tomorrow morning. We are using casualty litters attached to the hold of the ship for beds. Pulled out into the bay at 5:30 p.m. waiting for the convoy to form. It is 6:30 p.m., and we are getting under way. Were issued life belts after supper. Only catch is you have to blow them up yourself when in need of them.

Sep. 15, Fri. – It's beautiful out today. You can hardly tell you are moving, the sea is so calm. We are getting pretty good meals so far. Passed a convoy back to Naples at 4:30 this afternoon. The hospital ship *Arcadia* was passing by at the same time. Bert mentioned that ship in one of his letters awhile ago. We can see land in the horizon which they say is Corsica. There are 15 LST's in our convoy with two destroyer escorts. We went through the straits of Corsica and Sardenia at 6:30 p.m. which took about an hour. The shores of both islands look very rocky though the field glasses. If this calm weather keeps up, we expect to hit France sometime tomorrow.

Sep. 16, Sat. – This is the second birthday I spent on the water. Last year at this time we were on the boats to Salerno. We sighted the coastline of France this morning. We were just off shore of Toulon but being as we are way ahead of schedule or something, they got different orders, turned around, and now we are heading west. It is 5:00 p.m. now and just finished supper. Can't see land at all now, so we'll be spending another nite on board.

Our truck coming off an LST. I'm standing on the running board.
Southern France

Sep. 17, Sun. – Pulled into the harbor of Marseille this morning. The docks are full here also, so they sent us out again. Going back where we came from yesterday.

Sep. 18, Mon. – We couldn't land at Toulon so went on to St. Tropez. The docks are filled there also, so we are making a beach landing a couple miles down from St. Tropez. This convoy is just like a lost caravan. Five boats are unloading now, so it shouldn't take long. It sure looks pretty from offshore. It rained almost all yesterday morning and this morning. The sea got rough last nite and really pitched us around. Quite a few of the fellows got sick. We set our watches back an hour last nite, but now we'll have to set it up again. We landed at 3:00 p.m. Took off in convoy for Saint-Maximin. They took the wrong road and when they found out, we were only about 40 miles from the Italian border. We were going over some mountains at the time, and the scenery was sure pretty. We caught up with the 2nd Platoon about 8:00 p.m. and bivouacked for the nite. The people and towns are very clean so far. A great difference from the Italians. And the beautiful girls lined along the roads. Very friendly too, that is from the road.

Sep. 19, Tue. – Left about 8:30 this morning, then it started raining and continued all day and is still raining. We are next to the La Jasse airport and will be here a few days. The highways to here were littered with German guns and equipment. There's a world of difference between France and Italy.

Sep. 20, Wed. – It continued raining all nite and stopped about 5:00 this morning. Dried out our equipment and got march order this afternoon. We convoyed to Port-de-Bouc and went into gun positions along a canal. The mosquitoes are terrible here, and the ground is all rocks and thistle bushes. We didn't have to dig in as we expect to move shortly.

Sep. 21, Thu. – Went on a recon. this evening farther out on the coast. The area we have to dig out positions in is all mined and barbed wire defenses strung all over. I have to put my guns on a German coastal defense system which has slit trenches and underground rooms running all over.

Sep. 22, Fri. – Pulled out at 7:20 this morning. A colonel from the 68th AAA Group came over to check the positions, and then we commenced to build them. We have to build up from the ground as it's all rock. Our phone was out of order all nite. When the communication (team) strung the lines, they threw it over a high tension wire which was supposedly dead. About 7:45 p.m. the juice was thrown on and 1,800 volts went through our telephone wires. Almost every crew who were on the phone at the time got an awful jolt from it. Tommy Cirillo from Todd's crew was electrocuted. He was given artificial respiration for about two hours, but they couldn't bring him back to life. The reason he was killed was because he was sitting on the guns and therefore grounding himself.

Sep. 23, Sat. – Service for Tommy was held this afternoon at Marseille. Our chaplain held a Catholic Mass for him. Finished our "40" and "50" pits today and have to finish the director pit tomorrow, after which passes for Marseille are supposed to start. Got five packages in the mail tonite.

Sep. 24, Sun. – Worked on the director and power plant pits and finished them today. The officers even had to admit we have a good pit. It's one for show purposes mostly. Curly finished the kitchen today also. Lt. Hancock came around this evening to say goodbye as he's going over to "B" Battery. We sure hate to see him go. Just got a call that we got march order. Moving out first thing in the morning. Just after we get everything fixed up, damn it!

Sep. 25, Mon. – Pulled out at 8:00 this morning and convoyed up to Toulon. We took over gun positions from the 433rd. My position is next to the water, and we live in an old fort which is a dandy set up. Rooms, beds, everything. There's a big seven horsepower engine down below which we run for lights. It's really a spooky place. Dungeons way down below, passages running all over, and German ammo and equipment galore. There's an awful strong wind blowing today which makes this place sound like a murder story. The historic scuttling of the French fleet took place in the harbor which we are protecting. We can see quite a few of them with just the upper part sticking out of the water. This is also the spot where the Germans had their big submarine base.

The scuttled French fleet. Our gun position is set up in an old medieval fort right at the entrance to the harbor. Toulon, France, 1944

Sep. 26, Tue. – Built up the gun pit as the "wip" thought it was too low. A sailor told us there are 60 French naval boats sunk in this harbor. The battleship *Dunkirk* was sunk in dry dock, so just the deck on up is sitting out of the water. There really are some monstrous guns on it.

Sep. 27, Wed. – The 433rd moved out of the fort, so we took over the rooms they used. They sure left a mess, but we scrubbed everything up and have a beautiful setup. I've got a small room all to myself.

Sep. 28, Thu. – We sold cans of "C" ration to the German prisoners who are working next to us and made quite a pile for ourselves. Also got some belts and swastikas off them. It rained hard after supper tonite.

Toulon, France, 1944

Sep. 29, Fri. – Spash and I went on pass this afternoon to Toulon. Blew off some German hand grenades and potato mashers this morning. Boy they really have the concussion when they explode.

Sep. 30, Sat. – Had artillery drill all morning. Have to make a good showing for the general as in a week he is coming to inspect, which we'll see whether we stay here or not. Sure hope so as we have about the best set up of the whole battery. Went over to a house and brought back a piano this evening. Some of the hammers and keys were broken, but we fixed it up and it plays perfect.

Oct. 1, Sun. – We were throwing hand grenades most of the day when off guard. Have quite a supply of them in the fort here.

Oct. 2, Mon. – Sent our trucks away this morning, and they are supposed to be gone about 90 days. We were warned today not to go into town at nite as nearly every nite a couple of G.I.s have been shot and some killed. A German was captured after killing a major and a captain. He was dressed in French clothes, wearing a

Our music room in the Fort we occupied. Toulon, France

I'm holding German hand grenades. Toulon, France

F.F.I. armband. There has been an awful gale blowing all day. A motor boat off an American cruiser in the harbor smashed into the rocks next to the fort here. We took the sailors inside. Nothing wrong except they were soaked to the skin. Quite a few boats of the French fleet, what is left of it, are anchored in the harbor. The battleship *Richelieu* is anchored in the harbor.

Oct. 3, Tue. – Bill threw a hand grenade over the wall which landed on about 10 one-gallon cans filled with H.C. It all went off, and boy it felt like the fort was going to fall. I've put the clamp on now, no more of them being thrown.

Oct. 4, Wed. – Major Cooper was around to inspect today. He said everything was fine. Passes started today again. From the looks of things, we'll be here for quite awhile, which sure don't make us mad.

Oct. 5, Thu. – The colonel came around to inspect this afternoon. Everyone was right on the ball.

Oct. 6, Fri. – It started raining early this morning and worked itself up into a terrible wind and rain storm. Most of our roof leaks. When they bombed this place, they did too good of a job. I put a new roof above my room, but it still leaks.

Fixing roofs

Oct. 7, Sat. – It rained nearly all nite, and finally it stopped and the wind died down after supper. One good thing, this is better than being out in the mud anyway. Made a ping pong table and set up in one of the rooms upstairs. The rain leaked through and warped the boards today. Our piano is quite in the same fix. We sold enough stuff to buy a radio which cost us $105. We bought it from Welter, an American G.I. radio.

Oct. 8, Sun. – Went to church with Kip at Toulon this morning. A naval chaplain conducted the service, and he was a wonderful speaker.

Oct. 9, Mon. – Major Lossen and a Major from the 105th Group came around today and decided they had a better spot for our "40" and "50," so now we have to move. We just fixed up all of our roofs so they won't leak too.

Oct. 10, Tue. – The general was supposed to inspect today but didn't show up. I got a detail of 12 German prisoners to help us move. I had six handling sandbags, and the sergeant in charge and five of his men I put to rebuilding a frame house for us. Boy, we all feel like big shots today. Boy, they sure are good workers, and they like to work for us as they hate working for the French.

Oct. 11, Wed. – We moved everything and are all set now. We moved about a 100 yards on top of the hill into a German 37 mm position. It's a concrete position, and we had quite a job knocking one side out which was cemented in. It's a beautiful pit now that we have it fixed up and a perfect field of fire. Had all the prisoners back today to clean up around here. We try and feed them the best we can, make coffee for them and give them "C" rations heated up.

Our gun position. I'm on the left, the barrel indicates how many German planes were shot down by "C" Battery (9 planes). Our battalion (consisting of platoons A, B, C, and D) shot down 36 German planes. Toulon, France, 1944

Oct. 12, Thu. – Had the carpenters back today to work on our shack. They're coming along good with it. The officers came around and were really pleased with our gun pits.

Oct. 13, Fri. – Had a red alert last nite. One plane, didn't do anything but take photographs. They dropped window also to throw the radars off. When Hagen blew the siren, Spash came tearing out of our hut and tripped and fell on a broken bottle. He cut a vein in his hand, gee it sure is an awful gash. We had to put a tourniquet on until the medics came. Rained today. Slipped into Toulon this afternoon with Kip to buy some film.

Oct. 14, Sat. – It's a beautiful day today. Had the carpenters back again today. Done a little looting this afternoon to pick up some lounge rugs and pictures for our recreation room. Eight of us are sleeping in a bomb proof shelter and have it fixed up perfect. One of the Germans working on our shack speaks English. His name is Ed and a heck of a nice fella. He straightened us out on a lot of things about the German Army.

Oct. 15, Sun. – The Jerries put tar paper on the shack today. I never thought they could fix it up as wrecked as it was. We're really going to have a swell setup here.

Oct. 16, Mon. – Moved our kitchen in our recreation room today. Set the ping pong table up, the piano, and picked up a round table for poker. Even put curtains up. Lt. Kenny called this evening and said the general was going to inspect my section and no. 4 tomorrow.

Oct. 17, Tue. – The prisoners came today, so I had them clean up all over, and boy we had everything in top shape for the general. He came right after dinner. We threw the works at him, and he was really satisfied and well pleased. We had to pass this one.

Oct. 18, Wed. – Went on pass to Toulon with Curly today.

Oct. 19, Thu. – Couldn't get the prisoners today, so we finished putting tar paper on our recreation room. Put up a stove in our dugout here. The general wanted more ventilation in here. Don't know how we are going to do it as this bomb-proof shelter is about six to eight feet thick all over.

Oct. 20, Fri. – Fired trial shots this morning. A sergeants meeting at the battery this evening. The whole battalion is organizing an enlisted men's club for just the 451st. They have a big house outside of town we are going to use.

Oct. 21, Sat. – Had quite a time at the CP last nite. There's a Red Cross coming to Toulon, so the battalion can't have the club. We are forming one at the battery CP which is in a large hotel. Had to give no. 3 one of my men today which was Gordon.

117

Oct. 22, Sun. – Had a meeting this evening to get the fellas interested in a glee club. They want us to sing for the opening of the club.

Oct. 23, Mon. – Rained all day today. Heard that U.S. troops invaded the Philippines. They hit at the Island of Leyte. Held a practice at the club room this evening. It sure is going to be nice.

Oct. 24, Tue. – Lt. Hedricks and Lt. McGuire took Ray F. and myself around to inspect the 2nd Platoon this morning. We asked a few questions and had them run through a few dry runs. Lt. Hedricks called this afternoon and said that Major General Pargiter, who is a British general and head of all coastal artillery in France, is going to be around to my position to inspect it on Thursday morning at 11:30. General Chopin will also be with him. Chopin's the one who wants the pits as small as possible, so we've got to get busy.

Oct. 25, Wed. – Finished the pit last nite, and boy it's really a beauty. It rained most of the day, so we have to work like hell to finish shining the gun up. Major Lossen came to check up this afternoon. I had him sign the inspection book, and for the remarks he put the best gun pit I have ever seen!

Oct. 26, Thu. – The old boy came right on schedule. It started raining at the same time, but he wasn't in a hurry to leave. He said it was ingenious the way we had things fixed up. He talked to me about Anzio, and he said he was mighty proud of the work our battalion did while there. He really had quite a staff of officers with him. Our officers and Col. Snyder were really happy the way we put the show over, and boy they sure are bragging about the "40" pit. This afternoon the order came down that all of the gun crews have to remake their pits to look like mine. Boy I can just see how happy that makes them. Kip and I got a weapons carrier this afternoon to go to Toulon to get some snaps we had in there. Went to the club at the battery this evening. It is called the "Para-Dice Club."

Me with the officers

Oct. 27, Fri. – Got quite a bit of mail last nite. It's about time we got some. Cloudy and rainy all day.

Oct. 28, Sat. – Going on a 24-hour pass to Hyeres, which is about 18 kilometers from Toulon, this afternoon with Kip.

Oct. 29, Sun. – Came back this afternoon from our pass. Had a swell time. We ate and slept at the Leutchia Hotel. It was really wonderful sleeping between sheets and in a bed that made you want to sleep forever. Went to a dance at the hotel last nite. Spash came back from the hospital today. He's been gone 16 days.

Oct. 30, Mon. – A rumor is going around that we are going to China, Burma, or India and that we are going to be relieved by the French in about 15 days. The French have relieved most of the ack-ack outfits in Marseille already.

Oct. 31, Tue. – Boy it's really been cold out on guard nites lately. Curly and I went and got permission to look in on French current this morning for our lights, but they don't want to take a chance on our wire, so we have to hunt up some heavier stuff.

Nov. 1, Wed. – The 4th Army just came over. They are at Marseille. I'll bet that's where Art is. I'm going to try and find out.

Nov. 2, Thu. – Got a bunch of letters and packages last nite. Went over to Kip's today.

Nov. 3, Fri. – Kip and I got a special 24-hour pass this afternoon to Hyeres again.

Nov. 4, Sat. – We really had a swell time on pass. Kip is really a lot of fun and the best pal I have over here.

Nov. 5, Sun. – Went to church this morning with Kip and George. George let me read a letter telling that Ruby got married to some guy from Florida. Sure was surprised. Red alert last nite. It was a recon. plane as he circled over our heads a few times. G.O.R. didn't give the order to fire though.

Nov. 6, Mon. – The last four days have really been beautiful. Just like summer. Fired trial shots this morning.

Nov. 7, Tue. – An awful strong wind has been blowing all day. Kip came over this afternoon and played ping pong. Went to the show at Toulon this evening with Kip. Saw *Air Force* with John Garfield and Gig Young.

Nov. 8, Wed. – Sgt. Michleson called and said I was going on a five-day provost detail. I've got quite a bit of work to do, so I asked if someone else would rather go so Kip went. It's in Toulon and a pretty nice setup although the shift is 16 hours on and eight off. Our battalion has taken over M.P. duty in Toulon. Roosevelt's in again.

Nov. 9, Thu. – A wind storm started yesterday and kept on all day and nite, and it's still going strong. Went to Toulon to visit Kip this afternoon.

Nov. 10, Fri. – The wind is still blowing strong as ever. Ripped the tar paper off our shack and took our latrine on a reconnaissance. Went to the battery tonite to mail some packages.

Nov. 11, Sat. – Went to the firing range this afternoon, but it was too windy, no plane. Going tomorrow morning again. Had a red alert last nite and early this evening. The 90's only fired on them as they were too high for us. We could see them firing at Marseille, and then they came here dropping five photo flares. A parade was held this morning with American and French troops participating. Churchill was in the parade in Paris.

Nov. 12, Sun. – Went out on the firing range and fired this morning. Boy the fellows really did some swell shooting. Went to church this afternoon. Got the Washington–Brooklyn football game on our radio this evening direct from New York.

Nov. 13, Mon. – Major Lossen was around today. Rained this afternoon. The news has sounded a bit more encouraging the last few days. Listened to the Sammy Angot–Daniels fight this evening. Daniels won by a decision.

Nov. 14, Tue. – Rained most of today. Bill got burned pretty bad today by a flare which was in the fire he had started to wash his clothes. Over the news last nite they said that British Lancasters sank the German battleship *Tirpitz*, the last of Germany's big warships.

Nov. 15, Wed. – The *Stars and Stripes* today said that Himmler has taken over Hitler's place in Germany. I think that Hitler was killed when they said he was only wounded in the assassination attempt.

Nov. 16, Thu. – Dance tonite at the club. Over the news this evening, a big offensive took place at 11:45 last nite. Six Allied armies from the Netherlands to the Swiss border are taking part on a 400-mile front. Our Armies have been standing still for the last two months, bringing up supplies and equipment for this big push.

Nov. 17, Fri. – Its been a beautiful warm day today. Washed clothes today. The news said the big drive is pushing ahead steadily but is hindered by snow and rain in some sectors.

Nov. 18, Sat. – Louie and I went to Hyeres on 24-hour pass this afternoon.

Nov. 19, Sun. – Came back from pass this afternoon. Had a swell time. Saw a pretty good fight between some Senegalese and French officers at a bar down there. Blood flying all over.

Nov. 20, Mon. – The wind started blowing again last nite and looks like another three days of it. When a wind storm comes up over here, it blows steady from three to nine days.

Nov. 21, Tue. – Went to the club this evening to see George. Kip came over this afternoon. He came off the M.P. detail Saturday.

Nov. 22, Wed. – Lt. Hedricks came over this afternoon and said that six generals would be over to inspect Friday at 1:30. This is the only section from "C" Battery. I've been catching them all, but it shows I have a darn good bunch of fellows on my crew, otherwise we wouldn't catch the responsibility of putting on a good show for the big brass hats. The colonel came over just before supper to look things over. He said there'll be five brigadier generals and one major general.

Nov. 23, Thu. – Painted our kitchen last nite yellow and green. It really looks good too. Painted the gun all over also. Went to the CP for a turkey supper. Boy and did I eat like a pig.

Nov. 24, Fri. – Got word that the generals wouldn't be here until Saturday afternoon now. Went to a dance last nite at the club. Went on pass with Kip to Toulon this afternoon.

Nov. 25, Sat. – Had an early chow and are waiting for the big shots now. Col. Snyder, Major Lossen, and Major Cooper along with our officers just came as they are going to meet the generals here. Well after sitting around until 3:00 p.m., the colonel got a call that they wouldn't have time to come here, so he has to meet them at "A" Battery. He was really disappointed 'cause he said everything was perfect. We were pretty disappointed also 'cause we worked darn hard getting things ready. When I had the colonel sign the inspection book he said, "I'm not going to post excellent 'cause it was better than that, it was superior!" Major Lossen put down, "Superior, as it always is." Major Lossen said what they should do is put our gun out of action for a day and let the whole crew go on pass. If the colonel and major could do it I know they would, but the group commander wouldn't approve of it I don't think. The colonel said I should keep things as they were and that he would bring the group commander around Monday just to show him what a good gun position and quarters looked like. Lt. Hedricks said he would get me a two-day pass, and he's going to try and get Kip one also.

Nov. 26, Sun. – Went to church this morning with Kip and Ray. The radio said this evening that Tokyo was bombed by B-29's.

Nov. 27, Mon. – We were all set for the big shot, but he didn't show up today. The colonel sent a bottle of his private stock of cognac over today which he promised us for last Saturday.

Nov. 28, Tue. – Major Lossen came around with Lt. Hancock from "B" Battery to inspect this afternoon.

Nov. 29, Wed. – The group commander came to inspect my gun this morning while his executive went to the other guns in the battery. Everything went perfect except Hagen had a dirty field jacket on with the bottoms open. The group commander was well pleased though and probably didn't notice it, but Col. Snyder informed me of it.

Nov. 30, Thu. – Lt. Hedricks came around today and told me that from the results of the inspection yesterday, which the whole battalion underwent, my gun crew tied with no. 5 in "A" Battery as being the best in the whole battalion, and if it hadn't been for Hagen that we would have been the best. Went to Marseilles with Sgt. Michleson this morning to look up Art but no luck. He is still further away than I expected. We went to U.S. headquarters there, and he is up near Epernay. We hitchhiked back this evening. Don't care to stay in that place very long as over 100 G.I.s have been found shot since the Americans took over Marseilles.

Dec. 1, Fri. – Went to Toulon with Kip this afternoon. Went to the show this evening. Saw *Desert Victory* which showed the exploits of the 8th Army in the desert of Africa. Had a raid the nite before last in which the 112th, a 90 outfit, did quite a bit of firing. We didn't get the order to fire. The Jerries dropped flares and also photo flash flares.

Dec. 2, Sat. – George came over this afternoon and stayed until this evening. We listened to the Army–Navy game which we got direct from New York. Army won 22 to 7.

Dec. 3, Sun. – Went to church this afternoon with Kip and George. The wind is starting to blow again.

Dec. 4, Mon. – Fired trial shots this morning. Went to Toulon with Kip this afternoon.

Dec. 5, Tue. – We are now connected with the 9th Air Force Group. Don't know what will come of it yet.

Dec. 6, Wed. – Went to Marseille with Kip today to see the stage show *The Barretts of Wimpole Street* with Kathryn Cornell and Brian Ahern.

Dec. 7, Thu. – Went to Toulon this afternoon with Buck and Pete.

Dec. 8, Fri. – Rumor going around that the 896th are going to take over our positions soon. They just came over from Sardonia. Went to Toulon again this afternoon with Kip. Had a clothing inspection this morning.

Dec. 9, Sat. – Two truck drivers from each crew went to Marseille today to get our trucks. The French have been using them, and every one is a wreck now. Don't know what we'll do if we have to go up to the front with them. Went to the club with Kip this evening. We felt pretty good so stopped in at the CP on the way back. Nobody was in, so we tore up Sgt. Michleson's and Spannates' and Lt. Hedricks' beds.

Dec. 10, Sun. – Heard that the whole CP is restricted, and Lt. Hedricks made everyone in there get up last nite and fix the beds. Ha–Ha. Went to church with Kip this afternoon. When we came back we had march order and have to have our gun out by 8:00 tomorrow morning. We are going to stay at the battery for three days, until we get trucks that will run, and then we are supposed to take around a 700-mile trip the other side of Paris. There's snow up there and cold as the dickens they say and us with just plain shoes. The battalion supply has turned in for shoe packs and combat jackets, but I don't imagine we'll get them for awhile yet. Gee, how we hate to leave this setup as it's been the best we've ever had since being overseas.

Dec. 11, Mon. – Moved our gun and stuff over to the battery CP. We are living in rooms in the hotel. Don't have to do anything all day. Had a movie here tonite, *Maisie Goes to Reno*. Frank Gulell came over from group and ran the projector. His transfer is in, and he's going to stay with the 105th Group permanently.

DEC. 1944

Battery "C"
451st AAA AW Bn
APO 758
% Postmaster NYC

Dear Mr and Mrs Anderson,

Once again as Yule Time approaches we are reminded of the Seasons wish, "Peace on Earth", and as we watch the progress of our struggle against those who wish to destroy our way of life we find that this wish will become a fact. "Peace on Earth".

Today as we push forward we can fully realize what the word cooperation means. To you at home it means sacrifice, giving up some of the little luxuries which we used to consider essential. It means longer hours of work and without a doubt the hardest thing is the temporary loss of our loved ones. Sergeant John Anderson has also had to make great sacrifices. This he has done without the slightest bit of complaint. So we find that because of this close cooperation between you at home and your loved ones in the field of battle we stand today ready to take our place in the new Post War World.

It seems that at this particular season our thoughts naturally turn more than ever to those who are near and dear to us. You at home must have this same feeling, so with this letter it is my pleasure to inform you that Sergeant Anderson is in the best of health and his morale is outstandingly high.

It is my sincere hope that before another Christmas Season comes he will be home with those he loves, knowing that he has done his part and that his sacrifices were not in vain.

In behalf of the other officers and myself, I wish to extend our wishes for a very Merry Christmas and a Happy New Year.

Respectfully yours,

Robert J Weiden

ROBERT J. WEIDEN
Captain Btry C
Commanding.

5th Edition

December 12, 1944 to August 11, 1945

Our campaign in France and Belgium continued and Germany

In December 1944, more than 200,000 German troops launched a counter-offensive known as the "Battle of the Bulge." After initial success by the Germans, the Allies with an estimated one million troops, including the famous General Patton and his 3rd Army, came out victorious. The 451st left France and headed north over 600 miles to Liege, Belgium where they would participate in this battle focused on protecting travel routes like bridges and shooting down German V-1 cruise missiles (Vengeance Weapon One) known as "buzz bombs" to the Soldiers. Years later, Jack shared what he remembered about the danger of German buzz bombs. If you heard the "putt putt" of the bomb out of one ear or the other, you were OK, but if you heard it out of both ears, you had to take cover. One of those bombs landed only 40 yards from his gun pit and created a crater as big as a truck. Not long after this battle, Germany surrendered on May 8 when Jack and his fellow Soldiers listened to Winston Churchill give his speech declaring the war in Europe officially over.

Dec. 12, Tue. – Got in a bit of a jam today. Sgt. Michleson and I took the weapons courier to Aix, the other side of Marseille. The M.P.'s stopped us and found the dispatch ticket improperly made out, so they thought that we stole the vehicle. We didn't have any means of identifying ourselves, so they took the vehicle and we had to hitch hike back which was about 75 miles. Boy, and was it cold!

Dec. 13, Wed. – I had to go back with Lt. McGuire to get the vehicle this morning. Michleson is in the soup but is talking his way out. Our trucks came back today. I got Carol back again, but she hasn't the power she used to have. The damn French really ruined all of our trucks. Everyone got a typhus shot this afternoon. We were all issued sweaters today and are going to get the new combat jacket and comforters issued tomorrow. We also got the 9th Air Force shoulder patch today.

Dec. 14, Thu. – Were issued comforters and combat jacket today. Cleaning the joint up this afternoon prior to leaving tomorrow.

Dec. 15, Fri. – Breakfast at 5:00 this morning, left at 7:30. Drove until 7:00 this evening, bivouacked in an airport in Saint Rambert. Cold as the dickens all day.

Dec. 16, Sat. – Crossed the Rhone River this morning and drove along the Rhone Valley most of the day. Went through Lyon. Drove until 5:30 this evening, bivouacked in the town of Dijon. Wasn't so cold riding today, so we are getting away from the coast.

Dec. 17, Sun. – Arrived at our destination at 4:00 this evening which is Chalons-sur-Marne. We are bivouacked about seven miles outside where we expect to stay until Wednesday. Some other "40" outfit has taken over our position which was guarding an airport. Our new assignment is that we are going into Belgium and fire at buzz bombs. The Belgian border is only 60 miles from here, but we expect another 200-mile trip which will take us quite a ways into Belgium. [Note: Battle of the Bulge took place.]

Dec. 18, Mon. – Rained all nite. Heard over the news today that the Germans staged a big counter-attack in Belgium. Played cards most of the day. Pulling out early tomorrow morning.

Dec. 19, Tue. – Left before dawn this morning. Went past the old battlegrounds of the Marne (World War I). The front line trenches are still there, and a huge monument is erected there. Crossed the Belgian border at the town of Dinant. Bivouacked outside of Huy for further orders. Jerry came over and dropped A.P.'s and strafed us. Nobody was touched though. The colonel and Major Lossen came back from brig. headquarters and said our positions had been changed again. We were supposed to have gone up into Germany. We are going to guard a bridge in Liege instead.

Dec. 20, Wed. – Left this morning and arrived in Liege about 3:30 this afternoon. This is really a beautiful city and seems like a big city back home. This is a part of the buzz bomb district also and quite a bit of the city is shattered. We are digging our position on top of a garbage dump. Got our first taste of the buzz bombs this evening. They make a loud chugging noise as they come in and leave a flame as they go across the sky. It has been foggy ever since we left France, but when the fog lifts we can see them good. They really let off a blast when they hit. Some go over, some short, and the rest you just hope and pray don't come any closer. Quite a few Germans have been caught in this town in G.I. clothes. Paratroopers are dropped nearly every nite.

Buzz bomb, Liege, Belgium

Dec. 21, Thu. – They threw buzz bombs over all nite long. We are living in tents, but dugouts wouldn't be much better if one landed close. A Belgian came over and told us six paratroopers were in a home not far from here last nite. The M.P.'s went over there, but they must have gotten wind of it as they were gone when they got there. Buzz bombs came over off and on all day. Over the news this evening they said that the Germans gained 35 miles in Belgium and had cut the main highway 14 miles from Liege. Things are looking pretty serious for us. The bridge along the Meuse River is all set to be blown in case the retreat comes this far. This fog and bad weather has hampered our planes.

Dec. 22, Fri. – Finished our position today. The fog lifted a little while today, so we saw some of the buzz bombs going over. One came directly down the valley over our heads. The motor cut out just over our heads, and it landed in the factory about 300 yards from us. It threw stuff all over. Turned in our French money for Belgian money. All we got back is 88 Belgian francs for each 100 we turned in.

Dec. 23, Sat. – Spent quite a nite last nite. Buzz bombs were coming over and then quiet about 1:00 a.m. It wasn't long and Jerry planes came over. They dropped flares first, then bombed and strafed all around here. The G.O.R. here is quite a screwed-up affair. There was a lot of air activity overhead this afternoon as the sun came out a while, but it froze all day today. There were eight P-47's over which dropped bombs on the city. They must have been captured by the Jerries. We had our gun apart at the time so couldn't fire on them. Went over to pick out anti-tank positions at a bridge which Kip's crew and mine have to hold in case the situation arises. I pray it doesn't as it's to be held at all cost, to the last man. Paratroopers are supposed to be dropped over the city tonite, intelligence reports.

Dec. 24, Sun. – Went to church this morning in Liege. Jerry came over off and on all day with Me 262's dropping glider bombs. It is a jet propelled plane and really is fast. The sun was out today as the sky was full of our bombers and fighter planes. We saw Jerry fighter planes attack our bombers, and we saw 23 planes go down in flames, ours and Jerries. There really was a mess of planes that went over. The drive was stopped also, and we are counter-attacking.

Dec. 25, Mon. – Christmas. We fired at Jerry planes that were dropping glider bombs all day. "D" Battery shot down a plane yesterday and captured the pilot. Three buzz bombs were dropped around Kip's position last nite killing three civilians. This afternoon Lt.'s Hedricks and Kenny took the 1st Platoon sergeants to a café in town to celebrate Christmas. Had turkey for supper tonite.

Dec. 26, Tue. – Buzz bombs have been dropping in all day. Been an extremely heavy fog all day today. Went over to the tunnel with the girls this evening. It's a coal mine tunnel in the side of the hill where people all around here go to and sleep. It's quite an experience to see how people have to live. It's damp and not very healthy. Some people have been in there since May as their homes were destroyed.

Dec. 27, Wed. – Our colonel, Major Lossen, a major from the 1st Army, and a British major were around inspecting this morning. They were well impressed with everything. The rest of us were issued our overshoes today which we sure need as it's cold as the dickens here. The frost is so heavy at nite that everything is coated white and stays that way all day as the sun doesn't get to us, and when it does come out there's a hill which blocks it.

Dec. 28, Thu. – Jerry was over last nite bombing and strafing. Gun no. 6 of our battery knocked down a Ju 88. Buzz bombs every day and nite since we've been here. We had to investigate one which landed within 300 yards of our pit and found a crater 30 feet in diameter and eight feet deep. A few U-2's landed in here also . They go around 300 miles an hour, and it hits way before the sound is heard. The receiving room of the 23rd General Hospital was hit last nite.

Dec. 29, Fri. – It was snowing this morning awhile. The buzz bombs have been coming too close for anything all day and more of them. Just before chow this evening, one dropped at the foot of the hill to the right of us. We went over to investigate, and the Polish kid was there who does a lot of work for us at the gun site. He was digging for his father and brother who were digging for coal at the time the bomb hit and were buried alive. We dug them both out and they came out of it in pretty good shape, but I don't see how as there was an awful bunch of rock and stone on them. Just after we got back to the gun two buzzers came over, one about 75 feet off the ground going like hell. It hit the side of the hill near the tunnel. Everyone is under an awful strain, and I don't doubt that some of the fellows crack pretty soon. It's an awful feeling you get every time you hear one coming. They say we have rockets also, but why don't we use them on the Germans like they are doing. Too damn much politics running this damn war!

German buzz bomb, Liege, Belgium

Dec. 30, Sat. – It snowed most of the day. Everything looks so white and pretty. Jerry sent over an awful bunch of buzz bombs last nite. None of us got much sleep. One landed the other side of the road at the foot of a coal mine throwing coal and rocks all over.

Dec. 31, Sun. – Hardly any buzz bombs all last nite, but Jerry planes were over all nite long bombing and strafing. We had action stations almost all nite, so sleep was very limited. We fired on the Me 262 (jet-propelled plane) this morning. Boy that thing is faster than any plane we have. P-47's started chasing it, but they couldn't get close. Beautiful morning and our planes were over all day. Jerry is catching hell again. Here comes a buzz bomb over now. They sound like a one-cylinder motorcycle. It landed over in the factory. We are connected with the 1st Army and are in the 31st A.A. Group. We were issued thermite bombs to destroy our equipment the other day. We have them taped on our gun, director, and power plant ready to set off in case the Jerries broke through. We are holding and counter-attacking in most sectors, so I don't think the situation will get bad enough to have to destroy our equipment.

Jan. 1, 1945, Mon. – Paratroopers were dropped again last nite. In a German radio broadcast to the Belgian people yesterday, they said because the Belgians hadn't helped in sabotaging us they were going to throw over many buzz bombs New Year's Day. They started coming in last nite four at a time. Our planes are over the launching area, so there haven't been so many so far today. It's a beautiful day today but still chilly. Having turkey for supper.

Jan. 2, Tue. – Snowed all day today. It really looks pretty. Kip and I went to the café with the girls this evening. Fired on an Me 262 this morning.

Jan. 3, Wed. – We could hear Brussels catching it last nite. Got two replacements for Bill and Hagen who are on detached service. Went with Kip to take a shower over in the coal mine. Zebras (buzz bombs) have been going over all day.

Jan. 4, Thu. – It half snowed and half rained today. Visibility was very poor.

Jan. 5, Fri. – Had another close one from a zebra this afternoon. Sounded like it was coming right at us but hit the coal mine just across the road. Some coal miners were trapped down in a caved-in shaft but were pulled out with ropes. Passes started today which start after the evening alert is over. Sure is a funny time for passes to start.

Jan. 6, Sat. – A zebra hit a streetcar last nite killing nearly everyone in it. Snowed all day.

Jan. 7, Sun. – Went to church this morning. Took a shower this afternoon over at the coal mine.

Jan. 8, Mon. – A Belgian fellow was over today who used to live in the States and speaks perfect English. He was an active member of the Underground. He really had some stories to tell.

Jan. 9, Tue. – Went to the dentist this morning to get my partial fixed, instead he filled two and pulled one. Made an appointment for the dental clinic at the 56th General Hospital for tomorrow. Jerry slowed down some with his buzz bombs for a few days but is starting to step them up again.

Jan. 10, Wed. – Was down at the 56th General Hospital all day. Got some mail this evening. First in three weeks.

Jan. 11, Thu. – Sub-zero weather all day. Spent the morning at the 56th General. A buzz bomb landed next to it while there. It shattered most of the windows, spraying glass all over us. Started snowing this evening. Also started snowing buzz bombs. They have been coming in about one or two every five minutes for the last two hours. They have been coming directly down the valley we are in and thank God, are dropping short or going over.

Buzz bomb hole, Liege, Belgium

Jan. 12, Fri. – Ordnance brought a Weiss sight over this morning and installed it on the gun. It takes the place of the stiffkey stick and director. Zebras been coming in all day.

Jan. 13, Sat. – Finished up with the dentist today. Cold as the dickens today. Got orders to dig our tents in. Going to get prisoners to do it.

Jan. 14, Sun. – Kip and I went on pass this evening. Had a pretty good time at the Polish café.

Jan. 15, Mon. – Snowed some more today. The news sounds pretty good lately. Russians' new offensive going strong. Had a really close call from a buzz bomb this evening. It landed about 40 yards away from our position. Two of the new fellows,

Johnny and Earl, were cut in the hand. The concussion snapped most of the ropes holding up our tents, scattered our food and pans all over the kitchen. Curly and a few of the other fellows who hadn't hit the ground when it cut off over us were knocked down when it hit. I was writing a letter, the concussion sprayed ink on me.

Buzz bomb hole. This landed 40 yards from our gun position. Liege, Belgium

Jan. 16, Tue. – German prisoners came over and dug our tents down today. They hit a spot in our tent which has quite an odor to it. Inspection tomorrow morning by the group commander, Col. Scott of the 31st Group.

German prisoners digging in our tents, Liege, Belgium

Jan. 17, Wed. – Inspection this morning by Col. Scott, Col. Snyder, and Major Lossen. Everything went over good. Cold and windy all day. Got four prisoners to finish up today. Went on pass this afternoon with Kip.

Buck Benoit, dug in tent, buzz bomb alley, Liege, Belgium

Jan. 18, Thu. – Had a 60-mile gale all last nite with a pounding rain. The tents all leaked like sieves. Some tents in some of the gun sections were blown away. Most of the snow is all gone, and this place really looks like the dump it is.

Jan. 19, Fri. – No buzz bombs all day today. We heard that Stalin threatened to drop German prisoners over Berlin without any parachutes if Jerry didn't stop throwing buzz bombs over Russia and Belgium. There may be something to it.

Jan. 20, Sat. – It froze and started snowing last nite. It snowed about six inches. No buzz bombs all last nite. Started throwing them in about 11:00 this noon, and they've been coming pretty steady all day. One that came directly down the valley cut off and started coming right at us. It flipped around twice and shot over us into the factory. I was caught at the latrine at the time. I was about to dive into the latrine, when it started up again and passed over. I had my camera so I snapped a picture as it shot down. Steel girders dropped around us, but no one got hit.

Jan. 21, Sun. – Got quite a bit of mail last nite, mostly all Christmas cards. Went to church with Kip this morning. Snowed last nite but today the sun was out, in fact it was the best day we've had so far.

Jan. 22, Mon. – The Russians are really driving, if they keep it up this way won't last much longer. Adolf must have gotten another truckload of buzz bombs in as he threw quite a few over today again.

Jan. 23, Tue. – A Belgian Prince passed by our position this morning on the way over to the tunnel on an inspection tour. It was a procession of about 12 American Buicks, Packards, Fords, and Chryslers, along with an M.P. escort and Belgian Police with guns out ready for use.

Jan. 24, Wed. – Got quite a bit of mail last nite. Letters, packages, and Xmas cards. Snowed last nite again. Cold as the dickens today. Earl and Johnny left, and Bill and Hagen came back. Two truck drivers are going to Paris from each crew tomorrow where they are supposed to pick up some new trucks and four-barreled 50 caliber. That's going to be heck 'cause we'll have to get rid of our trailers.

Jan. 25, Thu. – Kip and I went to town on pass today. Went to the show. Cold as the dickens all day.

Jan. 26, Fri. – Snowed most of the day. Ordnance was around checking the equipment this afternoon. Went to a meeting at the battery this evening. Battalion is cracking down again, so they cracked down on us. Thirty-day furloughs are going to start, 10 men and two officers each month. If the Russians keep on going, we won't have to wait for furloughs to get home.

Jan. 27, Sat. – Inspection by Capt. Weiden this morning. Everything went over good. About six buzz bombs came over today only most of them went way over. Started snowing again this evening.

Jan. 28, Sun. – Went to church this morning with Kip. Cold again today. Went on recon. to pick out our "50" M.G. position along the Meuse River protecting a bridge. Also found a house for the fellas to sleep in.

Jan. 29, Mon. – Snowed all day. A searchlight outfit are putting a light right next to our "50" so went over to put our claims on the house. Adolph threw over quite a few buzzers today. They are starting to drop in close again.

Jan. 30, Tue. – Everyone got a vaccination this morning. Had a real blizzard all day, toward evening it was closer to a rain. Cleaned most of the cosmoline off the four-barreled "50" this afternoon. Every piece has to be heated over a fire as everything is froze stiff.

Jan. 31, Wed. – Hitler gave a speech last nite. We listened to part of it and got what he said at the 11:00 p.m. news broadcast. He told the people peace would be hell and they should fight to the last. The Russians are 60 miles from Berlin and American troops are fighting and advancing through the Siegfried Line. Finished mantling the "50" today. Going to test fire it tomorrow. Rained all day.

Feb. 1, Thu. – The snow is all melted again, everything mud. Fired the "50" this afternoon. Boy it really throws out the lead. A big push is in the makings on the 9th or 1st Army front as troop movements have been going up all day. Brought the M-51 back to the 40 pit, going to go in position tomorrow morning.

Four-barreled 50 caliber

Feb. 2, Fri. – Worked on the "50" pit all day. Only half done with it. Rained all morning.

Feb. 3, Sat. – Finished the "50" pit today. Remodeled the 40 pit and all around it. The officers really like it. Rained this morning but was really beautiful this afternoon.

Feb. 4, Sun. – There's really a bunch of troops going up. Heard tanks going through all nite long. A 1,000-plane raid went over us to bomb the heart of Berlin last nite. There was really a racket all nite long. A buzz bomb landed close to the M-51 last nite. It broke the door in and windows in the room the fellows are sleeping in. Went to church this morning.

Feb. 5, Mon. – Rained most of the day. Got orders to move the "50" pit over a foot. Boy they really burn a guy up. They never know what they want in the first place. This is one time I'm not going to have it done. Inspection by group tomorrow. Got paid this afternoon.

Feb. 6, Tue. – Rained all day again and last nite. Tanks have been going through all day. Inspected by an officer from group this morning. It stopped raining just long enough so he could go through everything. He found everything OK and said I had a very good gun position.

Feb. 7, Wed. – Got a haircut this morning. Played football this afternoon and basketball this evening. The evenings are really nice. Bombers were over all nite.

Feb. 8, Thu. – A big push took off this morning on the British front. 1,500 bombers went over us to go and soften the lines up. Tanks have been going by all day and nite.

Feb. 9, Fri. – Rained all day. It's rained every day so far in February. No buzz bombs since the last part of January. And thank God for that.

Feb. 10, Sat. – Everybody had to see a movie today on non-fraternization with the German people. It really came out with the bare facts. Rained most of the day. Went with Kip and Alex to the café this morning.

Feb. 11, Sun. – Started out to be a nice day but started raining right after dinner. Went to church this afternoon with Kip.

Feb. 12, Mon. – Rained again all day. Took a shower over at the coal mine this afternoon.

Feb. 13, Tue. – Got a hair cut this morning. Rained this afternoon. Kip and I went over to Jeanin's place this evening (a tavern).

Feb. 14, Wed. – Major Lossen came around to inspect this morning. Beautiful day all day. Played some ball this afternoon. Went to the café this evening. Bombers over all day.

Buck Benoit doing KP while in gun positions. Curly Bluse made the mess kit cleaner from a 50-gallon drum cut in half. He sectioned it off into three sections: one for soapy water and two for rinse. Heated by gasoline from the five-gallon gas can. Liege, Belgium

Feb. 15, Thu. – Another perfect sunshine day. Jerry sent over three buzz bombs today, the first in a long time. The Belgian news said that Hitler was going to send 500 over in the next two days. I think they're crazy though. A mass of bombers were over today again. Kip and I screwed off this afternoon. Got a new man today. He's a replacement from the infantry. His name is Jim Moseley. Seems to be a pretty nice fella. I put him on the M-51.

Feb. 16, Fri. – The Meuse River had risen over two feet the past week flooding most of the basements around here. It has gone down now. It must have come from the dams that the Germans blew up on the Rhone River. Two trainloads of infantry, two of tanks, and one load of gas went through today. The radio said this evening that a large carrier task force went over and bombed hell out of Tokyo. The news hasn't given out too much lately on the front up here.

Feb. 17, Sat. – Col. Scott and Col. Snyder were around to inspect the M-51 this morning. Everything was excellent. More train loads of infantry and tanks went up again today. There's really something taking off pretty soon.

Feb. 18, Sun. – Went to church this afternoon with Kip. Been a foggy and rainy day. *Stars and Stripes* said today American forces landed on Iwo Jima 750 miles from Japan. More tanks and infantry went through again today.

Feb. 19, Mon. – Haven't gotten much news over the radio as just as BBC starts to give the news, a German propaganda station cuts in on the same wave length. Swell day today so worked over all our equipment and cleaned up the dump a bit. Went over to Kip's this evening.

Feb. 20, Tue. – Rained most of the day. Kip and I went to the theater in Liege and saw *Tall in the Saddle* with John Wayne. Went to the Red Cross after and took the train home.

Feb. 21, Wed. – Sixteen fellows are being transferred out to the infantry tomorrow. Hagen is going from my section. It really is a shame after sticking it out for over two years in ack-ack and then have to leave. It's really hard to see a fella go 'cause we're all just like brothers. 15% of the battalion have to go each time. Don't know whether it's weekly or monthly.

Feb. 22, Thu. – Hagen left early this morning. Alabam went also to drive one of the trucks to Paris. They are supposed to get six weeks infantry training and then go up on the lines. Our bombers were over all nite long. They must be softening the lines for a big push.

Feb. 23, Fri. – Heard that Alabam was in a wreck. He was sideswiped by a truck full of German prisoners. Alex was cut up, but they didn't say how bad. I hope it isn't serious. First thing the captain asked was if the truck was damaged. He sure as hell don't seem to give a damn about the men. 6,000 planes were over Germany in the biggest raid yet. Went over to Kip's this evening.

Feb. 24, Sat. – The 9th and 1st Armies took off in a drive across the Ruhr River. Turkey has come in at the 11th hour to declare war on Germany and Japan. The battalion is throwing an anniversary dance the 4th and 5th of March to celebrate our two years overseas. A booklet is coming out on the history of the battalion also. Kip and I went to a dance last nite over to a café across the river. Didn't have a pass, but we got by. The group commander is going to be around to inspect this afternoon. Curly left for the hospital to have his tonsils taken out. Alabam is back with us and is pretty well banged up. There was a gas explosion over in the coal mine which killed five Belgians last nite. Kip and I went to the show in Liege and saw *Mrs. Parkington* with Greer Garson and Walter Pidgeon.

Feb. 25, Sun. – News said this morning the drive has pushed four and a half miles across the Ruhr. Eisenhower had a speech last nite, also so did Adolph. Went to church this afternoon with Kip.

Feb. 26, Mon. – Went to a soccer game with Kip this afternoon. Two Belgian teams played. Cold as the dickens today.

Feb. 27, Tue. – Frank sent all his movie reels in to get them developed. Some guy in town is going to take them to Brussels to have them done. An order came out that no film can be developed unless censored by the Army. Hope they don't check up on the movie film. Kip and I took a jaunt over to the café this evening.

Feb. 28, Wed. – A bunch of bombers were over all nite in a raid on Berlin. The drive is going good. A rumor is out that another bunch are going to be transferred to the infantry.

Mar. 1, Thu. – Got paid today. Rained all day and had security guard. Kip and I went to the show this evening. Him and I talked our way into a special pass, which is good any time.

Mar. 2, Fri. – Sandbagged the outside of the director pit today. Kip and I got a haircut this afternoon. This evening we got our dates for the dances. Kip is taking Mariett from the café, and I'm taking Eleanor Bemelman who lives just across the field from my position.

Mar. 3, Sat. – Inspection today. A brigadier general is coming around. Bill left early this morning on a detail. They have to move an ack-ack outfit up to the front. The German air force has come out in strength in an attempt to stop the drive to the Rhine.

Mar. 4, Sun. – Went to a special memorial service this afternoon in honor of the fellows who were killed. Today marks the day we got on the boat at New York harbor.

Half of the crew are allowed to go to the dance this evening, which is being held at the Dominican in Liege. Frank went to Brussels yesterday on a 48-hour pass to try and pick up an 8 mm projector. He came back today with a 9 mm so we are going to try and convert it into an 8 mm.

Mar. 5, Mon. – Went to a sergeants meeting this afternoon. The officers are burnt up over something, so we caught hell and have to start pounding the guys again. Kip, Buck, and I went to the dance this evening with our dates. Really had a swell time, but it was so crowded you could hardly dance. Eleanor is really a lot of fun.

451st anniversary dance March 5, 1945

Mar. 6, Tue. – The officers are really busting our hump around here. We have to have a layout on the bunks from 9:00 a.m. to 4:00 p.m. every day. Gas masks have to be worn every Monday all day and put on for 15 minutes. Rained all day.

Mar. 7, Wed. – Rained all nite and all day again. One buzz bomb came over today. It sure put a funny feeling in one's stomach.

Mar. 8, Thu. – Rained all day again. Louie left for Paris yesterday on a 48-hour pass. The drive is really going strong. Cologne was captured, and our troops are on the Rhine. Now if they can only get across.

Mar. 9, Fri. – Got a news report late last nite that 1st Army troops crossed the Rhine. Boy home sure looks a lot closer now. Still raining today. Plugged in on Belgian current so we have lights and the radio playing all day. Kip and I went to a show in Liege this evening. This morning a couple from each gun section went over to the CP to brush up on our marching as a ceremony is going to be held to decorate fellows who have medals coming. This is taking place tomorrow.

Mar. 10, Sat. – The decoration ceremony was held this afternoon near battalion headquarters in Liege. It was a perfect day for it. Purple Hearts, Bronze Stars, and Silver Stars were issued by Gen. Bernell. It really was an impressive sight, especially when the battalion passed in review. Had a band to lead us which really put a guy in the mood for marching. Spash got his Purple Heart. The officers were around inspecting today, but they were all smiles. Their inspection has changed all of a sudden.

"A" Battery, "B" Battery, "Colors," "C"Battery, "D" Battery, Liege, Belgium

Mar. 11, Sun. – A drizzly day today. Went over to Kip's this afternoon, and then we grabbed a train and took off for Liege. They were selling novelties, and girls with tin cups were going around collecting for those made homeless from the buzz bombs. Went over to Kip's this evening.

Mar. 12, Mon. – Major Lossen came around to inspect this morning. He really went over everything. The way things sound, we might be on the move again. Just rumors though.

Mar. 13, Tue. – Large formation of our bombers were over all day. The news said that the beachhead across the Rhine is like an inland Anzio. Boy and I can imagine just how it is. The searchlight outfit that came in not long ago pulled out today. Bill had to go and help move them.

Mar. 14, Wed. – Got some more replacements in today. Our directors were taken away this afternoon. Boy and it don't make us mad. Only thing, we'll probably be without lights if they take the power plant when we move. Also put the wheels back on the gun, which usually has been a good indication of moving. Been a beautiful day today.

Gun position outside of Liege, Belgium

Mar. 15, Thu. – I had to give one of my men to no. 4 today in trade for one of the new replacements. I drew names and Spash was the one who had to go. This is the hardest part of this job when they ask for a man 'cause were all like brothers. The new fellow's name is Wally Shapiro. Right from the start I took a liking to him, and boy he seems to fit right in the picture. There's a world of difference between him and that other replacement I got.

Mar. 16, Fri. – For the last three days it's foggy nearly all morning, so thick you can't see anything but from 11:00 a.m. on. The old haymaker has been on the job. Spash called and wants to come back. Don't know how he's going to do it as I don't want to lose Wally.

Mar. 17, Sat. – Col. Scott came around to inspect this morning. Looked like rain so I didn't have the spare barrel out, and he asked for a tube changing drill. Only had six men also, so things didn't go so good. Have to do it all over again for our officers tomorrow.

Mar. 18, Sun. – Gun drill went off perfect this morning. Col. Snyder and Major Lossen are coming around tomorrow to check up as a general is expected to hit us Wednesday. Went to church this afternoon with Kip.

Mar. 19, Mon. – Our colonel and major came around this morning and everything went off perfect. The colonel had a sort of heart-to-heart talk with me in the tent. Boy, a fella couldn't wish for better officers than Col. Snyder and Major Lossen. Beaucoups of bombers went over today. Two buzz bombs went over last nite.

Mar. 20, Tue. – Been a beautiful day today. Nobody around to bother us either.

Mar. 21, Wed. – Another beautiful day. The news really has sounded wonderful lately. Kip and I met the girls in town this evening. Went dancing and took in a show.

Mar. 22, Thu. – Beaucoups of bombers were over all nite. The general is supposed to be around but not sure whether he will stop in. Beautiful today, in fact it's hot out. We stuck around all day, but the general didn't show up.

Mar. 23, Fri. – 8,000 planes were over Germany in the biggest bombing raid yet. Another perfect day. It gives a guy the spring fever right.

Buck Benoit on phone duty, me, Roger Cholette, Charlie Knez. Liege, Belgium, 1945

Mar. 24, Sat. – Lt. Kenny came around and woke me up early this morning. He had to inform all his men that we are not to fire on any enemy plane unless a hostile act is committed. This morning is "D" Day for the biggest Allied airborne offensive ever undertaken. Planes of all types are being used to drop men and equipment way in Germany. This will be for today and tomorrow. Boy it sure sounds good! Beaucoups of bombers went over us this afternoon. Kip and I went into Liege to a show. Saw *San Francisco* with Clark Gable, Spencer Tracy, and Jeanette MacDonald.

Mar. 25, Sun. – Not much was let out on the news about the airborne offensive, but it stated Montgomery's forces joined up with airborne troops in six hours. Six Allied armies are across the Rhine. Also 10,000 planes raided installations in Germany yesterday. How the German people can stand up under such a bombardment. It won't be long now though. Palm Sunday. Went to church with Kip this afternoon.

Mar. 26, Mon. – We manicured the dump today between the gun and tents. Hauled cinder, leveled the place off, and outlined walks with bricks. It was a lot of work, but it really looks good.

Mar. 27, Tue. – The officers came around and were really surprised and pleased with the way our area looked. Maybe the captain won't bother us for awhile now.

Mar. 28, Wed. – Rained today so not much doing. Bombers were over all nite. Jerry is really catching hell.

Mar. 29, Thu. – Turned in our thermite bombs which were attached to our equipment in case we had to destroy it, and also our rifle grenades, hand grenades, and bazooka ammo were turned in. Pretty windy today.

Me with 451st AAA "C" Battery sign

Mar. 30, Fri. – Went to church this evening. There's a blackout on most of the fronts, but we know they are still going strong.

Mar. 31, Sat. – Got paid today. It didn't last very long tho. Went over to Kip's this evening.

Apr. 1, Sun. – Easter. Windy and rainy all day. Went to church this afternoon with Kip. We were told early this morning that we were going to have an inspection, but after all the bitching was over with, it turned out to be an April Fool's joke.

Apr. 2, Mon. – Went to town with Eleanor this evening. Got in a fight with a Belgian civilian. It would just happen that Kip wasn't along as there were five of them. Boy, what fun we could have had. I did knock hell out of the one guy though, which added to my prestige.

Apr. 3, Tue. – Turned in some of our "40" H.E. and A.P. today. One of these days we'll be turning in our 40's. Sgt. Michleson and myself went to the National Ammo Factory just outside of Liege to see about getting a shotgun. Also went over to the Val Saint-Lambert Crystal Factory. Really saw some beautiful vases, bowl, and sets. If I can dig up the money, I'll be all set. Rained most of the day and really came down hard this evening.

Apr. 4, Wed. – Going to be an inspection tomorrow by 31st Group, so we got some clean up to do. 3rd Army is only 160 miles from Berlin. Formations of transports have been taking off from the airport near here all day long for the past few days loaded with gasoline and supplies for the front. They bring back wounded. Wally and I went and got a haircut this afternoon.

Apr. 5, Thu. – Inspected by group this morning. He asked a bunch of questions on the 40 and went away well satisfied. Started raining right after dinner.

Apr. 6, Fri. – Rained off and on all day. Went to a show with Kip this evening. A bunch of bombers went over today. One landed at the airport here on the way back, with two motors shot out.

Apr. 7, Sat. – I cosmolined my Mauser today, crated it, and sent it home. The mail situation has been pretty bad for the past week. We are going to have a battery dance at the battalion Monday nite.

Apr. 8, Sun. – The sun came up just beautiful this morning, but clouded up after breakfast and is staying that way all day. Went to a soccer game between an English team and a Belgian. Score was 1–1. It was the largest crowd I've seen since a Packer football game. Beaucoups of bombers were over all day. B-24's, B-17's, and Halifaxes. Rumors going around that we're going to get march order soon. Boy, we're sure going to hate to leave this place.

Apr. 9, Mon. – Beautiful day today. Bombers been going over all day. We got our bazooka ammo back today. Expect to move up to Duren, Germany before the week is over. Got the order to tear our pits down, take the guns out, ready to leave tomorrow morning. Have to be on the main road by 8:00. We are going to guard a pontoon bridge on the Rhine River. It is close to the Ruhr pocket. Kip and I went over to say goodbye to Eleanor and Lorette. Gee they hated to see us go. They cried and almost had us crying too.

Apr. 10, Tue. – Pulled out of our position at 8:00 on the head. It was almost like leaving home again. All of our friends we got to know quite well around there were there to see us go, and most of them were crying. Gee what a funny feeling I got. We left in convoy at 8:20, and the day was just perfect. We were going along good until about 15 miles from Aachen, and then trouble started. A piston rod and a piece of the crank shaft went through the crank case. Lt. Hedricks went up to Aachen and sent a wrecker back which towed us in. They had to put in another motor which took all day. Lorrie came back with the other truck about 8:00 p.m., so we transferred the load and left Bill with the truck. We had about 110 miles to go and got lost in Kripp. We finally found the gun we were relieving at 3:00 a.m. The pontoon bridge we were guarding is next to Remagen Bridge.

Pontoon Bridge near Remagen Bridge

Apr. 11, Wed. – Only got about an hour sleep as we had to get started on the pit at dawn this morning. We are about 400 yards off the river, and the "50" is right next

Remagen Bridge, Germany, after it was blown up

Gun position on the Rhine River, Germany

to it. Germany is really torn up and Duren there isn't a building left standing. We put our tents up today and just in time as it started raining. We almost got march orders this afternoon as another outfit came around on a recon., but orders were changed again. Boy and were we glad 'cause we really like it here. We are living in an apple orchard which is in full bloom.

Apr. 12, Thu. – Set up our kitchen and found some heavy veneer which we made floors in the tents with. Heard over the radio this morning that President Roosevelt died of a heart attack. It was quite a shock to us. Went over to see Kip this evening with the truck. We went over to the CP where we saw Lt. Deballian and got us some good red wine.

Apr. 13, Fri. – Here at nite is called nite watch on the Rhine. Searchlights are set up along the river, and tanks with smaller searchlights pull up at nite and light the river up all nite long. Everything that comes down the river is shot at with rifle and machine gun fire. Tracers can be seen ricocheting off the water way up into the air. My M-51 has orders to fire on objects or men coming down the river with intentions of blowing up the bridge. The other nite, four Germans were captured in rubber suits swimming down the river with TNT on their backs to blow the bridge. Truckloads of Jerry prisoners go by all day long coming back from the Ruhr pocket. German slave laborers which consist of Poles, Belgians, and French are loaded on trucks next to Kip's position and then taken back.

German prisoners being hauled over a pontoon bridge on the Rhine River. Our gun position is just on the left. Germany, 1945

Apr. 14, Sat. – Went looting in some of the houses near Kip. Picked up some utensils for the kitchen. The Germans had more stuff then any place we've been to yet. Found a baby grand piano in good condition. There's a cable stretched across the river just off of us which sets off mines every once in awhile which are floated down the river by the Germans. Hundreds of trucks went by today loaded with Jerry prisoners with about 50 to each truck. Boy they really are jammed in. Saw a German general go by in a Jeep. There's some pretty nice looking frauleins around here. We can't even give them a second look though as there's no fraternizing with German civilians whatsoever.

Apr. 15, Sun. – Heard that we are going to move again Tuesday. It's supposed to be a long trip. Kip and I went over to the CP this afternoon and stayed up in the officers' room drinking wine all afternoon. Went over to the tannery and picked us up a sleeping bag.

Apr. 16, Mon. – We pulled our gun out today. Going to leave in the morning. This is the kind of march order I like when you have plenty of time.

Pontoon bridge just above the Remagen Bridge on the Rhine River. Our 40 mm and truck just reaching the other side. Germany, 1945

Apr. 17, Tue. – Left at 8:00 this morning. We crossed on the east side of the Rhine just below the Remagen Bridge. Followed the Rhine most of the way, and it's the most beautiful drive we've been through yet. Crossed back on the west side of the Rhine at Bingen. Bivouacked outside of the city for the nite.

I took this picture while we were crossing the Rhine River. Kip's gun is the one ahead of me. The Remagen Bridge which collapsed is just to the right of this pontoon bridge. Germany, 1945

Apr. 18, Wed. – Expected to leave this morning, but Major Cooper didn't get back until this evening with our orders. We are going up to Heilbronn, which was taken three days ago. Our bombers have been going over all day.

Apr. 19, Thu. – Left at 7:00 this morning. We hit the Autobahn about 9:30 and really made good time while on it. We were batting along 50–55 most of the way. Ate dinner in Heidelberg. Arrived in Heilbronn about 4:00 and went on a recon. to pick out our positions. Mine is right next to a pontoon bridge which we are protecting, which is on the Neckar River. This bridge is the main supply route for the 7th Army.

Apr. 20, Fri. – Jerry was over at 11:00 last nite strafing. The front is eight miles away. Artillery fire is pretty plain. Finished our pits today. We are with the VI Corps and under 35th Brigade. Our battery is the furthest one up. The 194 Field Artillery is just outside of town. We were connected to them on Anzio. Went over to Kip's this evening. I found me a whole case of good cigars, so I brought a box over to him. He showed me where I could get some gas engines and also some good vermouth.

Took two gas engines which we plan on fixing up to furnish light for the "40" and "50" crews. They are brand new and run perfect. We are living in tents. There are houses close by, but every room is wrecked. A cigar factory is just across the river and also a shoe factory.

Apr. 21, Sat. – Bed check Jerry was over at 11:00 again last nite strafing. Mick and I went for a walk today. I found a flag with a big swastika in the center in a general headquarters building. Also found 1,730 dollars worth of mark notes. Don't know if they are any good. I sure hope so though. Wally and I ran across a good Jerry rifle, which was booby-trapped to a bazooka round. Our food rations have been very good since we came up here. Our PX ration is free again since we are up in combat area. The German people are very friendly, and it's pretty hard to keep from fraternizing with them. There is quite a bit of firing going on around town at nite, so we have to go armed wherever we go. Today is Hitler's birthday, and he asked all the German people to kill one American for a birthday present for him, for which we had to double the guard for last nite and tonite. The German people are only allowed out between the hours of 7–9 in the morning and 3–5 in the afternoon. Rained most of the afternoon and evening. Heard over the news that the Russians are shelling Berlin. Sure sounds good, but it looks like the Nazi party is going to fight to the last.

Apr. 22, Sun. – Almost a steady stream of guns and supplies cross the bridge all day and nite. Not much sleep when the tanks go across. Bill and Louie have been on trucking details every day hauling infantry up to the front. Rained off and on all day. The sun would come out just as bright for five minutes, and then it would rain or hail.

Apr. 23, Mon. – Rained most of the day and cold as the dickens.

Apr. 24, Tue. – The colonel and major were supposed to come around to inspect today. Worked all morning cleaning up, and just after dinner we got march order. Curly got a pass to see a friend of his this morning, and he won't be back until tomorrow. Pulled over to the CP at 2:30. Left in convoy at 3:00. We pulled in at an airport outside of Goppingen. Unloaded all our trucks and stored our 40 away in a hanger. We are put up in German pilots' barracks.

Apr. 25, Wed. – Had a meeting at 11:30 last nite. It looks like we are through with ack-ack. We are going to be security guard for the VI Corps and guard captured supply trains, P.W. enclosures, roads, and this D.P.C. (disposed persons center) which is next to us. We guard these things until the Army comes up and takes over. There are pockets of Germans still around here. Last nite, snipers were firing up at the gate. Armored cars are patrolling the woods. Patrols of the 100th Division came in this afternoon to clear them out. A bunch of Jerrys were captured in a barn not far from here. Yesterday there were only cub planes at this airport. Today it was loaded with C-47's bringing in supplies. Cleaned up our 40's for storage. This evening we moved all our stuff to another hanger. Our M-51 goes with us wherever we go as anti-personnel protection. Sergeant of the guard starting 6:00 this evening until 6:00 tomorrow evening.

Apr. 26, Thu. – The 2nd Platoon is guarding a liquor train, so everyone has all they want to drink. It's very good cognac. We expect to be relieved today by 7th Army M.P.s. This guard is really a screwed up mess 'cause nobody seems to know anything about what's going on. Names for passes were taken today, and some fellows are going to get furloughs home. Kip and I fixed it so we would get a pass together as we intend to go back to Liege. Refugees have been streaming in here all day and nite. They consist of every nationality, and there's always trouble at the main gate with them. Boy they really are a sorry looking bunch of people. The A.M.G. (Allied Military Government) takes them over and sends them back to their countries. Russian soldiers have been streaming in also which were prisoners of the Germans.

Apr. 27, Fri. – Snipers were firing last nite again. The link up between the Russians and Americans was let out over the radio today. The link up took place last Wednesday. Rained most of the afternoon. Had a little shooting last nite next door to us with some drunken refugees.

Apr. 28, Sat. – We had to send a 40 mm with all its ammo late last nite to "A" Battery as they are going up to wipe out a pocket. The 2nd Platoon moved up to a town about 20 miles from here. They are guarding an underground factory, and also are cleaning out a pocket of Jerries. They shake down the prisoners they capture so they have accumulated quite a few souvenirs. Curly finally found us today.

Apr. 29, Sun. – Snowed very hard today. We are situated just on the outskirts of the Bavarian Mountains. The Alps aren't so very far from here. Sergeant of the guard today. A peace plan by Himmler was given to the Americans and British, but it was rejected 'cause it didn't include Russia. The Germans are surrendering by the thousands. The radio said Hitler is suffering from hemorrhage on the brain and wasn't expected to live. He is in Berlin. Curly got a 20-minute notice to pack up and leave for home.

Apr. 30, Mon. – Mussolini was executed by his own people in Milan. He was shot with 17 of his stooges and then swung from gallows so the people could view them. Went out to see George at the 2nd Platoon this afternoon. Picked up some souvenirs. We were relieved from the D.P.C. guard today. We expect to move, and the rumor is that we are going to the other side of the Danube into Austria.

May 1, Tue. – Went out and inspected the train guard with Roy and Lt. Hedricks. The trains have 88's, ammo, and food on them. Snowed again today. A news flash came over at 10:26 this evening that Adolph Hitler was dead.

May 2, Wed. – Got paid in German marks this morning. Snowing again. General Eisenhower went through here yesterday in a big black Packard with eight staff cars. Field Marshal Gerd von Rundstedt is a prisoner here at the airport. All the Germans in Italy surrendered unconditionally. The papers were signed Sunday but didn't come out until today. Berlin surrendered also. The way Jerry has been giving up all over I think the papers for the surrender of Germany are also signed already too.

May 3, Thu. – Kip and I went to battalion headquarters with Lt. Deballian this morning. It's 101 miles from here across the Danube River near the Swiss border. We saw the Alps from there. Quite a bit of snow up there. On the way back, it snowed so hard you couldn't see three feet ahead. We are supposed to move up and relieve "B" Battery tomorrow. Got a rumor while up at battalion headquarters in which our outfit is slated to go home and a possible discharge.

May 4, Fri. – The orders have been changed so often, now the whole battalion are supposed to meet and go into bivouac. We are leaving at 7:00 tomorrow morning with our personnel stuff and M-51. Got a news flash this evening which stated the whole of N.W. Germany surrendered along with Holland and Denmark.

White flags. Germany surrenders.

May 5, Sat. – Left at 7:00 this morning and arrived at battalion at noon which is in Kaufbeuren. Capt. Weiden went and picked out a big apartment house for us as we expect to be here a few days. There were German civilians living in it, but he gave them an hour to pack their stuff and get out. It seems pretty cruel, but their people are going to get a lesson this time. We have three apartments to two gun sections, and boy it's really nice. The Germans from this building moved in the building next door, but a little while later "A" Battery moved in there, so out they had to move again.

May 6, Sun. – Went to church with Kip and George this morning. We are guarding the Messerschmitt factory, radio tower, creamery, ammo train, and the Royal Bavarian family which is just across the Austrian border in a big castle. Two of the fellows went out and shot two deer this evening. Beautiful day today.

May 7, Mon. – Beautiful day today. Expect to move to a town about eight miles from here. Capt. Weiden went to VI Corps headquarters yesterday, but isn't back yet. Radio said Churchill would make an announcement in a day or so that the war was completely over in Europe. The 1st Platoon moved this afternoon to the town of Marktoberdorf. We are pulling the same guard but are here to occupy the town. This really is a nice setup.

"C" Battery on the move through Germany

May 8, Tue. – Beautiful day. Everybody comes to us with their trouble, so we have set an office up for them to really make it look like the real thing. Went out to check on the guard out at the castle. What a beautiful place it is. Listened to Churchill give his speech declaring the war officially over in Europe.

May 9, Wed. – We did a little celebrating last nite. Six of us went on a patrol this evening to wipe out a pocket of S.S. troops who have been knocking off Russians. We stood just outside the woods and really poured the lead to them. We stopped off at the Russian D.P.C. and had quite a feast on the way back. They were really grateful to us for cleaning the Jerries out.

May 10, Thu. – Boxed up three rifles, washed clothes today. Boy what a day for a sunburn. Men are starting to leave our outfit for the States already. Staff Sgt. Michleson and 1st Sgt. Sharp are leaving. We have 541 combat days to our credit, so we stand a good chance of going home soon. Kip and I took a stroll through town this evening and the beautiful fraternizing stuff we got a glimpse of. Took a walk through a park that was on a hill in a spruce tree forest. It was just beautiful with the snow covered Alps in the background. Sergeant of the guard this evening. Kip and I went back out to the creamery and got the first fresh milk we've had since the States. Fresh and it was delicious! Getting 25 new men in the battery tomorrow. They are supposed to have just come over from the States.

May 11, Fri. – Got some mail today, and there's supposed to be beaucoups of it at the battalion not sorted yet. Boy and it's about time. We've really got a racket here. When we are sergeant of the guard, we take our guards out and otherwise we sleep most of the time.

May 12, Sat. – Went over into Austria today. The scenery is just beautiful. Got more mail this evening.

May 13, Sun. – Got 11 new men on our platoon. Just been over for a month from the States, and they are just starting as they'll be the army of occupation. Heard how we are going to be discharged which is according to the point system. 85 and over are the lucky ones now. I've got 78.

May 14, Mon. – Sergeant of the guard today. Went over to the brewery and got a keg of beer for eight marks. Pretty good beer too.

May 15, Tue. – Major Lossen was here last nite, and Kip and I had quite a talk with him. He said we had a very good chance of going home soon. He also said we had the highest record of any Bofors (40 mm) outfit with the official number of planes actually knocked down. We were relieved of creamery guard today by the 36th Division.

May 16, Wed. – Went on a recon. with Lt. Hedricks this afternoon to find a CP as we expect to move in a day or so. Sgt. Michleson left which he thought was for his trip to the States, but when he got to battalion it was for his application which he put in back in Liege for infantry officer. He almost sucked me in on the same deal back in Liege. Kip and I did some fraternizing so to speak this evening.

May 17, Thu. – Half the platoon went to battalion to get a physical check-up which was supposed to have been done a year ago. We also went to S-1 where we were told the number of points we had. I've got 78. Came back and we got march order. I'm taking over the train guard with 14 men. The rest of the platoon are moving to Fussen about 30 miles from here. Some of the fellows are with the C.I.C.

May 18, Fri. – This is really perfect out here. Living in tents and doing our own cooking. We are out in the lonely woods surrounded by spruce trees about 50 feet high. No brass around to bother us, which makes it so nice. Kip came out with the mail this evening.

May 19, Sat. – Rained like mad last nite. The days are really beautiful. Kip came down this evening and said the restriction was lifted which was placed on all sergeants and officers the other day for passes on account of "A" Battery and no. 8 crew of 2nd Platoon screwing up on the road blocks. The restriction was placed the day Kip and I were scheduled to go to rest camp at Nancy from which we were going to screw off to Liege. Boy were we burned up 'cause we never had anything to do with it. We put our names in for a furlough to Liege instead. We have to be on the lookout for Himmler as he is on the loose. Rained this evening.

May 20, Sun. – Kip came out this morning, so I went back to the CP with him where we took in a show this afternoon. Took the truck back out and brought the fellows in this evening. We are going to be relieved tomorrow by the 141st Infantry.

May 21, Mon. – We were relieved at 10:00 this morning. Staying at the CP which is right alongside of the main roadblock. 1st Sgt. Sharp left for the States today. Kip's and my pass to Nancy went through, and we leave 6:30 tomorrow morning.

May 22, Tue. – Left at 7:30 this morning. Went through Ulm, Stuttgart, Strasburg. Rained all the way. Arrived in Nancy 7:30 this evening. Made 350 miles in 12 hours over the roughest roads imaginable. Ate supper at unlisted men's transit mess in Nancy. Going to Liege in the morning with the truck driver.

May 23, Wed. – Got our passes, PX, and all new clothes this morning. Ate dinner and took off with Kip and the truck driver in his truck. Went through Metz, Luxembourg, Bastogne, and the Ardennes. Knocked out German and American tanks along the road, and the road was torn up which really made it a tough ride. Arrived in Liege at 7:30 this evening. Are spending the nite at Bemelman's.

May 24, Thu. – Things aren't the way I expected them, and I really feel sorry for Eleanor. We went over and took a shower at the coal mine this morning. Rained this afternoon.

May 25, Fri. – Took a walk with Kip and Lorette this afternoon. Played mailman for the fellows who have girls here. Went over to Ordett's house. They have our pictures on the wall and have pinned fresh flowers on them every day since we left Liege in April.

May 26, Sat. – Bill left this morning, and Eleanor is really a changed girl. She didn't eat anything while he was here, and she was the saddest looking girl I've ever seen. She really is happy now. Went for a walk with the girls to a peak overlooking Liege. These people treat us just like one of the family, and boy it's been just like home.

May 27, Sun. – Left back for Nancy this noon. Got back at Rest Camp at 8:00 this evening. Took a shower and went to bed.

May 28, Mon. – Slept all morning. Played ping pong most of the afternoon with Kip. Went to the show this evening. Saw *Frisco Sal*.

May 29, Tue. – Left right after breakfast this morning back for Fussen. Took us 12 ½ hours to get back. Got back at 10:00 this evening and have to get up at 3:00 a.m. as the whole battalion is moving back to Mannheim which is about another 200-mile ride.

May 30, Wed. – Left at 5:00 this morning. Had perfect weather until we got to the other side of Stuttgart where it started raining, and it's been keeping off and on ever since. At Stuttgart we hit a trolley car which knocked us into a weapons carrier. We knocked the trolley car off the track. It hit our M-51 machine gun trailer which weighs 5,700 pounds. It knocked one wheel out of line, and after three hours of driving all the rubber was worn off right down to the cord. We are bivouacking for the nite just outside of Mannheim. Hicks from battalion headquarters said we have the fifth star now. They are working on the sixth one and a possible seventh. I'll have 83 points with the fifth one.

May 31, Thu. – Reveille at 6:30 this morning and inspection of rifles and bunks at 8:30. Laid around the rest of the day. Went to a show in Mannheim this evening.

Jun. 1, Fri. – The sergeants didn't have to get up this morning. "A" Battery got march orders and are moving back to Munich. The battalion is going to be scattered out between Mannheim and Munich. Were issued our E.T.O. jackets today. They really are keen looking. Went to the show again last nite. Went to the Red Cross across the Rhine River. We crossed the Ernie Piel Memorial Bridge to get there.

Jun. 2, Sat. – Our platoon got some gin someplace, so when we got back everyone was near drunk last nite. Going to pull out this afternoon. We are going to Karlsruhe. Left at 2:00 p.m. and are set up in some barracks near the depot. Our job is liaison sergeants at the depot, and the men guard the train. We are the only G.I.s in Karlsruhe, which is under the French. Nobody has any use for these French. They fraternize with the German girls, they pull a lot of dirty deals over on the Americans, and 16 American Soldiers were killed in Stuttgart the other nite when the French were ordered out, and on the way out they stole everything they could.

Jun. 3, Sun. – Guard started at noon today. Going back to Goppingen tomorrow to get our 40's. One reason is just in case these French got hostile. I go on guard at 2:00 this afternoon.

Jun. 4, Mon. – Went on guard at 8:00 this morning until noon. Went to the show in town this evening. Saw *Objective, Burma!* with Errol Flynn. Very good picture. It lasted two and a half hours. Our 40's came back today.

Jun. 5, Tue. – This train guard is really a headache. Turned in some of our equipment this morning. Prisoners cleared the swimming pool out, and we turned the water on this evening. It should be filled by morning. Had to put M.P. on our helmets and were issued M.P. arm bands for this train guard. Going on guard at 2:00 in the morning with Mick who came back to us yesterday.

Jun. 6, Wed. – Slept all morning. Went swimming this afternoon and was the water cold. Went to the show this evening. Saw *Eadie Was a Lady* with Ann Miller. Go on guard at 10:00–2:00.

Boy, what form. Good thing the picture is dark so nobody can tell it's me. Karlsruhe, Germany. July 1945

Jun. 7, Thu. – Swimming this afternoon and also after Buck and I came off guard at 10:00 this evening. Too hot to sleep, so we took a dip and then slept like a log. General Patch's (7th Army commander) train pulled in at 8:30 and was serviced at the depot here. Boy what a luxurious train it was. It used to be Goebbels' private train.

Jun. 8, Fri. – Rained like mad this morning but cooled things off. Going on guard at 2:00 this afternoon until 6:00.

Jun. 9, Sat. – Guard from 10:00–2:00. Washed the 40 down, and there was so much pressure on the hose the joint came off also. Went swimming this evening.

Jun. 10, Sun. – Guard 6:00–10:00 this morning. Tore the 40 down and greased it all up this afternoon. Got our PX rations.

Jun. 11, Mon. – Rained this morning. Off guard for 40 hours. Went to the show with Kip this evening. Saw *Molly and Me* with Gracie Fields and Monty Woolley. Haven't gotten any mail in the battery for the past week.

Jun. 12, Tue. – Went on guard at 2:00 this morning till 6:00. Rained most of the day and nite.

Jun. 13, Wed. – "Bank nite" tonite at the Santa Fe theater. Didn't even come close. Tickets cost 10 marks or $1. Swimming this afternoon.

Jun. 14, Thu. – Turned in some of our equipment today. The depot is loaded with refugees all the time who ride freight trains with all their children and luggage. S.S. troops or prisoners go through every day back to France. Our troops are going through every day bound for China–Burma–India.

Jun. 15, Fri. – Guard as usual. Heard today all the data is in for the sixth star and are waiting word on it. Rained today.

Jun. 16, Sat. – Went to the show this evening. Guard as usual.

Jun. 17, Sun. – Kip and I went to Heidelberg on pass today. Not much to do in there except play ping pong at the Red Cross.

Jun. 18, Mon. – We played an engineering outfit in baseball this afternoon and beat them 11–0. Played battalion headquarters this evening and beat them 7–1. Went swimming this evening.

Jun. 19, Tue. – We can wear our fifth star now and are pretty sure we'll get the sixth also. Hot as the dickens this evening, and the mosquitoes are terrible. One of the women refugees who was waiting for a train gave birth to a baby in the depot while I was on guard.

Jun. 20, Wed. – One of the trains which had gasoline on broke loose outside of Worth last nite and burned up. A brake man was killed, and we have to wait until the wreckage is cleared away as two of our guards were thought to be on it. Went to the show this evening. Also saw a stage show which I sure didn't enjoy very much. Lillis from 2nd Platoon won the first prize of $170 for bank nite which was tonite also.

Jun. 21, Thu. – Painted our 40 today. Went swimming all afternoon. Rained this evening. PX rations today.

Jun. 22, Fri. – Came off guard at 10:00 this morning and am off for 36 hours. Went to the show this evening where we saw a stage show consisting of all European talent, and it was the best U.S.O. show I saw since coming overseas. After the U.S.O. show, we saw the movie *Thunderhead, Son of Flicka*.

Jun. 23, Sat. – Played baseball this afternoon and got beat 8–3. Went swimming with Kip this evening and then went for a walk.

Jun. 24, Sun. – Came off guard at 6:00 this morning, slept till noon. We were told we had six stars now and that our unit would be going home together between now and September sometime. Boy it sure sounds good.

Kip and me. This is taken not long after getting up after a big nite.
Karlsruhe, Germany.

Jun. 25, Mon. – Got a letter from Mother today saying Minerva was getting married the 16th of this month. Don and Bev were also married the 16th. Swimming this evening.

Jun. 26, Tue. – The Germans have taken over running the railroads now and boy what a time we have trying to get guards on trains on time. Their system is different from the American system and a lot slower. They have no competition over here like they have in the States, in fact, they have no competition at all, so that accounts for it.

Jun. 27, Wed. – Show this evening. Bank nite also, no luck.

Jun. 28, Thu. – Guard as usual. Rained most of the day.

Jun. 29, Fri. – Played baseball this evening again and got beat 7–2. They had a new pitcher which we just couldn't hit.

Jun. 30, Sat. – Guard as usual. Inspection this morning which I slept through as I came off guard at 6:00. Played the 713th Railway Battalion this evening and lost again. Another fastball pitcher.

Jul. 1, Sun. – Church this morning. Guard as usual. Wilson our battery clerk was around today where   we signed for two more battle stars. I have 88 points now. Our six battle stars are official now. They are for Naples to Foggia, Rome-Arno, southern France, Rhineland, Ardennes, and Central Europe.

Jul. 2, Mon. – Played the 713th this evening and beat them 8–6. We put in a pinch hitter, Matalahio, in the last inning with two men on bases, and he clouts out a homer.

Jul. 3, Tue. – Rained most of the day. Kip, Spinnata, and I took a ride to Ettlingen this evening about 15 miles from here, and without choice we walked back. The truck broke down, and to top it off, it rained most of the way. We made it in two hours and 50 minutes.

Jul. 4, Wed. – Came off guard at 10:00 this morning. Played headquarters battery this afternoon and beat them again, 5–4. Went to Ettlingen this evening with Kip, Alberts, and Spinnata.

Jul. 5, Thu. – Went to the show this evening. Saw *The Merry Monahans* with Peggy Ryan, Donald O'Connor, and Jack Oakie.

Jul. 6, Fri. – Came off guard at 6:00 this morning so slept most of the morning. Turned in our "40" and "50" ammunition this afternoon.

Jul. 7, Sat. – Inspection this morning. Show this evening.

Jul. 8, Sun. – Got 42 fellows from the 67th Gun Battalion who have over 100 points. The fellas under 85 points are leaving us the 11th and those under 75 are leaving the same day to go into an outfit scheduled for the Pacific. Took the truck out this evening, and it took three of us to drive it back. Lost the spring for the gas feed, so Alberts did the steering, I sat on the left fender regulating the gas, and Kip sat on the right side holding up the hood.

Jul. 9, Mon. – Went on guard at 10:00 this morning. The 84th Division M.P.s have taken over M.P. duty in Karlsruhe.

Jul. 10, Tue. – Left with 20 other fellows on a trip to Dachau to see the concentration camp at which so many atrocities were committed. Went through the building with the gas chamber, cremation, and slaughterhouse in. The latter which had blood all over the walls, and the odor was terrific. Went up to Munich before we came back. On the Autobahn between Augsburg and Stuttgart, we stopped where there were a bunch of jet-propelled Me 262s just off the road. The Jerries had used the Autobahn for an airstrip. The middle section which usually has grass or shrubbery separating the four lanes had concrete and was painted green so you could hardly tell it wasn't grass. The trip covered about 400 miles, and to top it off it started raining about half way home.

Me 262, German jet on the Autobon used for a runway

Jul. 11, Wed. – Kip pulled my guard for me today. Wally left this morning for the 67th Gun Battalion. Everyone got a typhoid shot this afternoon, and boy what a sore arm everyone has now.

Jul. 12, Thu. – Nobody got much sleep with the oversized arm they have today. Didn't feel like doing anything, so slept most of the day. Played ping pong this evening. We had the Jerries make a table for us, and it's really a dandy.

Jul. 13, Fri. – Played "C" Co. of the 713th Railway Battalion last nite and got beat 6–2. Played "B" Co. this afternoon and beat them 4–2. Went on guard at 6:00 this evening. The trains that went west today were troop trains. We really have a time guarding the ration trains when a troop train is in the yards. There was an accident at 9:30 this morning in which two troop trains were involved. Six G.I.s were killed and 40 some wounded near Durlach.

Entrance to Dachau Concentration Camp, Germany 1945

Dachau Concentration Camp, Germany 1945

Jul. 14, Sat. – The usual Saturday morning inspection this morning. Eighty men are leaving the battalion for the States tomorrow or Monday. Seventeen are leaving from here, but most of them are guys who came in about a week ago from the 67th Gun Battalion and have over 100 points.

Jul. 15, Sun. – Went on guard at 10:00 this morning. Sgt. Michleson left with the fellas for the States this morning.

Jul. 16, Mon. – Played 713th this afternoon and beat them. Went to the show this evening. Saw *Here Come the Waves* with Bing Crosby and Betty Hutton.

Jul. 17, Tue. – Went on guard at 6:00 this morning and are off for 40 hours now. Kip and I are pulling together. Went to Ettlingen during our time off.

Jul. 18, Wed. – Came back at 20:00 this evening. Go on duty at 2:00 in the morning.

Jul. 19, Thu. – Kip and I spent the afternoon at the pool and acquired quite a tan. Went to the show this evening. Saw *Winged Victory*. Bank nite was also and first prize was $223 but didn't quite make it.

Jul. 20, Fri. – Kip and I went on duty at 18:00 this evening and were on the go until 22:00. The 45th Division was coming through, and three train loads were in the yard. The yard was also jammed with kids hanging around the troop trains. There was such a congestion of kids that the switch engine couldn't switch cars around, so we were kept busy chasing kids all the while. Had a meeting this evening, and at 4:00 in the morning a big shakedown is going to take place of all German civilians and G.I.s on the streets. It's going to last for 48 hours. Our battery stops and checks everything that comes in at Karlsruhe West here and at the main station in town.

Jul. 21, Sat. – No inspection this morning. Went on duty at 2:00 this afternoon.

Jul. 22, Sun. – Went swimming most of the day. Played ping pong with Buck this evening.

Jul. 23, Mon. – Went up to Ettlingen with Kip.

Jul. 24, Tue. – A fellow from "A" Battery was electrocuted when, while he was walking on top of a box car chasing civilians off the train, his rifle touched a low hanging wire which burnt his whole left side and knocked him clear off the car.

Jul. 25, Wed. – Went on duty at 2:00 this morning till 6:00. Slept all morning, went swimming all afternoon. Played the 713th this evening and got beat in the 11th inning. Good game.

Jul. 26, Thu. – Went swimming all day. Went to the show this evening.

Jul. 27, Fri. – Two Russians, two Poles, an Arab, and a German were seriously hurt down at the depot this morning. One of them made a fire over a hand grenade which blew up.

Jul. 28, Sat. – Inspection this morning. Rained all afternoon.

Jul. 29, Sun. – Went on duty at 6:00 this morning after which we have 40 hours off. Played ping pong with George all afternoon. Cooked ourselves up some fresh corn this evening.

Jul. 30, Mon. – Jack Benny's show is going to be in Karlsruhe tomorrow at the Ardennes Stadium. We were issued a new E.T.O. ribbon, good conduct ribbon, and the Silver Star in place of five Bronze Stars. Went to the show with Kip and George this evening. Saw *Gypsy Wildcat* with Maria Montez and Jon Hall.

Jul. 31, Tue. – Slept all morning. Jack Benny's U.S.O. show played in Karlsruhe this afternoon. Didn't get to sign up for it, so Kip and I went to see it this evening in Bruchsal. We left early enough as it was 20 miles away, but the drive shaft broke going to the rear wheels which took half an hour to disconnect. We still got a pretty good seat though and was really a good show. Ingrid Bergman, who won the Academy Award, was there and boy was she nice. Martha Tilton sang, and Larry Adler, the worlds best mouth organ player. David Lee Winter played the piano.

Jack Benny, Bruchsal, Germany, July 31, 1945

Aug. 1, Wed. – Got paid this morning. Rained most of the day. Another quota of 118 men are leaving the battalion for the States Friday. It's all those with 100 and over and a few exceptional 99's. Kip is leaving which makes me glad he is going to get home, but it gives me a kind of a lost feeling. Him and I sure have had a lot of fun together these past three years.

Aug. 2, Thu. – Kip and I played horseshoes most of the morning. Went on duty at 14:00. Went over to the RTO with Kip and Ray and stopped off at the officers' quarters on the way back. We are going to throw a party for Kip and Sparky Saturday nite at the officers' quarters. The guys who were going to leave tomorrow aren't going till Wednesday.

Aug. 3, Fri. – Went on duty at 10:00 this morning until 14:00. Went to Ettlingen this evening.

Aug. 4, Sat. – Inspection this morning. We cosmolined our "40's" and "50's" this morning also. Kip and I printed a bunch of pictures this afternoon. We are having a party at the officers' quarters this evening for Kip, Chapman, and Adams.

Aug. 5, Sun. – Really had a quite a time last nite at the party. It didn't break up until 5:00 this morning. Major Lossen was there, two other captains from headquarters, our officers, two C.I.D. (Criminal Investigation Department) men, and all of the sergeants. Had a swell time. Slept all day.

Aug. 6, Mon. – Slept all morning as I came off duty at 6:00. Kip and I went swimming all afternoon. Went to show this evening. Saw *Lake Placid Serenade*.

Aug. 7, Tue. – Rained all day. Went to the show with Kip this evening. Saw *Practically Yours* with Fred MacMurray and Claudette Colbert.

Aug. 8, Wed. – Heard over the radio last nite that we have an atomic bomb which is equivalent to 20,000 tons of TNT or 2,000 superfortress loads. One was dropped on Japan. It's something in the Buck–Rogers stage. Rained all day again. Over the radio this evening they said Russia declared war on Japan which goes in effect at midnite. Kip and I took a walk over to the 713th Railway Battalion this evening to say so long to Swede and Jack. They are leaving Saturday.

Aug. 9, Thu. – Kip and the other boys left at 7:30 this morning. It's sure going to seem different without Kip around. Rained all day. Went to the show with Kapp and Frank this evening. Saw *Earl Carroll Vanities* with Dennis O'Keefe and Constance Moore. It was very good.

Aug. 10, Fri. – Rained all day, so everybody slept all day. The wind blew all the tents down and ruined a lot of crops.

Aug. 11, Sat. – Rained all morning so there wasn't much of an inspection. Went to the show this evening.

6th Edition

August 12 to November 14, 1945

The war is over, and I'm coming home

In August 1945, the United States dropped the first and second atomic bombs on Hiroshima and Nagasaki, leading to Japan's unconditional surrender on August 15. By the end of October, Jack along with over 1,800 other Soldiers boarded the USS *Oneida* bound for the United States, and after 11 days at sea arrived on U.S. soil on November 6, 1945. Jack and George received a pass for the weekend so they could attend George's brother's wedding on the weekend, but only until Monday, so they had to return for a few more days. Jack was excited to go home after being discharged, but also sad to leave those who he served with — a "swell bunch of fellas" as he described them.

Aug. 12, Sun. – Came off duty at 6:00 this morning so slept until noon. Everyone is in on every news broadcast 'cause we figure Japan will throw in the towel any moment. This new atomic bomb has put a scare into her and everyone else. One bomb knocks out a whole city of 250,000. There's a heavy rumor going around that we're to be relieved in a week.

Aug. 13, Mon. – Came off duty at 2:00 this morning so slept till noon. Boy a guy sure gets plenty of sleep. Heard a news flash that Japan had surrendered, but it was false. Go on duty at 22:00 this evening.

Aug. 14, Tue. – Everyone has their ear to the radio waiting for the big news flash. I went to Heidelberg this morning and looked up Art. Didn't have much trouble finding him. Sure was nice seeing him. I hitchhiked back this evening. Rained most of the day.

Aug. 15, Wed. – We had the radio on all nite long, and at 1:30 this morning we got the official Jap surrender which was announced by President Truman. Everybody in camp was awakened, rifles were fired and yelling going on all over. There's a rifle inspection this morning for the sections at which empty cartridge cases were found outside their barracks. Went to the show with George and Nachtwey this evening: *Escape in the Desert*.

Aug. 16, Thu. – Went on 6:00 this morning till 10:00. Went to the show this evening. Saw *Together Again* with Irene Dunne and Charles Boyer. It was good.

Aug. 17, Fri. – The Japs are acting pretty funny with the surrender terms and fired on some of our observation planes. Played ping pong all day.

Aug. 18, Sat. – Inspection this morning. Rained all afternoon. Saw *Ship Fields* this evening at the Ardennen Stadium in Karlsruhe here.

Aug. 19, Sun. – Rained all day and nite. Sure is miserable, laying around with nothing to do.

Aug. 20, Mon. – Rained most of the day. Went to the show this evening. Saw *To Have and Have Not* with Humphrey Bogart and Lauren Bacall.

Aug. 21, Tue. – We heard today that we are connected with the 2nd MRS now, and they don't intend to release us. Boy what a dirty deal that is. Every guy is fighting mad now after hearing that. Wally dropped in for a few hours this afternoon. Rained all afternoon.

Aug. 22, Wed. – Major Lossen, who is now our battalion commander as the colonel went home, went down to MRS headquarters and raised hell. He almost got in the soup himself for it, but they finally saw his point so now if we can find an outfit to relieve us, we'll be leaving in a few days. Boy what a happy bunch of fellas we are now!! It rained most of the day again, but who cares!

Aug. 23, Thu. – We turned in our M-51 today. Mine has been in for some time already. They are down to Paris to get an outfit to relieve us. Went to the show this evening. Saw *The Climax* with Boris Karloff and Susanna Foster.

Aug. 24, Fri. – Turned in our 40's and power plants this morning. After everything was turned in I still had a big pit of junk and stuff in my pile, so Dixon had everybody pitch in and get rid of it. Don't know where it all came from. Now all that is left for us to take care of are our own personal things and trucks. Gee, I sure miss Kip. I can't seem to find anything to do to amuse myself. He and I always found something to do.

Aug. 25, Sat. – Inspection this morning. Looks like we're stuck here now. They can't find anybody to relieve us. Boy and all the outfits around with under the number of points and doing nothing. The trouble is they feel they might have a chance to go home as a lot of guys with below 85 points are being taken to fill out quotas going home. We really are taking a screwing. Made some Anzio patches this evening just to have something to do. We aren't authorized to wear them, but I'm going to anyway.

Aug. 26, Sun. – Went to church this morning over at 106th headquarters. I had my Anzio patch on, and it really took notice. I've started something in the battery now. Got two letters from Kip this morning. He was still at the holding camp near Antwerp but is probably on his way home by now. Sure wish I was with him.

Aug. 27, Mon. – Capt. Weiden wrote a letter for the *Stars and Stripes* in regard to our not going home which everyone signed their name to. There's going to be a battery commanders meeting this afternoon after which we will know the good or bad news. Well, all we found out is that we aren't essential and that we go as soon as we're relieved. We sure didn't learn much. Went to the show this evening. Saw *A Tree Grows in Brooklyn*.

Aug. 28, Tue. – Went to a hardball game at the Ardennen Stadium between the 106th and the 36th. 106th won 9–2. Went to the Red Cross theatre this evening and saw the U.S.O. show *Kiss and Tell*. It really was good! The weather has been beautiful the last four days.

Aug. 29, Wed. – Took a walk out to the airport this morning. Went to a ballgame again this afternoon. (Sergeant and Bill left for the States.) 106 and 36 played again. 106th Division beat 2–1. Hear this evening we are sending trucks down to Paris to bring up an outfit to relieve us. It's supposed to be official this time. I got a nice long letter from Pat this evening.

Aug. 30, Thu. – Rained off and on all day. Went to the show with Pete this evening. Saw *My Reputation* with Barbara Stanwyck and George Brent.

Aug. 31, Fri. – Rained all day. Got paid today. S.S. prisoners were in the yards waiting to go to France to work in the mines. They were guarded by G.I.s, and after dark some made a break but were shot. The last group that went through there were about 300 who tried to jump off the train. 150 were shot.

Sep. 1, Sat. – Inspection this morning. An advance detail pulled in this afternoon from the outfit that's going to relieve us. They are the 385th M.P.s. Went to the show this evening. Saw *Swing Out, Sister* with Billie Burke and Arthur Treacher.

Sep. 2, Sun. – Pretty chilly this morning. Our trucks are leaving early tomorrow morning, so they should have them back and us relieved by Wednesday. We might get in with the 106th Division as they are scheduled to leave the 5th.

Sep. 3, Mon. – A beautiful day all day. Went on duty at 6:00 this morning till 10:00. Went to the show this evening with Pete, Kapp, and Torchy. Saw *Hollywood Canteen*. It was about the best show I've seen for a long time! Joan Leslie took a leading part.

Sep. 4, Tue. – Fifty of our trucks went down to Verdeen yesterday morning and this evening came back with the 385th M.P.s.

Sep. 5, Wed. – Went on at 2:00 this morning till 6:00. Slept most of the day. Rained all day.

Liberated Russian PWs serving chow to George, Karlsruhe, Germany, 1945

Sep. 6, Thu. – Steinke and I went on at 6:00 this evening and were relieved by the 385th at 8:00, so now we are officially relieved and are going to move into a theatre in Ettlingen Saturday morning. There's a pretty good rumor going around that we leave there the 13th. Gee what a wonderful feeling, knowing we are started on our way home.

Sep. 7, Fri. – Rained all day. Went to the show this evening. Saw *The Suspect* with Charles Laughton.

Sep. 8, Sat. – Breakfast at 6:00 this morning, and we left at 8:00. We are set up in a theatre which is a part of a college which is next door.

Sep. 9, Sun. – Went to church with George and Sam this morning. It was held in Karlsruhe. Went to the Red Cross in Karlsruhe this evening for coffee and doughnuts.

Sep. 10, Mon. – Showdown inspection this morning and a physical this afternoon. A number of cases of trench mouth and scabies have broken out in the battalion. Any who had either are going in isolation tomorrow for a few days to get rid of it.

Sep. 11, Tue. – The first sergeant announced at breakfast that we have to be at Camp Pittsburgh on the 20th, so that means we'll be leaving here in a week. PX today and boy it's about time as it was overdue, and everybody was out of cigarettes. Turned in our rifles and ammunition this afternoon. All the sergeants went to headquarters where we had our records checked. The whole battery will go tomorrow.

Sep. 12, Wed. – Played ball most of the day. Took a walk with Buck and Sam this evening and covered just about all of Ettlingen.

"Seasoned Veterans," Karlsruhe, Germany 1945

Sep. 13, Thu. – Drove Lt. Henry this morning. Went to the show in Karlsruhe this evening. Saw *Roughly Speaking* with Rosalind Russell, Jack Carson, and Alan Hale. It was very good. The mornings are pretty chilly, but it's really nice sleeping at nite. We have a 15-minute orientation lecture every morning on the G.I. Bill of Rights. We are going to be issued overcoats and winter underwear while we are here.

Sep. 14, Fri. – Cloudy all day. Rained a little this afternoon. Sixty new men are coming in tomorrow, so all the beds have to be closer together. George came back from battalion headquarters and moved up next to my cot.

Sep. 15, Sat. – The new men came in this morning. Most of them have only two overseas bars, but they are all old men over 35. Played football this afternoon. Went to the show this evening at the Santa Fe. Saw *Pan Americana*. A very good picture.

Sep. 16, Sun. – Today marks the third birthday I've spent in the Army. Went to church this morning which was held in the Protestant church next door. Went to the show this evening in town. It was a 16 mm film and kept breaking down all through the picture. Turned back the clocks one hour today.

Sep. 17, Mon. – Was on CQ from 3:00 to 5:00 this morning. We are going to leave here Wednesday morning instead of tomorrow. Can't get convoy priority on the road for the whole battalion. Went to the show with Kapp and Alabam this evening. Saw Olsen and Johnson in *See My Lawyer*.

Sep. 18, Tue. – Got a letter from Kip saying he hit the States on the 6th of this month. Packed our bags this evening. Breakfast is at 5:30, and we have to be on the road by 7:00.

Sep. 19, Wed. – Left at 7:00 this morning. Pulled into the Nancy bivouac area at 7:15 this evening. This really is a beautiful spot. It's run by the 112th Gun Battalion. We are sleeping in tents with cots already set up. Chow at any hour. All the Coke, beer, and doughnuts one wants. A band concert, movies, ping pong, horseshoes, boy there's everything here. It's just like a place in the States and fixed up beautiful. We have to be ready to leave at 6:00 in the morning. It started raining just after we left Germany which was early this afternoon. We went through the Siegfried Line. Had quite a congestion at Metz where a number of convoys got tied up in a traffic jam.

Sep. 20, Thu. – Left at 7:15 this morning. We arrived at Camp Pittsburgh in Reims, France at 1:15 this afternoon. We are living in big tents with an area and mess hall for each battery. Took a shower in the dark this evening.

Sep. 21, Fri. – Reveille at 6:30 this morning, breakfast at 7:00. Turned in our German marks in exchange for French money. Only your base pay plus 10% could be turned in. A lot of guys are getting stuck with over $1,000, which they accumulated through black market. Registered our pistols and turned them in. Battalion headquarters is going to hold them until we leave. Got a physical this morning. Got a shot this afternoon. Turned in our dog tags to be stamped. Got PX cards but can't use them until we get our French money.

Camp Pittsburgh, Reims, France, September 1945

Sep. 22, Sat. – Showdown inspection this morning. Stenciled our duffel bags. Took an oath this morning stating that we had no firearms in our possession and weren't going to smuggle any U.S. equipment other than issued to the States. Sergeant of the guard tonite. Heard that the port of Le Havre is under quarantine.

Sep. 23, Sun. – Played some football this morning. Turned cold today. Got a shot this afternoon and turned in our dog tags to be stamped.

Sep. 24, Mon. – Got our records checked this morning. Rained most of the day. Boy, was it cold in bed last nite! Got coffee and doughnuts from the Red Cross.

Sep. 25, Tue. – Turned in our sizes for overcoats. Went to see a movie, *Your America*, which everybody had to see. Everyone got their $17 from the French government this morning. Went to the Stanley Theatre this evening. Saw *Week-end at the Waldorf* with Ginger Rogers, Walter Pidgeon, Lana Turner, and Van Johnson. It was very good.

Sep. 26, Wed. – We have a training schedule which started yesterday. Half hour calisthenics, one hour lecture every morning. Rained today so we only had the lecture. The battalion had a parade review this afternoon for officers and enlisted men who were awarded the Bronze Star. The camp commander presented them. Went to the show this evening. Saw Gary Cooper in *Along Came Jones*.

Sep. 27, Thu. – Rained most of the day. Played pinochle with Louis and Buck all morning and afternoon. Issued stoves today.

Sep. 28, Fri. – Everyone had to go to a movie this morning on V.D. Cold as the dickens last nite. Went to the PX and got some Coke and ice cream this evening. Heard we're leaving here Wednesday for Marseille. Boy, that's going to be another long ride across country. Issued overcoats this evening.

Sep. 29, Sat. – Foggy all morning but cleared up beautiful this afternoon. Saw a football game just across from us between the 169th Ordnance and the 653rd Ordnance. The 169th won 12–0. Met George Krah at the game. He's a 1st lieutenant.

Sep. 30, Sun. – Got paid this morning. Started to get our added pay for three years in the service. Went to the Red Cross this evening with George and Norbert.

Oct. 1, Mon. – Here's the first of October, and we're still here. Now the latest is we don't leave until Saturday. Boy nobody knows nothing. Went to a U.S.O. show this evening. *The Amsterdam Follies* which was all Hollanders. When the doors were opened there was one mad rush just like a bunch of animals. Millet and I held the crowd back while I pulled one fellow out from under our feet. He would have gotten trampled to death.

Oct. 2, Tue. – Boy, was it cold this morning. Went to the show this afternoon. Saw *Dime a Dance*. Went to the show this evening. Saw *The Corn Is Green* with Bette Davis. She did some very good acting, but it was a dry picture.

Oct. 3, Wed. – Got issued some more equipment this morning. Went to the show this afternoon. Saw *Blonde Reason* it was very good. Went this evening again. Saw *Her Highness and the Bellboy* with Hedy Lamarr, June Allyson, and Robert Walker. It was really good, but we had to stand for the whole show.

Oct. 4, Thu. – Registered our cameras and field glasses this morning. Got a physical this afternoon. Nobody leaves the area. We're finally pulling out of here. We leave 11:30 this evening. After packing our bags, we were allowed to go to the PX. Alex, Pete, Buck, and I went over to the "Barn" where we indulged in Coke and ice cream. Cold as the dickens this evening. Listened to part of the World Series. Detroit won 4–1. The Cubs won yesterday 9–0.

Oct. 5, Fri. – Big semi-trucks came at 1:15 this morning and took us to the train. Boy, it was a relief to get off the trucks as we were packed like cattle. We were the last to get off the trucks so there were no seats left. We finally pulled out at 5:00. The Red Cross passed out coffee and doughnuts before we left. Cold as the dickens. We ate dinner at a transient mess in Joinville. Ate supper in Beaune, which was at 9:00 this evening. 320 miles to Marseille yet.

Oct. 6, Sat. – Ate breakfast in Villefranche at 5:00 this morning. Boy what a rugged ride this is. Stayed in Lyon for two and a half hours. No dinner. Stopped at a mess place for supper, but just after the whole battalion got in line, which is over a thousand men, they said we had to get back on the train as it was leaving in a little while. Boy, was everyone burned up.

Oct. 7, Sun. – We stopped for supper at 11:00 last nite. Boy, their trains really are slow. We got off the train at 11:15 this morning about 25 kilometers outside of Marseille. Ate cereal and powdered eggs at a transient mess close by, and it was the worst one we encountered on our trip. After eating, we loaded on semi-trucks which took us to the "Coles" staging area. The camp is on top of a big hill, and it really is a big camp. Windy as the dickens with red dust covering everything. We are living in tents, 18 to a tent. A part of the 45th Division and the 106th are still here yet.

Oct. 8, Mon. – Went to the show last nite at the Shangri-La Theater which is an open air job. Saw *Out of this World* with Eddie Bracken. Boy, was it cold early this morning. The water is shut off for three days, so I guess we smell like goats until then. We manage to swipe enough from the mess kit water to wash our face in. Turned in sizes for winter underwear, gloves, and fatigue hat this afternoon. Boy, more junk to fill up a bag. Listened to the World Series at the Red Cross this evening. Cubs won 8–7 in 12 innings which ties them up with Detroit.

Oct. 9, Tue. – Filled out customs papers today and turned in our money which we get back in gold seal green backs six hours prior to sailing. Sweated out the PX line this afternoon. Boy, I've gotten so sick of seeing lines. Lines to the Red Cross, lines to the PX, lines for chow, and lines to the latrine! Went to the show this evening with Buck, Kapp, and George.

Oct. 10, Wed. – A training schedule started this morning. I had to take the battery out for calisthenics for a half hour, then a lecture by Lt. Hollingsworth, another lecture by Sgt. Smith, and this afternoon a showdown inspection. Listened to the Series this evening. Detroit took it 9–3.

Oct. 11, Thu. – Went to Marseille on pass with George, Buck, and Pete today. We were issued our Good Conduct medals when we came back. Went to the show this evening.

Oct. 12, Fri. – An outfit with less points and who came in here after we did left this morning. We got our call to leave last Tuesday, but some guys didn't have all their clothing, so we couldn't leave. Now they say we won't leave before the 17th. Boy, we're really getting a royal screwing. The shipping strike in New York is holding up a lot of ships from coming over here. Boy, there's a lot of people who don't care whether we get back or not. Now that the war is over the G.I. doesn't mean a thing. Took a shower this afternoon, but the water was ice cold as usual. The water situation is really pitiful around here.

Oct. 13, Sat. – We had to see a training film this morning. Pete and I took off for Marseille just before dinner and just made it for chow at the transient mess in Marseille. It's about 15 miles from camp to Marseille and takes the bus about 45 minutes. Took in a show *Our Vines Have Tender Grapes* with Edward G. Robinson, Margaret O'Brien, and James Craig. Went to the Red Cross this evening.

Harlon Peterson and me, Marseille, France, 1945

Oct. 14, Sun. – Went to the church this morning at the Shangri-La Theater. Washed some clothes this afternoon. Went to the show this evening. Saw *A Thousand and One Nights*. Pretty good. There must have been 15,000 G.I.s at the show. Boy, what a crowd.

Oct. 15, Mon. – Calisthenics and an orientation lecture this morning. I see I'm on fire guard starting at 5:00 this evening for 24 hours. Sweated out the PX line right after dinner. Also, the doughnut line this afternoon. Went to the Beer Garden

Theater this evening, which is another outdoor theater. Saw *Salty O'Rourke* with Alan Ladd. There's over 65,000 G.I.s in the camp and truck loads coming in every day, and I don't see very many going out tho. It's really discouraging being stuck here and not knowing when we'll get home now.

Oct. 16, Tue. – Close order drill this morning and a lecture. Played cards all day. Saw all the shows for the evening. Went to Red Cross.

Oct. 17, Wed. – Police call, calisthenics, and close order drill this morning. Went to see a training film this afternoon. These training films cover the battlegrounds of the Pacific and over here and are very interesting. Went over to the Beer Garden Theater this evening. There's heavy rumors going around we're leaving here Sunday. There's also a rumor which we got direct from the chaplain that some newspapers in the States are printing articles saying that the reason the rest of the high pointers aren't home yet is because of court martial or V.D. Boy, everybody is plenty wild about it too 'cause if it's true there's going to have to be a lot of explaining to do.

Oct. 18, Thu. – The usual stuff this morning. Training film this afternoon. Went to the Beer Garden Theater this evening. Saw *The Falcon in San Francisco*. We went right after supper, but it was crowded already. Gee, I hope we get out of here soon. There were five outfits alerted today, but we weren't one of the five.

Oct. 19, Fri. – Police call, calisthenics, close order drill, and a quiz class this morning. Lt. Hollingsworth also told us we were to be alerted in the next three days. Played cards all afternoon and evening. The P.W.s must have had a show in the stockade last nite 'cause they were really doing a lot of clapping and yelling. The engineers set off a bunch of demolition this afternoon which really shook this hill. The P.W.s are setting up poles for lights, but by the time they are in there won't be anyone left in this camp. Went to the Red Cross and sweated out the cake and doughnut line.

Oct. 20, Sat. – Inspection this morning. A rumor is going around that we were taken off the alert. It's got everybody pacing the floor cussing this damn Army. Went to the Red Cross this evening. What a beautiful nite it is with the brightest full moon I've ever seen.

Oct. 21, Sun. – Rained hard nearly all day, and boy what a good mud it makes. Major Lossen said today that we are supposed to be alerted tomorrow and leave by the 25th and our boat is the *Oneida*. He also said, you know how the Army works, which means that they could change it and take us off just like that. Being a separate battalion is just no good.

Oct. 22, Mon. – Well our name is on the board down at the CP headquarters so things are really looking good. Rained most of the day. Drew our PX rations this afternoon. Boy, what a time it was trying to find enough francs to pay for it. We don't get our money back until six hours before sailing. Went to the Red Cross this evening.

Oct. 23, Tue. – We were told we are restricted to the area tomorrow, so we should pull out tomorrow nite some time. Our boat is the *Oneida*, a Victory ship. All battalion records, battery records, and the officers footlockers were loaded on this evening. Boy, those officers sure cart around a pile of junk.

Oct. 24, Wed. – Stuck around the area all day. Got our customs papers back. Got a haircut.

Oct. 25, Thu. – The wind blew so hard last nite it almost took our tent away and then it turned cold as the dickens. Formations all day long. We got our numbers checked on our backs. Mine is no. 5. Physical right after supper. Turned in our helmets and linens. Got our pistols back. Drew "K" ration for our first meal on the boat. Our battery drew MP guard while on the boat. It will enable everyone of us in the battery to have a bunk 'cause the boat is going to be crowded, and the other batteries will get to sleep two nites out of three. We turn in our comforters in the morning. Breakfast at 5:00, reveille at 4:30.

Oct. 26, Fri. – Got up at 4:30 this morning. The trucks didn't come until 7:15. We loaded on big semi-trucks which took us right to the boat. Arrived at the dock at 9:00 and went on board at 10:00. The Red Cross girls passed out doughnuts and coffee while we were lined up on the dock, then while going up the gang plank every guy was handed a bag with cigarettes, candy, soap, and a sewing kit. Boy, what a staggering time we had with our pack on our back, our duffel bag over our shoulder, and then they handed us that bag. Well, we made it anyway. We are down two floors in hatch no. 4. We are sleeping on cots, and every bit of room is taken up. Some fellows have had to take turns sleeping as the ship is 30% overloaded. There are 1,857 troops on board. We get two big meals a day and a lunch at noon. Boy and the food is wonderful. Our battery are the M.P.s during the trip and as usual, I caught sergeant of the guard first so I had to go around with a lieutenant from the ship and find the guard posts. There are 20 in all, and after I came to post my guard it took me another two hours to find the post. I'm on for 24 hours so shouldn't catch it again the rest of the trip. Two tugs pulled us out of the dock at 5:00 this evening and then we took off for home! Took a shower this evening but what a time trying to get the soap to lather in salt water, and it was cold too. The hot water is on at certain hours only.

Oct. 27, Sat. – First day out. A beautiful day. We passed the Balearia Isle this afternoon and came in sight of the coast of Spain. From here it appears to be very mountainous country. Had an abandon ship drill this morning. Yesterday just after getting on board, we were given our money back in gold seal currency, so today we paid for and ordered our tobacco ration. Also were issued red lights to attach to our life belts. We have a ration ticket for our meals, and each time we eat our ticket is punched so nobody gets seconds. The meal you get is plenty. For lunch this noon we had soup, a quart of milk, and ginger snaps. Boy, did that milk taste good!! The crews from the ship said this is the fastest boat of its class and the fourth fastest on the Atlantic. It's about 450 and some feet long, so it isn't so big but it sure can cut the water. It was built last year. The shipper is going to try and break the record going back. We passed up three ships last nite and another one this evening. So far the trip has been wonderful with the ship rocking hardly at all. We don't have to use any of our mess equipment for chow. We eat off tin plates with silverware and drink out of paper cups.

Oct. 28, Sun. – Second day at sea. Passed up more ships last nite. We went past the Rock of Gibraltar and through the Straits between 8:00 and noon. We could see land on both sides very good. The African side was the prettiest, but both the Spanish and African sides were very mountainous. As we got closer to the Straits the water got rougher, and now that we are out in the Atlantic we have been pitching and rolling since noon, and it's after 10:00 p.m. now. Half of the fellows on board are sick already. Hardly any chow line for supper this evening. Catholic services this morning and Protestant this afternoon.

Oct. 29, Mon. – Third day at sea. Boy, what an awful nite it was last nite. Didn't get any sleep at all as I was knocked from one side of my cot to the other. More guys dropped out of the chow line today. They would just get a smell of the food and away they'd run. Hasn't bothered me as yet. Set our watch back another hour last nite. This rough weather hasn't let up since we left the Straits.

Out on the Atlantic on our way home

Oct. 30, Tue. – Fourth day at sea. The boat pitched and tossed all nite, but from breakfast on it's been pretty nice sailing all day. The ship still rocks an awful lot. The reason is because it hasn't any load and is sitting high in the water. There's a plotting board in the companion way just above our stairway which tells how many knots we average, how many miles we've gone, and how many left to go. We've gone 1,226 miles so far and are only one-third of the way. Been averaging 15 knots. Started an hour orientation lecture today. Went to a show in the mess hall this evening.

Oct. 31, Wed. – Fifth day at sea. Passed St. Agnes Island at 1:00 this morning. Ran into swells off and on all day. Boy, this sea air really gives one an appetite.

Nov. 1, Thu. – Sixth day at sea. Been pretty nice sailing all day today. We are past the halfway mark now and only have 1,944 miles left to go. Only! Moved our watch back an hour last nite.

Nov. 2, Fri. – Seventh day at sea. Moved back another hour at 12:00 last nite. Ran into a strong southeast wind, and it's been raining all day. Nobody is allowed on deck.

Nov. 3, Sat. – Eighth day at sea. Entered the gulf stream sometime last nite where it is considerably warmer, 70 ° the water is, so the air is very warm also. It's really stuffy down in the hold where we sleep. The current is with us now, so we have averaged 16 knots. Had a fire drill and abandon ship drill this morning.

Nov. 4, Sun. – Ninth day at sea. Moved the clocks back an hour last nite. Beautiful day today. Saw a school of flying fish off the port side. Ran into some funny rains all day, which would come all of a sudden and then were gone. Seeing rainbows all day. Running into a lot of seaweed floating over the water. Been seeing it for the past four days. Only 750 miles left to go. Church this afternoon in the mess hall.

Nov. 5, Mon. – Tenth day at sea. Ran into a bad storm about 3:00 this morning which continued all day and nearly all nite. All doors were closed and nobody allowed on deck all day. Nearly everybody got sick all over again. Went down in the engine room where a merchant marine fellow showed me all around. We were listing about 30 ° back and forth most of the day. The cots were sliding all over the floor, and breakfast and supper were really a calamity. Coffee spilling all over trays; you were eating everybody else's chow but your own. It really was funny though. The engines were wide open, but we were only doing about 10 knots. We ran into the storm where we left the Gulf Stream, and boy did it turn cold. Spray would come over the ship and covered the whole ship at once.

Nov. 6, Tue. – Eleventh day at sea. Everybody up at 5:00 this morning. The sea was as calm as the Mediterranean all the rest of the trip. We sighted land at 9:00 this morning, pulled into Chesapeake Bay at 9:30. Waited off Norfolk for a health boarding party and after their reports were filled out, we took off up the bay again.

A tug came out and pulled us into dock with band playing and people cheering. Docked at 12:00 noon, stepped onto U.S. soil at 12:45, boarded a train right at the dock which took us to Camp Patrick Henry. Arrival there at 1:45. WAACs were at the docks to direct us to the train, and the Red Cross gave us milk and doughnuts. A band met us in camp and lead us to the theater where we had a short lecture, after which we were assigned barracks and then got a steak dinner at 3:00. Took a shower after eating, and boy it really felt good as the ship's showers were salt water, which is better not to wash at all. George and I then went over and put in phone calls home. Put them in at 5:45 p.m. Gee, it was the biggest thrill I've ever had when I talked to them! Received a letter from Kip this evening.

Nov. 7, Wed. – Boy, it really got cold early this morning. We sleep in double-deck spring beds with mattresses, and it was almost too soft. George and I went shopping at the main PX this morning. Called Bert – had to wait three hours, but it really was worth it! Gee, this is so wonderful I can hardly believe it. Had a battalion formation this afternoon where some officers and enlisted men were presented Bronze Stars. The 451st is now no more. We were put in groups, and I'm in charge of 56 men from our battery going to Fort Sheridan. There are 258 from the battalion going there. We aren't leaving until tomorrow nite at 7:30. Those who travel more than 30 hours to the reception center get Pullman cars, so we're pretty sure we'll get Pullman. George and I went to the "Dairy Bar" this evening and indulged in milkshakes and sodas.

George, Federwitz, and me just back from overseas. Camp Patrick Henry, Norfolk, Virginia, 1945

Nov. 8, Thu. – Bought an OD cap this morning and had dinner at the service club with George and Nachtwey. Loaded our duffel bags in a truck this afternoon, which were put in a baggage car. Those going to Fort Dix left at 5:30 this evening. Buck and Frank went in that bunch. Alerted at 6:30 this evening. Had a leader meeting at 7:00. Assembled at 7:30 where we said goodbye to our officers. We marched down to the train at 8:00 with a band leading us. There were over a thousand who boarded our train. Well, as usual for the Army, we didn't get Pullman. We rode an old day coach with window, which opened only if you broke them. We were 62 to a car. The first town we came to we had to stop and change cars as we had a hot leak on ours.

Nov. 9, Fri. – Didn't sleep much last nite. Went through Silver Springs, Maryland, Charleston, West Virginia at noon. Crossed the Ohio River and passed though Columbus, Ohio by evening. We eat on paper plates, wooden spoons, paper cups. Chow isn't bad at all.

Nov. 10, Sat, – Went through Toledo, Ohio last nite. Arrived in Chicago at 4:00 this morning. Sheridan is full, so we had to go to Camp Grant. Arrived at 7:30 this morning, cold as the dickens. Ate breakfast, then had our records checked and stamped by 11:00. Assigned to barracks, and then George and I went to the personnel section to see about a pass. Finally finagled one out, but only until Monday morning at 6:00. Bought a round trip ticket and took off for Chicago at 2:00 p.m. Arrived in Chicago at 4:00, dashed over to the Northwestern Station, just boarded the "400" and it took off. Met Ray Wolfe on the train who was also going to Lee's wedding. The aisles were jammed after we left Milwaukee, so we stood up the rest of the way home. Arrived in Marinette at 10:10 p.m., and everybody was there to meet us. Gee, what a reception it was and how wonderful it was to see everybody!!! Practice for the wedding and didn't get to bed until 2:00. Boy, what excitement!! Called Marion also.

Nov. 11, Sun. – Went to Coleman to pick up Minerva and then to Oconto Falls to meet the Petersons and pick up Marion. Gee, what a sweet girl she is!!! Don and Bev took us. Too much excitement so could hardly eat all day. Boy, how Marcy has grown. Wedding was at 4:00 p.m. Boy, we were all about as nervous as Lee and Jewell. It was a pretty wedding, after which we went to Bakers for pictures, then to the Cholette House for super, then out to the hospital to see Ma Nault and then to the dance. We had to leave for camp at 10:00, and boy we sure hated to leave. Didn't have any clean clothes to wear, so we borrowed from Lee and Don. Don, Jerry, and Ray drove us back.

Nov. 12, Monday – Arrived at 4:30 this morning, so slept till noon. Picked up our bags. Boy, we were really burned up as we wouldn't have had to be back until tomorrow as we were just put on the list. Rained hard this afternoon. Went to service club for supper and then to a show.

Nov. 13, Tue. – Turned in our extra clothes and were issued some new stuff. German P.W.s sewed our patches and discharge emblem on our blouses. Gee, it seems so good to be this close to home and yet, it seems strange too. Said goodbye to Sam and Pete tonite as they have been processed and received their discharge already. I want to get home so bad, and yet I hate to see these fellas go. All I can say is that I was pretty lucky in having such a swell bunch of fellas as I had.

Nov. 14, Wed. – Had our final physical check up today. Finished our processing and received our discharge at 4:30 this evening. Hurrah!

Conclusion

I hope you enjoyed reading Jack Anderson's World War II diary that he wrote to provide his parents a journal of his experience serving in the United States Army. Over 20 years ago, my uncle, mom and I helped him take his hand written books to an electronic, then printed format that's been read by many family members and friends. Over 80 years after the original, I brought his diary to you with the goal of sharing a first hand account of World War II, keeping my grandfather's story alive, and honoring his service and all of those that served with him including those that made the ultimate sacrifice like Major Cook and others.

During his time overseas, his battalion chalked up 541 combat days and were awarded six battle stars indicating their engagement in combat under grave danger. They got credit for shooting down 36 planes and likely more that were shot down during barrage fire at night. According to Jack's notes, they shot down more planes than any other anti-aircraft battalion. During World War II, he spent five months and 22 days in the United States, and two years, eight months, and two days overseas for a total of over three years of service.

There were scary and chaotic days of fighting where danger was imminent, and other days where playing a tune on the piano, taking a swim in the Mediterranean, riding a horse, or seeing the sites on a day pass with his buddies, Kip, Spash, or George provided needed respite. He mentioned these three friends almost 300 times throughout the diary. George Hemminger became his brother-in-law, and I recently connected with Spash Esposito's daughter who said her dad used to talk about his buddy Jack. I even found a letter Kip sent to Jack back in 1981 when Kip's wife Mina was diagnosed with terminal cancer. Here's what Kip wrote:

"I guess when you get 72, you lose a little gusto. I remember when I was in the war and my dad died and I knew a guy who sure made it easier. And I lived in Marinette when Mina broke her back and that same guy made it easier for me. Now I sure know that if that same guy had been around in this case it would have helped me one helluva lot. There, that's what you mean to me Jack. Love Kip"

When I read Kip's letter, I was overcome with emotion as I thought about what it must have been like to be at war when your father passed away, and how Jack Anderson must have demonstrated a genuine warmth and empathy to have caused Kip to write this letter when he was faced with his wife's terminal cancer. I am so thankful that I had the opportunity to feel that same warmth, empathy, and positive energy that I will take with me the rest of my life. If you never met him, I hope you enjoyed learning more about him, and if we cross paths, I will do my best to model his character and maybe even sing a tune with you!

Afterword

Messages of tribute by friends and family

I still remember going to the train station in Marinette to welcome back my brother George and Jack from their service overseas. My brother Rod was set to be married the following day, Armistice Day, and I was paired with Jack to stand up in the wedding. We had a great time at the wedding, and six weeks later he proposed to me on Christmas Eve, and the rest is history. I am thankful for the 63 years we had together. There are too many memories to list here, but here are a few that come to mind. He always came over to my side of the bed to kiss me good night. He always called me "Sug" for sugar. He was an amazing husband and father. I miss him very much. It happened so fast when he passed away. I remember being at the hospital with my daughter Barb, where we held his hand one last time. I look forward to see him again someday, although I am thankful to be living in the house Jack and I built together with Barb and Gary (son-in-law) watching over me and my family and friends staying connected to me online and through regular family gatherings.
— *Annette Anderson (Jack's wife)*

Grampa would always call me Mildred! And every time he would see me he would say, "Megan, Megan, I've been thinking!" (He would tell me to say, "With what!") What a real nice girl you are!" Hard to believe it's been over 14 years since I heard that. :(But it's always fresh in my mind, and I can hear his voice saying it.
— *Megan Buenning*

A Soldier's Song

In my mind, what made Jack such a special person was his never-ending focus on making any person he was around feel special. In addition, his love of music was infectious. At our wedding reception, Jack initiated impromptu sing-a-longs whenever the band took a break. I will remember how special that was to our celebration for as long as I live.

— *Steve Lemerand*

My grandpa was truly one of a kind. I have so many memories riding home from our cottage in his little white truck. I would always help drive down the cottage road, then we would sing campfire songs all the way home. He was a great man who would be so proud of all his grandkids and great grandkids.

— *Kirsten Tuyls*

Jack was like family to me. He and Annette were dear friends of my parents. I have wonderful memories of the Andersons and Saleskys singing barbershop in our kitchen every Friday night (Jack had a beautiful tenor voice), of him dressing up and putting on "shows" during vacations at the cottage in Chassell (such a dry sense of humor), to being willing to help anyone whenever help was needed. He was a one-of-a kind gentle, caring, talented, funny, honest person. I will always respect and love Jack. I am thankful to have had him in my life.

— *Jane Salesky Rettke*

Your grandfather's singing voice was amazing! I had the privilege of singing in the choir with him at Zion Lutheran Church in Marinette, Wisconsin. My father sang with him in a barbershop quartet. My dad died when I was in grade school. Jack gave me a cassette tape of them practicing which is the only recording of my dad's voice known in the family. I played a selection of that tape at my mother's funeral.

— *Ann Buscher*

Great Uncle Jack is responsible for fostering a love of music: playing on the organ in his basement, singing tunes around the campfire at the Cottage and Maiden Lake, and playing the autoharp. He influenced me to study the clarinet and learn to read music beginning in 5th grade.

He taught me the notes and lyrics to barbershop classics like "The Green Green Grass of Home," "Harvest Moon," and how to stand/sit to every B in "My Bonnie Lies Over the Ocean." Lyrics I still cherish and sing to my young sons. Some of my favorite childhood memories are around the fire and listening to him sing harmony. His encouragement helped me stick with clarinet through high school even when I wanted to quit band for more free time.

Afterword

I'll always cherish the fond memories of Uncle Jack leading the group in song, in appreciating and making music as a family.

— Bailey O'Leske

Jack touched my life in so many ways (and still does) — every old video played at the Cottage, hearing "Silver Bells" at Christmas, sitting around the Cottage campfire, watching or reading anything about WWII. He's the reason I know lyrics to dozens of songs from the 1940's and 50's. He was such a wonderful role model — patient, fun-loving, always ready for a good time, and a great listener. I can still hear his laugh. New Year's Eves were extra-special because we got to dress in costumes and party at Uncle Jack's!

I even got to know my own Dad better because of him. They shared years of WWII and were a comfort to each other. George hated to remember the war and his journals are cryptic and hurting. Jack was able to find something good in even the most terrible things, and his journals (about the very same happenings) are actually uplifting. Reading them filled in the blanks for me. I would never have known that he and my Dad stood in the same places I did in Dachau and Rome — now I feel so connected to both of them when I'm there. One of my dearest memories of him is the day we spent a few years before he died. He helped me label dozens and dozens of photos and items from the war and told stories about them. He was sure that my Dad made the best pancakes in history and told some great tales about Soldiers lining up for them. I love those pictures! And my favorite pic from that box is framed in my dining room: Jack playing a piano in a bombed out house and making something awful look a little better.

I'm so thankful he married my Dad's beautiful sister and became my future uncle! And I sure hope he knows how much we all loved him.

— Carol Lemerand

Jack was my uncle. I remember his always taking pictures. He was so incredibly talented with music. I always enjoyed listening to him play the autoharp. When I first went to work at Luther Home in 1979 I knew the words to all the old songs from listening to Jack sing around the campfire. The first time, and many times after, I shared the picture and story about him and the piano in the bombed building with the residents at Luther Home. They were very touched by it.

— Denise Bretl

Jack Anderson. Wow lots of memories. When I was a teenager freezing in an open air deer stand, I walked over to Jack's stand (enclosed and heated), and he always welcomed me. We were probably the only not too serious hunters back then. We ate sandwiches and he pulled out a bunch of diaries, small books. He asked me to read through them to try to get them in order of time. Also on another note, Stephanie and I switch lying with our kids every night. We talk and sing songs. Gordon's regular request is "Swing Low, Sweet Chariot" that I sing in my best Jack Anderson voice I have.

— Al MacIntyre

When I remember my dad, I smile each time, especially when music or grandkids are involved! He was a friend to many and when asked how he was, he always answered "I'm OK now!" He was an honest, humble man whom everyone admired. When I think about how young he was when he entered and served all those years in the war, I'm filled with pride! I am grateful I got to call him my dad.

— Barb Grom

My Uncle Jack was a true gentleman and a mentor. And for anyone who chose to try to follow his example, it would be to follow a path leading to success as well as a life well lived. He was a true hero of the greatest generation, and I was fortunate to have received his personal support and guidance.

— John Sturdy

So what I remember the most about Jack was how he was always so welcoming to everyone who came to the cottage, and then just videotaping all the festivities. He was always happy and loved to share the videos! And also how he would start the singing, along with all the war stories with my dad. So interesting and such great memories! I just loved listening to his stories about the war!

— Patti Hefler

Jack Anderson was my father-in-law, and my first memory of him was the day I met him and the rest of the family. Steve and I were both recently discharged from the military and traveling to his hometown, Marinette, Wisconsin with a stop in Chicago, Illinois to visit my family and get married. I met them one day before our marriage. Jack immediately welcomed me to the family with open arms. Jack was always kind, loving, patient and willing to share many memories of his interesting life. He was a wonderful role model for our two sons.

— Kathi Anderson

Jack was the husband of my mother's cousin (Nette). Such a wonderful family! Jack was truly a very humble gentleman. When Jack would greet me (or anyone for that matter), he made me feel like I was the only person in the room (and we have a big family!). He would ask questions not to just make you feel welcome, but because he really cared about your response. It felt to me like it was Jack's "job" to let you know how very welcome and important you were and how much he appreciated that you took the time to come visit. To me, he was a "gold standard" man, a person who's character many people could never attain. He was so respectful, courteous, and he spoke with kindness and generosity.

— *Jill Struzik*

Jack and I were at our land, carrying a 16 foot ladder deer stand with a platform on top. I was at the front with the platform, and Jack was at the end of the ladder. I stepped over a log, but neglected to tell Jack. He tripped on the log, his glasses flew off and they landed in a pine tree. He didn't get mad, laughing he just said, "You could have told me."

I was hauling wood from my Grandpa's land, using Jack's white Toyota pickup to haul the wood. I couldn't get the truck to move, so I called Jack to come and figure out what was wrong. When he got there and checked the truck he said, "Did you check the parking brake?" That was it!! He didn't get mad, and we laughed about it!!

Jack would split wood with me at the land. He operated the handle on the splitter like a pro, and although we never had eye contact, he never pinched my fingers! We would take a lunch break, and he would enjoy a short nap in the truck. I always appreciated his help and our time together.

Jack was a friend to everyone, but when he passed away, not only did I lose my father-in-law, I lost my best friend.

— *Gary Grom*

I would have never had a love for golf if it wasn't for him. It wasn't pressure as much as it was just the internal want to make him proud in everything you did. Still to this day, the hot and cold water signs in the cottage bathroom is one example or the three-page cottage shutdown list. He always had the answer or the steps to get anything done, and you still get reminders every day.

— *Drew Andrist*

Jack was nice to be around. I remember him sitting on a bench with me at Maiden Lake, "That stress... it'll kill ya." He was always so positive. I never heard him say an unkind word about anyone.

— *Nancy Bintz*

Jack was an illuminator. He always put others before himself and made you feel great. His typical greeting when asked how he was doing was, "I'm doing better now that you are here." He also coined the old school phrase, "She's a peach." He was well known for his parties, especially costume parties. If you didn't have a costume to wear, he had an outfit for you.

Jack was an incredible role model. When I moved to Marinette, he took me under his wing. He got me summer jobs at the paper mill and facilitated my becoming a goalie for the UW Marinette Soccer Team. He was also the partner you always wanted in horseshoes or jarts.

Marinette was a magical place for me to grow up. Uncle Jack was committed to family and had a gentle soul. He was indeed, a very special guy — telling his war stories, sharing his memory of the first and last name of every guy in his Anti-Aircraft Unit, to his great sense of humor. Jack shared his love of singing, and boy did he have a beautiful voice! He loved to sing barber shop, lead family sing-a-longs, and performed many solos.

I think Jack added to the lives of everyone he met. He came from humble beginnings, which resonate with me. Jack was not only my uncle but also my friend. Love that guy.

— Craig Anderson

I'll always remember his memories he told to me about things like how bad the flies were in North Africa. Or as they made their way thru Europe "Das For Jockey!" as I was told many times by Grandma. And I'll always remember the great times when my dad held me so close to his chest that all I could hear was the perfect harmony of the next song. It was great.

— Steve Anderson

Growing up without a father (mine passed away when I was six), I was always in awe of this kind, sweet man. He was the father figure I hoped my own father would have been had he lived. Jack was so accepting of everyone he met. He made me feel like I was part of his family from the first time I met him. His love for family and his love for music was so inspiring. I will always remember how patient and kind he was with all the children that were around him all the time. My own included. The life lessons he taught and the campfire sing-a-longs that were so heartwarming. This world would be in such a great place if there were more men like Jack Anderson in it.

— Judy Hahn Bogenschutz

I have such fond memories of my "Uncle Jack" starting from when I was a young girl. Whenever someone would see him and ask, "How are you doing?" he would reply, "Well, I'm fine now that you're here." It would always put a smile on our faces and make us feel so special.

Uncle Jack was such a fun-loving person, entertaining many with his beautiful voice. I remember many times from my younger days to my grown up years sitting around the campfire with him and many extended family members singing songs for hours. He had a true heart for the young and old and everyone in between. In the Bible, it talks about the Fruits of the Spirit being love, joy, peace, patience, kindness, goodness, faithfulness, gentleness, and self-control.

Afterword

Thank you, Uncle Jack, for sharing with all of us these attributes that you so wonderfully exemplified.

— Lori Scott

The "Greatest Generation" is a term coined to describe those Americans who grew up during a time of great change and turmoil. These men and women who were born in the early years of the past century witnessed first hand the War to End All Wars, the Great Depression, WWII, and technological progress never seen by man. These Americans served their country without hesitation and with great pride. My life and the lives of many of my former students were enriched by the tales shared by my wife's Uncle Jack. Jack Anderson was full of unbridled pride in how he served our country during WWII. His excitement of serving like he did could be captured in both his oral and written accounts of events such as using "geometry" in order to make their anti-aircraft guns more efficient to the "nights out on the town." Uncle Jack's character had no facade. His character shined with honesty, respect, true humility, and an inner faith that enriched the world around him. When Jack Anderson left this world, he left it a much better place than when he found it.

— Mark Scott

Jack had an old wood sailboat with retractable dagger boards at The Shore. The mast and rigging were there, but never installed probably because the wood hull was questionable. But with a motor on the transom, it made a great fishing boat. Bud, Jack, my Dad and I (that I can remember) took it out on Green Bay to fish for perch. I'm guessing this is late 1950's. There were still perch. We'd motor over to where there were commercial fishermen's nets to fish with hook and line and worms. Jack, Bud and Rod knew that the commercial fishermen had a much better idea where the perch were than we did. We'd catch plenty, but not stay too long at one spot, and then move on to where there were more buoys.

Mary and my wedding reception, December 16, 1972. We both had gotten jobs in West Bend that fall. Mary's parents lived in Cedarburg 14 miles away, so we were in a hurry. Jack sang the solo "Somewhere" from *West Side Story*. He and Sandy Knuth, the church organist practiced before the service.

At the reception at The Port Washington Country Club, Mary's mother had arranged for an organist to play. We could reserve the Country Club for only three hours because of our late plans. Jack had printed song sheets to distribute to everyone there. He met with the organist, and the two of them set up a sing-a-long play list. It was fantastic.

Finally the box of Scott products for Christmas. We still use several of the boxes to store Christmas ornaments.

— Bruce Hemminger

The MacIntyre family arrived in Edwin Street, Marinette, in May 1982 straight from Scotland.

We were made very welcome by our neighbors, and soon we realized the patriarch in our little part of the street was Jack Anderson. All our kids loved him, he would drive them around in the trailer of his riding lawnmower, and often they would arrive home with a fresh new haircut, Army style.

Jack was a wonderful singer and had perfect tenor harmony to my baritone voice, and there was nothing quite like an evening at the cottage on the Bay standing around the fire pit singing "On Wisconsin" and my personal favorite "Swing Low, Sweet Chariot," and if we did a good job he would announce to anyone within listening distance, "If you don't like that, then you don't like home cooking."

It was a privilege to know and be friends with Jack Anderson, he was a gentleman.

— *John MacIntyre and Family*

I got home from the service in May of 1970. We were at a family gathering at George's house. George, Rod, and Jack tried to get to know me better by taking me off the corner for a talk. George started by giving me some advice. "Don't borrow money from family!" I responded, "Isn't that what banks are for?" Jack said, "I am starting to like him already!"

In the fall of 1983, I was helping Jack put the dock and boat lift away. When we pulled up the boat lift, Jack chained it to a tree. He shared a funny little tip that he promised would cause me to remember the combination. When spring rolled around there were major ice shoves that were coming up on shore and were about to crush all the items near the shoreline. Gary and I were moving items away from the shore, and we came upon the boat lift that was chained to the tree. Gary was ready to give up on the boat lift, and I said I remembered the combination based upon what Jack shared with me. The boat lift was saved!

Being a shift worker for 34 years, I always loved his line "Give me an hour and I'll be good." Never knew him to miss a gathering regardless of shift work. Even after he retired, he would comment on how he had to go in for midnights.

Jack always made you feel good. He was focused on you — your life, your skills, your interests. Every gathering included a song — he could play anything! And he never talked about politics. He was always in a good mood. As a fellow veteran of war, I appreciated the stories he shared, especially the fun one's like "These boots are for Jacque!"

— *Don Strojny*

My mom, Helen Campbell, was Aunt Nette's sister who was married to Uncle Jack. Growing up in the Hemminger family was a blessing! You spent a lot of time with your grandparents, aunts, uncles, and cousins. Friday nights at grandma and grandpas, Sunday at the cottage, Christmas at Uncle Bud and Aunt Neetz, and then continue to other relatives when we were younger. I remember Uncle Jack in their basement singing with all my aunts and uncles. He could play the piano and sing and the family would gather all around him (with an old fashioned or Manhattan in hand). A favorite memory as I grew older that I have of Uncle Jack is what he said. Wherever it was, Christmas at Neetz, holiday party at moms, seeing him at Anderson's cottage or Kelly Lake, I would go up to Uncle Jack to say hello and give him a hug and I would say, how are you? He always said, "Better, now that you are here." What a special uncle he was and very missed.

— *Tari Kobriger*

No one emulated kindness, compassion and sincerity more than Uncle Jack. Whether he knew you for one day or his entire life, you were treated with amazing kindness. His catch phrase to make you feel special each time the two of you met went something like this; when asked how he was doing he usually responded, with a smile and a happy voice saying, "I'm okay now that you're here!" He made you feel like you were the only person in the room when he interacted with you.

Jack was a role model for many and brought out the best in others. He was quick to laugh and smile, and he enjoyed sharing stories. His sense of humor was priceless, especially costume parties at his house or on vacation, wearing the darndest silly wigs. Jack knew how to have a good time and made sure others were having fun too. We all enjoyed football weekends, tailgating and happy hour with Jack.

Jack shared many memories of his military service. They were fascinating and incredible. He and his platoon made so many sacrifices for our country. The Battle of the Bulge is one of the most touching stories I remember him talking about. He shared stories of the memorabilia he had, along with where or how he acquired items. The most touching picture I have seen was of him playing the piano in a blown-up building during the war.

Another gift Jack had mastered was music. He had such a beautiful tenor voice and could harmonize better than most. Campfire sing-a-longs with family at the cottage at Breezy Point or family vacations will always be cherished memories. His singing would give you goose bumps or take your breath away. Hearing his solos or duets sometimes brought tears to my eyes, especially The Lord's Prayer.

Jack was a priceless, one-of-a-kind man. He was sincere, compassionate, of strong faith, and incredibly gifted. Jack was a natural leader who continues to be missed and loved by many. I feel most fortunate and blessed to have known him.

— *Sherry Anderson*

Jack frequently fried his version of Shaffer's Chicken in a fryer at The Cottage. I remember one time Mike Christian and I sat with Jack while he was frying the chickens enjoying some Manhattans. After the first batch was done, Mike tested out the chicken and commented that it was overdone and maybe the next batch should be cooked less. Jack didn't take too kindly to the suggestion based on his experience frying the chicken for many years. We decided to take it into our own hands and when Jack turned around, we took a few minutes off the timer. Mike and I laughed about that story for many years after. I had many good times with both Mike and Jack.

— *Kurt Hemminger*

Your Grandpa Jack was truly a Grandpa to all the kids on Edwin Street! He would take them on wagon rides, out to the cottage and play St. Nick to all our kids. Such a special man. Glad our family was able to be a part of his family!

— *Karen Dill*

Reflecting on a cherished memory with Grandpa Jack is no easy task, but one day from the early summer of 1982 stands out vividly in my mind. At the age of six, he invited my dad, a few other family members, and me for a boat ride on his wooden boat called the "Ace." We cruised around the lighthouse and up the Peshtigo River. When we turned back downriver Grandpa Jack, with a twinkle in his eye, looked at me and said, "Hey, old timer, do you want to take the wheel?"

Thrilled by the opportunity, I eagerly hopped in the driver's seat, feeling like a king as I gripped the steering wheel. With focused determination, I steered the boat, left and right, yearning to make my Grandpa proud. After about five minutes, Grandpa Jack, ever patient, had me hop up as he took the wheel again. He had me turn around and look at the bubble path in the water that the boat had made while I was driving. It looked a zig zagging road on the mostly straight river.

"You did a great job, old timer. Next time though, relax and try to not over-correct so much, trust that the boat will come back to center on her own. That way, you can enjoy the ride more." That afternoon Grandpa Jack imparted wisdom that went beyond boating and was more of a life lesson — it's a poignant memory that resonates deeply with me to this day. Miss you Grandpa.

— *Chris Anderson*

Afterword

The Bench beside the Bay

A special place of solace is this bench beside the bay
A breezy point to ponder all that nature has to say
A place where I've the privilege to enjoy a moment's stay
And the simple act of friendship is the only price I pay

My soul absorbs the wonder from this bench both day and night
Where the sun reflects its brilliance with a billion sparks of light
Where the pelicans and whooping cranes so softly take to flight
A lighthouse beams as ships drive safely in then out of sight

Starlight grows from dim to bright against the darkening skies
Sometimes a streaking fiery glow commands my watchful eyes
Glitter glistens off the bay as the moon begins its rise
And dazzling hues of northern light may thrill me with surprise

A log may crackle crisply in the stones behind this chair
And a hint of sweet vibrato may linger in the air
It's the place of song and laughter and a warming fire to share
Fond moments fill the memories of all who gather there

I've seen life go full circle from the bench beside the bay
I've seen children watch their children watch their children's children play
For good cheer, good food and spirits and best friendships I will say
That I've been truly blessed to find this bench beside the bay

For Jack

Above our flag slaps proudly near once a hero stood
The great and gentle steward of this special space of good
A kindly man who shared his gifts the way that all men should
I will oft remember him from this agelong length of wood

— *The Craig and Tammy Martin Family*

197

Acknowledgements

This project started over 80 years ago when my great-grandma Esther wrote a letter to her son upon hearing he was drafted into the U.S. Army to serve our country during World War II. From there, they wrote to each other on a regular basis, although he felt compelled to journal his daily experiences to provide her and my great-grandpa John a view into his life in the service. These six little booklets, along with dozens of pictures and souvenirs, provided an amazing "conversation piece" as my grandpa always used to say. Without that original letter and my grandpa's commitment to daily journaling, this book would not have been possible.

From there, my uncle Steve Anderson and my mom, Barb Grom, and I started and ultimately finished an original transcription of the booklets into an electronic format that my grandpa reviewed and validated for accuracy. I still have the original floppy disk that I am not sure can be read by any current computers out there. Without my grandpa's willingness to transition his original writing into the electronic version, and my uncle Steve and my mom's efforts to type each and every word verbatim, this book would not have been possible.

Over the years, many people have expressed interest in reading his diary including family, friends, co-workers and more. I highlighted in the preface Mark Scott who used the diary as part of his World War II history class. In addition, I shared excerpts from the diary on social media with a warm response from those who read the posts. I even found a World War II forum for the 451st Anti-Aircraft Artillery when I saw a thread about someone looking for information on Major Cook who was killed in action. Without the ongoing interest from so many, this book would not have been possible.

As an avid reader, I had thought about publishing a book, but thought it was not possible. That all changed when Steve Rosenbaum and Mary Connaughty-Sullivan generously provided guidance on the process after publishing their own books *Faster, Better, Cheaper How to Improve Any Learning Organization* and *Nudges From the Other Side*. Without their advice and encouragement, this book would not have been possible.

Faced with an already full schedule and over 180+ pages of editing/formatting not to mention cover design and more, I reached out to Kim Rodgers. We worked together previously, and I had always admired her "popcorn thinking" and design skills. She willingly jumped into the project and has spent countless hours to make this book a reality. Without her efforts, this book would not have been possible.

I need to thank my family for their support as I pursued this passion project to bring my grandpa's World War II history to the world. I tried to limit my focus on the project to the early mornings, but it sometimes bled into other times of the day. Without your support and patience, this book would not have been possible.

In closing, I am thankful God has given me the blessing of everyone named above as well as the motivation, talents, and skills to bring this to life.

About the Authors

Jack was born on September 16, 1921 and graduated from Marinette High School.

He served in the United States Army during World War II as a sergeant with the 451st Anti-Aircraft Artillery. After marrying Annette in 1946 and starting his career at Scott Paper Company, he re-enlisted in the Army, including a year of active duty in the 317th Army Band stationed at Camp McCoy, Wisconsin.

Jack and Annette raised their two children Barb and Steve who, along with their spouses Gary and Kathi, blessed them with five grandchildren: Kirsten, Chris, Jason, Mark, and Megan. While Jack didn't get to meet all his great-grandchildren, he had a special bond with all of them, including three that were named in his honor.

Jack was a lifelong member of Zion Lutheran Church, singing in the church choir since the age of 12. He was also active in barbershop quartets and chorus groups and orchestrated hundreds of sing-a-longs at gatherings with family and friends, especially around the campfire at The Cottage.

Jack passed away in December 2009, although his voice can still be heard in the hearts and minds of those who knew him.

Jason Charles from the house of Grom. First of his name. Champion of harmony. Learning guru. Husband to the OG problem solver. Father of two impressive kids. Driver of continuous improvement. Seeker of good habits. Learn in the flow of life.

Jason Grom currently resides in Maplewood, Minnesota with his wife Heather and two children, Hannah and Jack. He's a learning and development leader in financial services, with expertise in learning strategy, design, facilitation, and coaching. He writes a weekly learning blog called Learn In the Flow of Life and has been a guest on multiple podcasts sharing his expertise and ideas.

He grew up in northeast Wisconsin which he still calls home based upon his connection with his family and the area. He followed in his grandpa Jack's footsteps playing the tuba in school which led to an opportunity to join the University of Wisconsin Marching Band, performing at two Rose Parades and Bowls during his tenure.

If he's not working or attending Hannah or Jack's after school activities, you can find him enjoying family activities including golfing, fishing, and anything Disney, especially Star Wars, learning every step of the way!

Glossary

50: M2 Browning .50 caliber heavy machine gun

88: German 88 mm anti-aircraft and anti-tank artillery gun

A-20: Douglas A-20 Havoc American light bomber, night fighter, reconnaissance aircraft

Ack-ack: Slang for anti-aircraft gunfire

Allied Military Currency: A form of currency issued to troops to use in local liberated or newly-occupied territories.

Anzio Express: German Krupp K5 heavy railway gun with a 71-foot-long gun barrel in a fixed mounting with only vertical elevation of the weapon

A.P. (anti-personnel): Device designed to kill or injure people rather than destroy buildings, vehicles, etc.

Axis Sally: American broadcaster employed by Nazi Germany to disseminate Axis propaganda.

B-17: Boeing B-17 Flying Fortress American four-engine heavy bomber plane

B-24/Liberators: Consolidated B-24 Liberator American heavy bomber

B-25: North American B-25 Mitchell medium bomber

B-26: Martin B-26 Marauder American twin-engined medium bomber

B-29: Boeing B-29 Superfortress American four-engined propeller-driven heavy bomber

Beaufighter: British Bristol Beaufighter airplane (aka the Beau)

Bivouac: Temporary living quarters built by the Army for Soldiers (also known as a camp or encampment).

Bofors/40: 40 mm automatic anti-aircraft gun

C-47: Douglas C-47 Skytrain military transport aircraft

CP (Command Post): Activities involved in controlling and sustaining current operations and planning future operations.

CQ (Charge of Quarters): Tasked duty in which a Soldier is to guard the front entrance to the barracks, among other duties.

Director: Calculates firing solutions for use against a moving target and transmits data to the crew; usually used in conjunction with other fire control equipment.

DUKW (aka Duck) Boat: Six-wheel-drive amphibious modification of a 2.5-ton truck

E.T.O. (European Theater of Operations): Responsible for directing U.S. Army operations throughout the European theatre.

Fw 190: Focke-Wulf Fw 190 German single-seat single engine fighter aircraft

Garand: M1 Garand semi-automatic service rifle

General Grant tank: Medium tank (aka M3 Lee or M3 Grant depending on the turret pattern)

G.I.: Nickname for an American Soldier

Gig/Gigged: An unfavorable report / repercussions of unfavorable report

Goldbricked: Avoided work or engaged in personal activities while at work

G.O.R.: Gun Operations Room

Halifax: Handley Page Halifax British Royal Air Force four-engined heavy bomber

He 112: Heinkel He 112 German fighter aircraft

Howitzer: Artillery weapon that falls between a cannon (or field gun) and a mortar; generally aimed lower than a mortar but higher than a cannon.

Hutment: Encampment of small dwellings of simple construction

IP (Initial Point): An identifiable landmark about 20 miles from the target

Jerry/Jerries: Nickname for a German person or fighter pilot

Ju 88: Junkers Ju 88 German twin-engined combat aircraft

KP: Kitchen Patrol

L-5: Stinson L-5 Sentinel liaison or observation plane with green paint for camouflage

Limey: Slang for a British sailor

Long Tom: 155 mm field gun

LST (Landing Ship Tank): Ship that supports amphibious operations by carrying tanks, vehicles, cargo, and landing troops directly onto a low-slope beach with no docks or piers.

Luftwaffe: Refers to Germany's aerial warfare branch

M-51: Quad .50 caliber machine gun mount and trailer

Me 109: Messerschmitt Bf 109 German fighter aircraft (referred to as Me 109 by Allied forces)

Me 262: Messerschmitt Me 262 German fighter aircraft and fighter bomber

Glossary

M.P.: Military Police

MRS (Military Railway Service): Railway administration, dispatching, supply, communications, and maintenance in the theater of operations.

OD (Olive Drab): Cloth of an olive drab color, used often for military uniforms

OP: Observation Post (or Operations Post)

Ordnance (Ordnance Corps): Supplies Army combat units with weapons and ammunition, including at times their procurement and maintenance.

P-38: Lockheed P-38 Lightning American single-seat, twin piston-engined fighter aircraft

P-39: Bell P-39 Airacobra fighter

P-51: North American Aviation P-51 Mustang long-range, single-seat fighter and fighter-bomber

Power Plant: Refers to the power plant operator of an anti-aircraft gun

P.W.: Prisoner of War

PX (Post Exchange): Store for merchandise and services for military personnel and authorized civilians at a military installation

Sergeant of the guard: The senior non-commissioned officer of the guard who supervises enlisted members of the guard and is responsible to the commander of the guard.

Spitfire (Spit): Supermarine Spitfire British single-seat fighter aircraft

S.S. troops (Schutzstaffel): Protection squads originally established as Hitler's personal bodyguard unit, but later became elite guard of Nazi Reich.

Stuka: Junkers Ju 87 German dive bomber and ground-attack aircraft

U-2: Polikarpov Po-2 all-weather multi-role Soviet biplane

U.S.O.: American charitable corporation providing live entertainment and social facilities

Very pistol: Flare gun

WAAC/WAC (Women's Army Auxiliary Corps/Women's Army Corps): WAAC was established in 1942 "for the purpose of making available to the national defense the knowledge, skill, and special training of women of the nation." In 1943, the "auxiliary" status was dropped because changes were made to allow enlistment and commissioning of women in the Army, thus making the WAC a part of the U.S. Army.

Made in the USA
Monee, IL
03 April 2024

56317270R00125